AF606074

Approaches to Teaching Emily Brontë's *Wuthering Heights*

Approaches to Teaching World Literature

Joseph Gibaldi, series editor

For a complete listing of titles, see the last pages of this book.

Approaches to Teaching Emily Brontë's *Wuthering Heights*

Edited by

Sue Lonoff

and

Terri A. Hasseler

The Modern Language Association of America

New York 2006

Library of Congress Cataloging-in-Publication Data
Approaches to teaching Emily Brontë's Wuthering Heights / edited by Sue Lonoff and Terri A. Hasseler.
p. cm.—(Approaches to teaching world literature ; 89)
Includes bibliographical references.
ISBN-13: 978-0-87352-992-1 (alk. paper)
ISBN-10: 0-87352-992-8 (alk. paper)
ISBN-13: 978-0-87352-993-8 (pbk. : alk. paper)
ISBN-10: 0-87352-993-6 (pbk. : alk. paper)
1. Brontë, Emily, 1818–1848. Wuthering Heights. 2. Brontë, Emily, 1818–1848—Study and teaching. I. Lonoff de Cuevas, Sue. II. Hasseler, Terri A., 1964– III. Series.
PR4172.W73A86 2006
823'.8—dc22 2005032967
ISSN 1059-1133

Cover illustration of the paperback edition: still from the 1920 silent film *Wuthering Heights*, with Milton Rosmer as Heathcliff and Anne Trevor as Cathy. Courtesy of the Brontë Society

Published by The Modern Language Association of America
26 Broadway, New York, NY 10004-1789
www.mla.org

CONTENTS

PREFACE TO THE SERIES

In *The Art of Teaching* Gilbert Highet wrote, "Bad teaching wastes a great deal of effort, and spoils many lives which might have been full of energy and happiness." All too many teachers have failed in their work, Highet argued, simply "because they have not thought about it." We hope that the Approaches to Teaching World Literature series, sponsored by the Modern Language Association's Publications Committee, will not only improve the craft—as well as the art—of teaching but also encourage serious and continuing discussion of the aims and methods of teaching literature.

The principal objective of the series is to collect within each volume different points of view on teaching a specific literary work, a literary tradition, or a writer widely taught at the undergraduate level. The preparation of each volume begins with a wide-ranging survey of instructors, thus enabling us to include in the volume the philosophies and approaches, thoughts and methods of scores of experienced teachers. The result is a sourcebook of material, information, and ideas on teaching the subject of the volume to undergraduates.

The series is intended to serve nonspecialists as well as specialists, inexperienced as well as experienced teachers, graduate students who wish to learn effective ways of teaching as well as senior professors who wish to compare their approaches with the approaches of colleagues in other schools. Of course, no volume in the series can ever substitute for erudition, intelligence, creativity, and sensitivity in teaching. We hope merely that each book will point readers in useful directions; at most each will offer only a first step in the long journey to successful teaching.

Joseph Gibaldi
Series Editor

PREFACE TO THE VOLUME

> I love here what I loathe, what frightens me, what causes my being to recoil. . . . [*Wuthering Heights*] is a home of the damned, and yet . . . [like] Lockwood, I am drawn back.
>
> —A student's comment[1]

Responses to *Wuthering Heights* are never neutral, a fact that accounts for the challenges it poses as well as for its enduring classroom presence. The novel is regularly featured in syllabi on Victorian, gothic, and Romantic literature; in English and women's studies departments; in courses on composition, theory, and film and at levels from high school through doctoral. Movie and television versions have made the name Heathcliff so familiar that students who know nothing about the book may arrive with their expectations primed.

Yet despite its high position in academic and popular culture, it is not an easy novel to teach. The narrative is complex, the narrators unreliable, the dialect off-putting, and the context often baffling. While students still respond to its passionate intensity, they are frequently troubled by its violence and the absence of conventionally appealing characters. They may also have to grapple with the conflicts between the text and the film versions they have seen.

Beyond these student-based difficulties are the ones dissemination imposes. At least a dozen publishers market the novel for classroom use. Under *Wuthering Heights*, Amazon.com, as of this writing, lists 448 books and a profusion of related items. Students can download the text from the Web, buy it as an e-book, listen to audio versions, and view it on videocassette. Conscientious teachers will be hard-pressed to evaluate these offerings, much less the hundreds of critical, contextual, and biographical studies that begin with the reviews in 1847 and continue to proliferate. Guidance through this thicket is urgently needed, as are firsthand accounts of teaching the novel to diversified student populations. And so, when Joseph Gibaldi asked us to fill "one of the more glaring gaps" in the Approaches to Teaching World Literature series, we agreed to take the project on.

From the outset, we had several goals: to indicate the best resources for teaching, to focus on the issues most important to teachers, to present an array of approaches that could be adapted or replicated elsewhere, and to hear more directly from students. The first three goals are common to all volumes in the series. Traditionally, the "Materials" section reports the results of a survey of teachers, reviews and compares editions of the text, and provides an instructor's library; we follow this precedent. In the "Approaches" section, too, we follow the prototype, presenting eighteen essays by contributors. One respondent to our teacher's survey wrote, "This is such an open text that it excludes no point of view," and we have tried to make that diversity manifest by including approaches from every kind of course in which the novel is taught.

With our fourth goal, however, we wanted to move in a new pedagogical direction, one that reflects an academy-wide shift from teacher-based to learner-centered pedagogy. From its inception, the volumes in this series have emphasized what teachers say to students. Although instructions sent to all contributors urge them to "discuss actual classroom experiences, including student contributions and reactions," teachers necessarily report on those experiences from subjective positions. Furthermore, aside from direct quotations, the evidence of student responses to instructors' strategies is mediated through indirect discourse: "our students say," "they tell me," and so forth. In other words, the evidence for the success of any method or approach almost always comes from those invested in having it succeed.

While it may be impossible to measure outcomes of a teaching method by scientific standards, we believe that input from students is crucial in determining what works in the classroom. We have therefore implemented several original procedures. First, we designed a student survey that was conducted over more than two years; the results appear in the "Materials" section. Second, we asked some of our contributors to quote or reproduce their students' work—for instance, brief samples of writing. Third, we include other essays because they consider not only the teaching of *Wuthering Heights* but also the problematics of a changing student base and evolving departmental priorities. Thus, although the majority of essays continue to represent teachers' approaches, they also make students more prominent.

We would like to acknowledge the guidance and support of Joseph Gibaldi (general series editor) and Sonia Kane (aquisitions editor) of the Modern Language Association; in particular, we thank them for supporting the distribution of the student survey, which proved invaluable for measuring student responses to the text and to various teaching methods. We are deeply grateful to the numerous colleagues who participated in the teacher survey, providing detailed and helpful comments as well as information on their students' perception of or reactions to *Wuthering Heights*. We were pleased to receive thoughtful comments from the numerous peer reviewers of the manuscript, including the MLA Publications Committee. We would like to acknowledge Glenn Everett for his advice on Web-based technologies, which helped us in the development of the Webography. Sue Lonoff wishes to thank James D. Wilkinson, who first encouraged her interest in surveying students, and Jan Civian and Erin Driver-Jones, who provided expertise in the preparation of the student survey. Lonoff also expresses appreciation to John de Cuevas for his suggestions on her articles and his unwavering encouragement. Terri A. Hasseler recognizes the financial and clerical assistance provided by Bryant

University, and she would like to thank Ken Abrams for his support throughout the process—putting up with a number of all-nighters and making some computer magic when documents disappeared.

SL and TAH

NOTE

[1]All student quotations in this volume are used with permission.

Part One

MATERIALS

Courses and Course Designs

When we proposed this volume, we claimed that *Wuthering Heights* was taught in an exceptional variety of courses. Responses to our survey fully justify that claim. In fact, a number of instructors report that they teach it in several courses and across a range of student populations.

Twenty-seven percent of our respondents include *Wuthering Heights* in a course on the nineteenth-century British and Victorian novel.[1] Sixteen percent teach it as part of a required English literature or novel survey, usually in the second half. Eight percent teach it in courses on cultural or literary studies. John P. Farrell' says that he uses it as a "foundational text" on "the cultural and political history of the Victorian period," testifying to the novel's altered status: the novel that an older generation represented as radically unorthodox has now assumed a central position in courses on period and genre. Three respondents teach it in their critical approaches courses, where it becomes a case in point for explicating theory, and three include it in courses in which students learn the basics of college-level writing. The feminist movement too has promoted the novel's transfer to the academic mainstream. Ten percent of our respondents offer it in women's studies courses, and another ten percent in Brontë seminars, graduate and undergraduate. Three respondents feature *Wuthering Heights* in courses on the gothic and one in a course on dark Romanticism. The wide availability of video versions facilitates its use in courses on the media. Two respondents teach it in their classes on literature and film (or film theory), and several others contrast the work with one or more film versions. The novel is also a popular choice for theme-based courses—among them Violence and the Victorian Imagination, Sexual Transgression in Victorian Prose, Rites of Passage, the Victorian Animal as Social Critique, Victorian Fantasy, and Women Nature Writers.

While the number and range of courses vary widely, the amount of teaching time that the novel occupies tends to be more consistent. Sixty-two percent of respondents say that they spend two weeks on it, twenty-six percent indicate that they teach the novel for a week to a week and a half, and twelve percent devote three weeks to it. These figures do not take into account the number of weekly class meetings (one to three) or the length of each session, which varies from fifty minutes to three hours. On average, our respondents allot slightly less than six hours to *Wuthering Heights*, with a minimum of two and a half hours in a required survey course and a maximum of fifteen hours in a year-long Brontë seminar.

Decisions about when to teach the novel depend largely on the course, and instructors who offer it in several courses vary its position accordingly. Sixty percent of our respondents present it in chronological order (earlier texts before, later after), and a third of them teach it first or early on; typically, they use it to introduce topics pursued for the rest of the term. In one survey of nineteenth-century literature, *Wuthering Heights* follows a novel by Walter Scott or Jane Austen and so enables instructors to trace the evolution from Romantic or gothic to Victorian realism. Respondents offering theme or theory courses that are less concerned with chronological development might first teach a story or novel that establishes the issues they continue to explore in *Wuthering Heights*. Thirty percent of our respondents say that they have taught it in conjunction with another Brontë novel, most frequently *Jane Eyre* and then *Villette*. Two respondents also cite Anne Brontë's *Tenant of Wildfell Hall*. Emily Brontë's poetry, her diary papers, her Belgian essays, Charlotte Brontë's 1850 preface, and reviews from the period are all mentioned as contexts, although only by one or two respondents. Several report choosing editions because they include such materials.

Editions

The Clarendon edition of *Wuthering Heights* remains the standard reference for scholars. But as its editors, Hilda Marsden and Ian Jack, point out, there can be no strictly authoritative version, because neither Emily Brontë's manuscript nor any correspondence with her publisher, Newby, has survived. In addition, according to Charlotte Brontë, Newby's 1847 edition "abounded in errors of the press" (Wise and Symington 2: 162), and the publisher failed to incorporate corrections that Emily had made in the proof sheets. Charlotte Brontë imposed corrections on the subsequent edition, in 1850, but since her sister was no longer alive, her authority for making those changes remains open to question. Marsden and Jack and nearly all other modern editors therefore use Newby's edition as their copy-text. However, they correct the obvious flaws and note or incorporate aspects of Charlotte Brontë's edition wherever those changes seem warranted. Many editions also eliminate the original division of the novel into volume 1 (chs. 1–14) and volume 2 (chs. 1–20); instead, they number the chapters consecutively to 34.

Thanks to these more scrupulous editing practices and to the novel's academic popularity, reliable editions now abound. Our respondents reported using nine of them, and many said that they had tried several. Although three stood out as the most frequently selected—Richard J. Dunn's, Linda H. Peterson's, and Pauline Nestor's—no edition obtained a majority vote. Rather, there was a bifurcation between texts with supplementary material and texts described as reasonably priced. Teachers seeking contextual and critical articles opted for the Dunn and the Peterson and, in fewer numbers, for Diane Long Hoeveler's and Christopher Heywood's editions. Instructors who wanted only notes and an introduction opted for Nestor's edition, Ian Jack's edition, and, in one case, Candace Ward's edition. One respondent had used the Bantam edition in the past. Another, who teaches at a community college, recommended Irene M. Feltham's Amsco edition "because it provides interpretive comments and vocabulary enrichment." All these editions, except Heywood's, Ward's, and Bantam's, include Charlotte Brontë's two essays of 1850, "Biographical Notice of Ellis and Acton Bell" and "Editor's Preface to the New Edition of *Wuthering Heights*."

In 2003, the three leading publishers issued new editions of the novel. While users of Nestor's edition will find minor alterations—a new preface, a revised introduction, and an updated list of further readings—the changes in the others are more substantive. In pre-2003 editions, Norton (ed. Sale and Dunn) and Bedford (ed. Peterson) differed significantly from each other in their approach to *Wuthering Heights*. Because of its selection of Emily Brontë's poems, her diary papers, period reviews, and half a dozen articles, the 1990 Norton edition was preferred by teachers who wanted to contextualize the novel. As three of our respondents noted, however, current essays were scanty and the volume needed an update. In contrast, Peterson's 1992 edition was favored by teachers who focused on theory and wanted a variety of perspectives in one compact source. Like other volumes in the Bedford series, it features five critical approaches and a history of the novel's reception. Respondents who used this edition liked it. One noted that Peterson's summaries were helpful, although another said that students found the cultural-criticism section "incomprehensible."

The alterations in the subsequent Norton (ed. Dunn) and Bedford (ed. Peterson) editions have moderated the contrast. The Norton retains the poems and period reviews, enlarging the background section with Edward Chitham's essay on the novel's composition and further texts by Emily and Charlotte Brontë (see "The Instructor's Library"). Two articles on the novel's chronology have vanished, together with Sales's essay on the history of Gondal. However, it now features critical articles (by J. Hillis Miller, Sandra M. Gilbert and Susan Gubar, Martha Nussbaum, and Lin Haire-Sargeant) that several respondents rate highly. The changes in Peterson's Bedford edition, which are even more striking, reflect the recent emphasis on cultural studies, together with an effort to place the novel in historical context by including period documents and im ages. Peterson has kept the psychoanalytic, Marxist, and cultural studies approaches (by Philip K. Wion, Terry Eagleton, and Nancy Armstrong, respectively), but she has dropped Hillis Miller's deconstruction, replaced Margaret Homans's feminist approach with one by Lyn Pykett, and added an essay by Susan L. Meyer that shows how theoretical approaches can be combined. These changes make the Bedford more attractive to teachers who want both contextual and critical materials. Several respondents to our student surveys also singled out its essays as "useful." As Sarah Fermi's review in *Brontë Studies* points out, though, "the choice of the particular 'contexts' is rather confused and not entirely apposite" (90), especially when their bearing on the novel is debatable.

Two other editions cited by teachers incorporate contextual and critical studies. Hoeveler's edition includes a selection of Emily Brontë's poems and "The Bridegroom of Barna," a story from which she may have taken aspects of her plot. It also features articles not reprinted elsewhere, among them Mary Visick's analysis of Gondal, Maja-Lisa Von Sneidern's study of the Liverpool slave trade, Chitham's on the Brontës' Irish roots, and Hoeveler's on the novel's gothic feminism. Heywood's edition for Broadview, which restructures Emily Brontë's chapter divisions, is more controversial than the others. While his close examination of the Yorkshire landscape remains unrivaled, his insistence on Heathcliff's African identity and his assumptions about Brontë's intentions have been almost unanimously criticized. Still, one respondent reports that her students "appreciate the text's voluminous notes and its radical approach." Broadview, apparently less enthusiastic, is issuing an alternative edition, edited by Beth Newman.

Among the lower-priced editions, both Nestor's and Jack's provide helpful introductions, copious notes, chronologies of Brontë's life, and genealogies of the characters. Although American respondents tend to favor Nestor's volume, we have asked our contributors to quote from Jack's edition because it reproduces the Clarendon text (ed. Marsden and Jack). Students may also find Jack's endnotes a bit more informative than those in Nestor, especially the translations of Joseph's speech; its Select Bibliography is also more comprehensive. However, as we discovered the hard way, Oxford issued two 1998 paperback editions with identical covers and ISBN numbers but with different pagination: in one, the text runs to 338 pages, in the other, to 300. For the quotations from *Wuthering Heights* in this volume, we cite the page numbers in the Oxford 300-page edition, which has thirty-nine lines of text to the page.

Since we conducted our surveys, several publishers have issued new low-priced editions of the novel or have updated old ones. The Barnes and Noble Classic edition, with an introduction by Daphne Merkin and notes by Tatiana M. Holway, offers useful supplementary material, including a section on fiction, films, and poems that *Wuthering Heights* has inspired. But it reprints the 1850 version of the text, which some teachers may consider a drawback. Signet Classics has reissued an older printing with a new introduction by Alice Hoffman; however, like The Modern Library edition, introduced by Diane Johnson, it provides no notes. Ward's edition offers minimal glosses of Joseph's speeches and a much briefer introduction than any of the others; yet it is by far the cheapest reliable version in print.

Teachers who, like one of our respondents, have many inexperienced readers in their classes may want to consider Feltham's edition. It includes a unique diagram of the structure as well as vocabulary enrichment exercises and copious questions on the novel's content, setting, structure, and poetic language. Answers appear in a teacher's edition. Curiously, for such a directive volume, it contains no notes.

Finally, teachers should be aware of the increasing availability of online texts (e-books) that can be downloaded; we list several on the annotated listing of

Internet resources. Some are electronic versions of reliable editions—for example, Nestor's Penguin—but others provide no indication of the copy-text or its reliability.

The Instructor's Library

An inescapable sense of disproportion haunts anyone who tackles *Wuthering Heights*: although all the known writings *by* Emily Jane Brontë would fit into a medium-size paperback, the totality of texts *about* her writings, life, and background would swamp most instructors' offices. Recognizing the need for guidance, all editors but Ward provide selective bibliographies; Peterson also includes a history of reader reception. We therefore limit this section to the following categories: the most reliable editions of Emily Brontë's other works, biographies and background studies particularly relevant to *Wuthering Heights*, critical and theoretical articles repeatedly noted by respondents and contributors, and additional contextual materials that instructors may find useful. In addition, later in this section, we include a guide to Internet resources, and in the Works Cited listing, we provide a filmography.

Other Works by Emily Brontë

Although Marsden and Jack's edition of *Wuthering Heights* appeared in 1976, reliable scholarly editions of Brontë's other works did not emerge until the end of the twentieth century. The one exception was C. W. Hatfield's *The Complete Poems of Emily Jane Brontë* (1941), which is based on close inspection of the manuscripts; however, Hatfield's attributions are not completely accurate and his notes are minimal. Then, between 1992 and 2000, half a dozen publications made all her extant work available in annotated critical editions.[2]

The first to appear was Janet Gezari's *Emily Jane Brontë: The Complete Poems*, which one reviewer described as "indispensable, complete and handy" (Leighton). It was followed by Derek Roper's Clarendon volume, *The Poems of Emily Brontë*. Both editions include information on Gondal, Emily and Anne Brontë's imaginary kingdom. As noted earlier, selected poems also appear in both Norton editions and the Riverside edition, and the Norton editions include Anne's and Emily's diary papers. These six little notes, two written jointly and two by each sister at four-year intervals, were first published in Thomas J. Wise and J. Alexander Symington's *The Brontës: Their Lives, Friendships and Correspondence* (1932); however, this edition is notoriously faulty. In contrast, the first two volumes of Margaret Smith's *The Letters of Charlotte Brontë, with a Selection of Letters by Family and Friends* provide accurate transcripts of the last four diary papers and of all letters by or pertaining to Emily through 1851. The diary papers and excerpts from Charlotte's correspondence with the novel's publishers also appear in Dunn's edition, although its back cover inaccurately attributes Charlotte's letters to Emily, and in Juliet Barker's *The Brontës: A Life in Letters*.

The sketches that accompany the diary papers—together with all the Brontës' artwork—are well reproduced in Christine Alexander and Jane Sellars's *The Art of the Brontës*. This catalog is a comprehensive source for Emily Brontë's animal drawings and the landscapes she sketched around Haworth and Brussels. During her eight months in Brussels, she wrote *devoirs*, essays in French that have been published in Sue Lonoff's bilingual edition, *Charlotte Brontë and Emily Brontë: The Belgian Essays*. One *devoir*, "The Butterfly," is included in the Norton editions, and that one and two others—"Portrait: King Harold" and "The Cat"—will appear in Newman's Broadview edition. The only other extant writing by Emily is the fragment of an account book that she kept, reproduced in appendix 1 of Chitham's *A Life of Emily Brontë*.

Biographies and Background Studies

On its publication in 1994, Barker's *The Brontës* became the definitive biography of all four Brontë siblings. It is the reference work most frequently cited by respondents to our teachers' survey. Barker's later article "The Haworth Context" provides a more succinct description of the town and, like her biography, challenges the myth of the Brontës as isolated geniuses. That myth, launched by Charlotte Brontë in 1850, is furthered in Elizabeth Gaskell's *The Life of Charlotte Brontë*, which nonetheless remains the seminal source of information on both sisters. Frances Beer's article in this volume suggests a way of using these sources in the classroom; it also provides brief summaries of other biographies that our respondents cited: Winifred Gérin's *Emily Brontë*, Chitham's *A Life of Emily Brontë*, and Stevie Davies's *Emily Brontë: Heretic*. Chitham has written two other books that provide contextual material, *The Brontës' Irish Background* and *The Birth of* Wuthering Heights*: Emily Brontë at Work*, both excerpted in Hoeveler's edition. A broader assessment of the novel in its period, as well as information on its literary context, can be found in Kathleen Tillotson's *Novels of the 1840s*.

Although we target resources for the instructor, many of the works listed here are suitable for students, especially the books with illustrations of the moors and other sites pertinent to the novel, including Phyllis Bentley's *The Brontës and Their World* (reprinted in paperback as *The Brontës*) and Brian Wilks's *The Brontës* and *The Illustrated Brontës of Haworth*. The editions of *Wuthering Heights* by Peterson and by Heywood also include black-and-white photographs. For teachers or students who want to identify names, themes, and places in Brontë texts and lives, Christine Alexander and Margaret Smith's *Oxford Companion to the Brontës* provides the most comprehensive compilation. Miriam Allott's *The Brontës: The Critical Heritage* is the standard source for nineteenth-century reviews and other period assessments of the novel and the poems; extracts are included in Dunn's edition. Information on a range of adaptations, from the mid-nineteenth through the twentieth century, can be found in Patsy Stoneman's *Brontë Transformations: The Cultural Dissemination of* Jane Eyre *and* Wuthering Heights and in Lucasta Miller's *The Brontë Myth*.

Critical and Theoretical Studies

In going through the contributors' essays and the responses to our teachers' survey, we noticed that a few titles kept recurring. The most popular was Sandra M. Gilbert and Susan Gubar's *The Madwoman in the Attic*, a by-now-classic feminist analysis. Also winning several votes were Terry Eagleton's *Myths of Power*, an influential Marxist study of the novel; Leo Bersani's *A Future for Astyanax*, among the first books to theorize the connections between parts 1 and 2 of Emily Brontë's novel; J. Hillis Miller's "*Wuthering Heights*: Repetition and the 'Uncanny,' " a seminal deconstructive reading; and Von Sneidern's "*Wuthering Heights* and the Liverpool Slave Trade," a post-colonial study. Three older sources were also cited by several teachers: David Cecil's *Early Victorian Novelists* (though one respondent said she wanted her students to argue against it); C. P. Sanger's "The Structure of *Wuthering Heights*"; and Dorothy Van Ghent's New Critical classic, *The English Novel: Form and Function*. For a grounding in theory, several teachers recommended Peter Barry's *Beginning Theory*, as well as Michel Foucault's "What Is an Author?" and Roland Barthes's "The Death of the Author."

Additional Contextual Materials

In this category, we include material in media other than print. Primary among them is *The Brontës*, a CD-ROM edited by Tom Winnifrith, which provides reliable texts of all the novels and poems and the capacity for searching, so that, for example, the recurrence of any word can instantly be traced. This CD also provides more than three thousand manuscript images as well as six volumes of letters and juvenilia (unfortunately, from the less than accurate Wise and Symington edition).

A respondent to our teacher's survey asked how to give students a sense of the moors, beyond showing them photographs. Janet Gezari suggests using the first eight to ten minutes of *An American Werewolf in London*. Although mild objections may be raised to the dialogue, the atmosphere is fittingly wild. For a discussion of teaching the novel through its film and television (or video) adaptations, see the essay and appendix by Kamilla Elliott in this volume. An audio version of the novel, read by Patricia Routledge, can give students a sense of its aural context, as Dean de la Motte argues in his essay in this volume. For a different kind of auditory experience, several teachers and students suggest Kate Bush's pop song "Wuthering Heights."

Finally, there are a number of Web resources for the Brontës and *Wuthering Heights*. As our colleague Glenn Everett has pointed out, Web-based materials tend to be ephemeral, Web sites frequently change addresses (URLs), and state-of-the-art technologies may become outdated within a few years. As a result, we cannot guarantee that any of the sites below will remain as listed. Nonetheless, at the time of publication, these are the most useful ones.

Brontë.Info. The Web site of the Brontë Parsonage Museum and Brontë Society. <www.bronte.org.uk>.

Information is sorted under News and Events, The Brontës, The Museum, The Brontë Society, Haworth, and Resources—Educational and Research. There is a brief biography of Emily, a synopsis of *Wuthering Heights*, and an account of the village of Haworth during the mid-nineteenth century.

The Brontë Sisters Web. Ed. Mitsuharu Matsuoka. Graduate School of Languages and Cultures, Nagoya U, Japan. <www.lang.nagoya-u.ac.jp/~matsuoka/Bronte.html>.

Under "Emily," information is sorted under three headings: Chronology, Works and E-texts, and Academic Resources (which include unvetted amateur Web sites). Under "Haworth," there are good photographs of the moors. Under "Concordance," there is a complete concordance to *Wuthering Heights*. The site links to an online version of the novel.

Archives of VICTORIA. Ed. Jian Liu. A subdivision of the Victoria Research Web. 1993–current. Indiana University. <http://listserv.indiana.edu/archives/victoria.html>.

The archive of "The Electronic Conference for Victorian Studies" preserves online discussions of issues pertaining to Emily Brontë and *Wuthering Heights*. It is well indexed and can be used by nonsubscribers as well as members of its Listserv.

The Victorian Web. Ed. George P. Landow. <www.victorianWeb.org/>.

In the Authors section, information on Emily Brontë is sorted under five headings: Biographical Materials, Works, Cultural Contexts, Theme and Technique, Related Web Resources. Although, at this time, most entries are commonplace and the related resources not wholly reliable, this site has many useful articles on the Victorian period, and it is frequently updated.

Wuthering Heights On-Line: The Online Books Page. <http://onlinebooks.library.upenn.edu/webbin/book/search?title=Wuthering+Heights&mode=words>.

The Online Books Page provides links to four electronic versions of the novel, from

Nagoya University (Matsuoka), the University of Virginia, Bibliomania, and Project Gutenberg. These versions do not include notes, and there is no guarantee that the transcriptions are reliable.

The following URLs are for sites directed to students. All contain detailed summaries of *Wuthering Heights*, contextual information, and bulletin boards for student discussion.

<www.novelguides.com/ClassicNotes/Titles/wutheringheights>. This site includes "Editing Services" for student papers.

<http://pinkmonkey.com/booknotes/monkeynotes/pmWuthering01.asp>. This site, edited by Diane Sauder, links to Barron's *Booknotes*-Wuthering Heights.

<www.sparknotes.com/lit/wuthering/>. This is the site most frequently named by the students in our survey.

NOTES

[1]The percentages for type of course are based on responses from teachers who filled out our Teacher Survey Form and from others whose students filled out the Student Survey Form, which also indicates the name of the course.

[2]We use the word "extant" because other writings—material on Gondal, *devoirs*, letters—have probably been lost or destroyed. She may also have had a second novel in progress; if so, it too has vanished.

Wuthering Heights: A Family Tree*

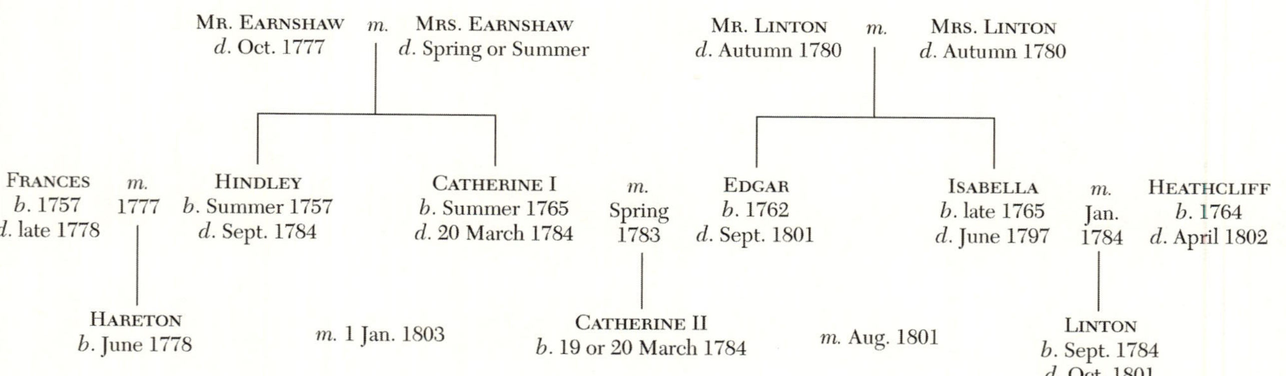

November 1801: Lockwood arrives at the Heights. Two days later, Ellen Dean begins her story.

*The genealogy of *Wuthering Heights* was first established by C. P. Sanger. Our chart includes a few modifications suggested by A. Stuart Daley.

What Students Say about Approaching *Wuthering Heights*

Because any book about teaching is, necessarily, a book about learning, we decided to go directly to the learners for responses to *Wuthering Heights*. To that end, when we were planning this volume, we designed a survey for students who had just read the novel in a college or university course. For over two years, responses have arrived from the United States, Canada, England, and Spain—in all, from 709 students in thirty-five courses. We have analyzed these data and, where relevant, compared them with statements from our teacher surveys. Although we do not claim that these findings are definitive, we hope they will give teachers information about the perspectives, concerns, and requests of students not unlike their own. (A sample form and an explanation of our methodology appears in the appendix following this article.)

Our aim throughout this section is to focus on the findings with the strongest implications for classroom practice. We present them first in a brief question-and-answer format. The explanations that follow are based on the evidence the surveys provided. We also include evidence from our teacher surveys wherever appropriate.

1. What do students want most when they are studying *Wuthering Heights*?

Our surveys offer two resounding answers: Give us a family tree, and let us talk.

The importance of a family tree first came up when we asked students whether they had had problems reading the novel and what helped, or would have helped, with those problems. Here are the five main areas they identified and the percentages of students citing them as problems.

Character confusion (keeping names and relationships straight)—38%
Joseph's dialect—30%
Confusing plot, chronology, narrative structure—12%
Difficult vocabulary—11%
Confusing shifts of narrators—9%

Of the students who indicated what could help eliminate character confusion, 84% responded "a family tree" or "genealogy." The importance of a family tree came up again when we asked students what resources connected to the novel they found most useful and what advice they would give to teachers. Their concern with keeping the characters straight was rarely corroborated by the teachers we surveyed or by most of the editors of *Wuthering Heights*.

Although most teachers are aware that Joseph's dialect is difficult and every reliable edition annotates it, only four of our respondents cited character confusion as an obstacle for their students, and only five editions (Nestor's, Jack's Feltman's, Barnes and Noble, and Modern Library) provide genealogical tables. (In Dunn, C. P. Sanger's genealogy is footnoted in Daley's article but not listed in the table of contents.) Three teachers said that they provided charts in the form of handouts or transparencies, and a few students similarly noted that they composed charts independently. One said, "To solve my confusion problem, I made a family tree of each family. For the women, I included maiden names in parenthesis. I also made a chart of who lived in each household and when."

A family tree can help with two other challenges that students identify: chronology and narrator confusion. However, a time line or narrative flowchart, like the one Leilani D. Riehle provides in her essay in this volume, more effectively addresses these concerns. In fact, half the students who admitted to narrative confusion said that a time line was (or would have been) helpful. Whether the source of confusion is chronology or the narrator's identity, students seem to benefit when the instructor goes over the charts with them, preferably early in the teaching process, and provides them with copies or has them make their own for subsequent reference and additions. A sample family tree appears at the end of the preceding section, "The Instructor's Library."

The importance of discussions came up when we asked students to rank the activities they found useful in their study of *Wuthering Heights*, with 1 as most and 4 as least useful. Following are the activities they ranked as most useful:

Discussion—59%
Lectures—31%
Papers/assignments—6%
Other activities—3%

Asked to explain their first and second choices, students replied overwhelmingly that discussion was useful for hearing other perspectives and ideas. They also indicated that discussion helped them understand and interpret the novel; that it brought out what they had not thought of or had missed; that it eliminated confusion; that it promoted closer reading. Their main point, however, was the value of exchange—of hearing, sharing, expressing, and refining ideas about *Wuthering Heights*. We quote several of their comments:

> Discussion is the most helpful because it's interactive. It exposes you to new and different readings, but also allows you to voice your own ideas, get feedback, and develop them. Good discussion keeps ideas from stagnating.

> I may not have agreed with the opinions presented, but they did cause me to read more carefully and think more critically about the text.
>
> Discussing, and to a lesser extent being lectured about, the novel brought up several points I had missed and forced me to think about them pretty carefully. Discussion especially, because you are held accountable for your thoughts.

These responses do not imply that a teacher's guidance is expendable. In fact, a number of students praised their professor's discussion-leading skills. They explained that lectures were useful because of the professor's knowledge and enthusiasm and that lectures promoted comprehension and insight, showed them what to look for, provided information on context and background, and taught them about various approaches to the novel. Still, of the thirty-five classes we have surveyed, only three rated lectures above discussion, a fact that suggests that students need to supplement the act of reading with oral communication.

2. What do students like about *Wuthering Heights*?

Our surveys show that nearly three-quarters like the novel—for its "love story," its drama, its character relationships, its narrative complexity, and (in fewer numbers) its language and its wild gothic atmosphere. These responses do not always accord with what teachers say about student preferences.

To determine how students respond to the novel, the survey form offered them a five-point scale. Following are the results of their ranking:

Really like—32%
Like—42%
Find it fair—17%
Don't like much—6%
Really dislike—3%

Since we did not identify gender, we do not know whether this distribution corroborates the claim of several teachers that women students like the novel far more than men do. It is also possible that disaffected students did not fill out the surveys. Nonetheless, the figures indicate that *Wuthering Heights* continues to engage undergraduate (and graduate) students.

The survey then asked students to indicate what they liked best about the novel. Since the teachers' survey posed a similar question (What do students find most engaging?), we looked for similarities and differences. In both sets of responses, the Catherine-Heathcliff "love story"—the drama of passion, conflict, loss, and vengeance—scored highest. Closely connected, particularly on the student surveys, is an interest in the characters and in their relationships. However, the surveys suggest contrasts between students' and teachers' responses. According to 40% of the teachers, students find Heathcliff compelling. One teacher wrote, "I am continually astonished about how many students, female and male, are seduced by Heathcliff in ways that replicate Isabella's infatuation." Half a dozen others referred to their students' love-hate relationship with him, and one noted that bringing those mixed feelings to the foreground can launch a productive discussion.

Yet among students who said they liked the characterization, only about a sixth cited Heathcliff by name and over half of those added qualifications. They found him fascinating as a character; they were drawn by the shift from victim to villain; his violence kept them engaged: "the characters are *so* extreme, you love to hate them, and *must* find out how the story ends." In fact, many if not most of these respondents drew distinctions between representation and reality, using terms they had learned in their courses. As one said, "I felt I was supposed to sympathize with [Heathcliff] and see him as a 'Byronic Hero,' but I saw him more as a gothic villain."

Even so, a substantial minority confirmed the observation by Maureen T. Reddy that students are "enamored of romance plots" and want to slot the characters into them. Pop-culture versions reinforce the expectations that make students like this one unhappy: "I came to the novel with the preconceived notion that . . . I would fall in love with Heathcliff. I didn't, and I read in constant anticipation of loving him, and was disappointed when I didn't."

In these surveys, though, naive readers were outnumbered by those who praised the novel for its formalistic qualities, especially the complex narrative structure (which ranks second under "What do you like best?") and the vivid language and imagery. Throughout, we found a mixture of emotional responses—"scary," "wild," "violent," "dark"—and attempts to use a more critical vocabulary: "framing narrators," "gothic" elements, "psychological realism." Several students showed an awareness of context, saying that they liked the novel because it defied Victorian norms.

3. What do students know about *Wuthering Heights* before taking their current course?

Thirty-four percent of the students we surveyed said that they had read the novel before, either in a class or on their own. From their responses, we could not determine how many had studied it in high school. However, in an online discussion of the novel's prominence in high school English courses, "a veteran teacher" noted "that *Wuthering Heights* is the title most often listed" among the works that students can select for the open-ended essay question on the Educational Testing Service's Advanced Placement English Literature exam (see Walters). While this observation suggests that an upper tier of high school students spends considerable class time on the novel, our findings indicate that most college students do not have this kind of preparation.

Still, 54% of our respondents said that they had heard of *Wuthering*

Heights. We asked them to describe what they had heard or seen. The commonest responses follow:

Film or video, whole or clip—39%
Former class, teacher, and/or criticism—24%
Reputation, rumor—18%
Relative or friend—11%
Other—8%

The films that students reported seeing vary—from the MGM classic, directed by William Wyler and featuring Laurence Olivier and Merle Oberon, through MTV's 2003 attempt at an update (directed by Suri Krishnamma)—but the fact that they receive their first impressions from this medium suggests that they will enter with misleading assumptions, like the "preconceived notion" of the student we quoted above. Two of our contributors, Patsy Stoneman and Kamilla Elliott, consider this issue in their essays.

4. What resources and activities do students find most useful?

Our respondents highlighted four resources that helped them in their study of the novel. Films and articles tied for top place, followed closely by handouts and then Web-based information.

Students from two-thirds of the classes in our survey reported viewing films or clips. In contrast, just under half of the teachers we surveyed reported showing them, and one added that he refrained "by design" from using film or video. While several factors—the nature of the course, time constraints, availability—can influence decisions to show or not to show films, the students' perspective can also be factored in. The ones we surveyed said films or clips helped them "see" the characters and context, provided opportunities for contrast, and offered other interpretations of the text. As one said, "Watching the old film version was interesting because it showed how culture mediates texts for us." No respondents, however, said they preferred a movie to the text, and a few noted that film had increased their appreciation of the novel.

Students from twenty-four of the thirty-five classes in our survey reported receiving handouts. The most popular (as noted earlier) were family trees and time lines. Also appreciated were handouts that illuminated character, structure, and theme or that guided them to key moments or areas. As one said, "I found that the handouts were the best because I didn't have to wade through entire articles to get the exact information I wanted or needed. For more in-depth I did my own follow-up."

Although fewer than 20% of all respondents explained why Web resources or articles were helpful, the contrasts are worth noting. Under "articles," students referred to a range of supplementary readings: biographical, contextual, and critical essays, as well as period reviews. Students found them useful for providing additional insight and knowledge and for promoting awareness of critical approaches and interpretations. In other words, articles deepen and complicate students' experience of the text. Web resources, too, embrace a range of possibilities: online information provided by the teacher, articles and study guides available through the Internet, and threaded discussions, or blackboards, that enable students to talk to one another. The leading reasons students gave for seeking Web resources—whether or not the teacher recommended them—were to get basic textual information and to "clarify" or sort out what confused them; they tended to use these resources to "summarize" and "simplify." While simplification runs counter to the aims of nearly all teachers of *Wuthering Heights,* students who believe there is a "right" way to read it may try to reduce their discomfort through resources increasingly available online. Eleven respondents recommended Sparknotes.com or said that it had helped them. Cliff Notes, York Notes, Coles Notes, and Pinkmonkey.com were also cited as aids. To combat reliance on such resources, teachers might attend to the advice these students offer:

> Make sure to emphasize how the book does not pass judgment on the story. . . . The whole gist of this book is to leave it up to the individual.

> Get students involved. We learn more through active participation, and it forces students to keep up with the reading.

5. What do students say about the use of theory? How do their attitudes toward theory compare with those of teachers?

We begin this answer with qualifications. Unless respondents volunteered the information, we did not necessarily know whether they were in classes that emphasized theory. Even when we had coordinate surveys from teachers, we could not always tell whether those teachers assigned theoretical articles directly, cited such approaches explicitly in lectures, or incorporated theory into classroom practice without attributing its origins. Furthermore, we asked students no direct questions about the use of critical approaches.

Nonetheless, given the current predominance of theory and the number of instructors who apply it to this novel, we would have expected students to allude to the topic in comments under several other categories—for example, useful resources and activities. In fact, only 6% referred to specific critics or articles or, alternatively, to the back-of-book essays in Peterson and in Sale and Dunn. Six cited Gilbert and Gubar's *The Madwoman in the Attic*, four cited Eagleton's "Myths of Power," and two cited Von Sneidern on the Liverpool slave trade. No other critic or critical essay was named by more than one respondent.

Does this result imply that most students were unconcerned with theory, or could there be other explanations? Comments on our surveys suggest that some students were indeed intrigued by critical approaches—feminist, gothic, narratological—but that they used a less professional vocabulary to express this interest. For instance, one called *Wuthering Heights* "the perfect novel to introduce [different literary themes] in because it can be read with them all." Then, too, students might have been unaware that many of the insights they gathered in class were grounded in the contributions theorists have made to the study of this text and of literature. Despite some engagement with theory, though, most respondents talked about traditional elements: character, plot, setting, theme, symbol, imagery. Another survey might be conducted to discover, from the students' perspective, how patterns of interest shift as undergraduates progress through the major and into graduate-level courses. Here, however, we have deliberately kept conjecture to a minimum, but we invite our readers to theorize about these results.

We concede that, although our sample is diverse, it represents only a small proportion of all courses on *Wuthering Heights* and that, since the survey was voluntary, some students chose not to take it. Still, we note that the novel itself provides a rationale for this project. As virtually all teachers point out, the book's narrative is mediated through tellers who may or may not be reliable. Readers must therefore consider the teller's stake in representing the events and the characters and adjust their perspectives accordingly.

While the narrative of classroom practice is rarely considered in the same terms as the plot of a novel, it is typically written by teachers who report on their students' responses—in other words, by mediators who may or may not be fully informed and who may or may not be invested in maintaining subjective positions. Although this essay, too, is mediated by an author whose selection and ordering of data are subjective, the surveys are archived and available for inspection. We close by suggesting that teachers of the novel administer the survey to their own students to see whether the results accord with these findings and, more important, to acquire the information that learners alone can provide.

APPENDIX
The Student Survey

The survey form that we distributed asks students to identify their school and their course. In a brief introduction, we explain that we want to make students' views better known to educators and help future teachers of the novel. We note that participation is voluntary and that the teacher will not see the forms until after final grades are submitted. We also ask students to indicate whether they will permit us to quote them anonymously. The questions are as follows:

1. Had you read *Wuthering Heights* before you took this course?
   Yes ______ No ______
2. Had you heard or seen anything related to it before this course?
   Yes ______ No ______
   If yes, please describe:
3. How would you rate your response to *Wuthering Heights* on the following scale?
   Really like ______ Like ______ Find it fair ______
   Don't like much ______ Dislike ______
4. What do you like best about the novel?
5. What do you dislike most about it?
6. In what ways, if any, did you have problems reading the novel?
7. What helped or would have helped you with those problems?
8. Which of the following did you find useful in your study of *Wuthering Heights*? Rank from 1 (most useful) to 4 (least useful) or leave blank if not applicable.
   Lectures ______ Discussions ______ Assignments/Papers ______
   Other Activities ______
   If you include "Other Activities," please describe.
9. What made your first and second choices in question 8 useful?
10. Which resources connected to the novel—handouts, articles or chapters, Web-based information, film versions, other—were most useful? Why?
11. Please use this space to offer any further comments or suggestions that would be helpful to people who teach *Wuthering Heights*.

We drew the teachers who administered the survey from three sources: our contributors, respondents to an ad placed on the Victorian Web, and respondents to announcements at conferences. Four teachers who taught *Wuthering Heights* in different contexts submitted surveys from two courses. The number of students in the courses ranged from two to forty-three; the average was twenty.

Part Two

APPROACHES

Introduction

In the process of developing this volume, we have been particularly interested in creating an anthology that responds to the breadth of approaches applied to the text. *Wuthering Heights* works well in numerous subject areas—women's writing, gothic narrative, and Victorian and nineteenth-century literature. Moreover, its narrative design and complex character development make it well suited to courses in theory. And its presence in courses on contemporary popular culture and on composition attests to its continuing popularity. In other words, *Wuthering Heights* remains a relevant and versatile text. However, the novel is not always accessible for students; many struggle with the genealogical elements, the complicated narrative structure, the historical moment, the violence, Joseph's dialect, and the problem of identifying with difficult characters, especially Heathcliff and Catherine. The essays in this volume respond to these concerns in ways that highlight the rich and vibrant readings available to students and instructors.

We have also responded to teachers' requests for information on theory and practice. These essays show how theories are applied in the classroom, and they offer practical ideas and methods that teachers can transfer to their courses. Seventy-one percent of instructors participating in the teacher survey noted that they use theory in their classes. They may teach it to a greater or lesser extent and may or may not assign critical articles, although the number who assign such readings is significantly smaller. The results of the student survey suggest, however, that students seem unaware of the theoretical approaches to which they are being introduced (a point we noted in item 5 under "What Students Say"). Few named a particular approach or identified a critical essay. The writers of the essays in this volume, by contrast, are drawn to the rich theoretical approaches offered by *Wuthering Heights*.

In many ways, the differences between student and teacher survey results capture the very challenge and pleasure of teaching *Wuthering Heights*. Although the work is easily adapted to a range of theoretical approaches, it tends to defy theory and complicate any analysis. As Beth Newman notes in her essay, critics respond to the mythic elements of the text, but they also work hard to root the text in its historical moment. Yet an appreciation for the historical does not undermine the significance of the mythic. The two operate in tandem. As they read *Wuthering Heights*, teachers and students must juggle competing approaches to the text: violence as destructive and violence as communicating affection; class, gender, and race as positions that define one another and are inseparable from narrative; and the canon and popular culture engaged in a mutually reinforcing relationship.

The authors of these essays self-consciously demonstrate how instructors can help students recognize that what they are engaging in—whether close reading or psychoanalytic criticism—is based on the application of a particular theoretical approach to the text. Students can thus be encouraged to see themselves as participating in a process of criticism. Similarly, the essays draw attention to the ways in which students question the very theories teachers value. Instructors learn from their students as often as students learn from their teachers, and these essays emphasize the reciprocal relationship that exists in the classroom.

We divide the essays into five sections: "Historical and Social Contexts," "Literary and Disciplinary Contexts," "Theories of Interpretation," "Imagining and Reimagining *Wuthering Heights*," and "Building Skills through Teaching *Wuthering Heights*." In addition to these thematic approaches, we provide, after the general overview, a series of alternative groupings that respond directly to other teacher and student concerns that emerged in the process of collecting the surveys.

Thematic Approaches

"Historical and Social Contexts" refers to the cultural moment of the text. We start here because of the importance of rooting the text in its history. *Wuthering Heights* has often seemed to defy historical analysis, many critics and teachers arguing that the book does not fit its time. Recent criticism has disputed that claim. The four essays in this section reveal the surprises hidden in *Wuthering Heights*—that race, gender, and class are moving targets located only through close analysis of the narrative in its sociohistorical context. Beth Newman's essay sets *Wuthering Heights* within the text's historical moment, paying special attention to the effects of industrialization, Liverpool as a site of the slave trade, the development of a rural middle class, the potential for downward and upward mobility in the elder Cathy's and Heathcliff's experiences, and the formation of a "fairly homogenous national culture" with the "weakening of regional differences." Carine M. Mardorossian's essay builds on Newman's suggestion that readers should delay any closure of Heathcliff's racial identity. Through creative close readings, Mardorossian teaches students to construe race, like gender and social class, as an unstable and incoherent position; she challenges the stable position we typically confer on race—an approach inherited from nineteenth-century pseudo-scientific thought. Mardorossian argues that characters are "blackened" and "whitened" when placed in relationship with each other. Cathy, for instance, when compared with Isabella, is blackened; in contrast, her stay at Thrushcross Grange whitens her.

As Mardorossian interrogates race, Barry V. Qualls similarly observes that *Wuthering Heights* calls basic categories of gender and class into question. Through an analysis of Victorian conduct books, Qualls argues that we should see the elder Catherine in the light of her subjection to the prescribed gender and class roles that she "cannot resist" and that thus drive her mad. He concludes that the "confinements of gender and class transform Heathcliff," kill Catherine, and construct Lockwood. Moreover, Qualls suggests, the ambiguities of gender (the narrative representation of Edgar's softness, yet Catherine's perception that he preys on her) reveal the more subtle forms of violence in the text, a point that serves as a transition to Catherine R. Hancock's essay on violence.

Hancock addresses the difficulty of teaching a novel filled with so much brutality, both subtle and apparent. Arguing that violence is a form of verbal and nonverbal communication, she considers how love and hate are expressed through violent language and actions. Looking at Heathcliff's manipulation of physical violence (mostly against women) and psychological violence (mostly against men), Hancock examines the ways in which women serve as the landscape on which male homosocial competition is played out. The theme of violence emerges in other essays, including those of Lisa Surridge (on Victorian legal and popular cultural responses to violence), Maureen T. Reddy (on violence's one-dimensionality in Hoffman's *Here on Earth*), Tamar Heller and Frances Beer (on the gothic and biographical elements of violence), and Diane Long Hoeveler (on beatings as a part of the masochistic-sadistic psychoanalytic framework).

The second section, "Literary and Disciplinary Contexts," provides solid teaching material on biography, gothic literature, and the discipline of English. In addition, the three essays help instructors introduce students to scholarly and critical debates about *Wuthering Heights* as a means of encouraging them to approach the text the way teachers do—as a vital narrative, open to multiple and competing interpretations. Heller's essay on female gothic literature considers the increased interest in a once-marginalized discipline. Like the writers in the first section, Heller comments on the ways in which boundaries of race and class are crossed; however, she places the crossing in the framework of gothic literature, which values boundary transgression, liminality, and character duality, as evidenced in the mother-daughter relationship. She, too, looks at the way gothic conventions depicted in the text (adulterous women, marital violence, and women's relationship to property) are products of the historical time period as well as the genre of gothic literature. In this way, Heller introduces students to an important genre.

Beer moves from genre to biography. She looks at standard Brontë family biographical issues such as death, loss, and cruelty, and she considers the biographical elements in other works by Emily Brontë, including the diary papers and the Belgian essays. Of particular note, Beer introduces students to the biographical debates, including Juliet Barker's and Elizabeth Gaskell's conflicting positions on Charlotte Brontë's interpretation of Emily, and Mary Visick's, Fannie E. Ratchford's, and Janet Gezari's differing conclusions on the Gondal poems. By placing the biographers' and critics' agendas in a kind of dialogue with each other, Beer teaches students how critics debate biography. Students are encouraged to participate in the debate by constructing a "composite portrait" after reading the various opinions.

Paula M. Krebs introduces students to the disciplinary debate on canonical literature and English studies. Her attention to numerous theoretical approaches (such as feminism, reception theory, cultural studies, race theory) helps students engage with the disciplinary conflicts on canon and theory. As a result, students learn how *Wuthering Heights* participates in these debates and how they, as readers and English majors, are members of a "discursive community of English studies."

In the third section, "Theories of Interpretation," we respond directly to teachers' requests for essays on general introductions to theory courses and on specific theoretical approaches, such as psychoanalysis, new historicism, narrative structure, film study, and deconstruction. Suzy Anger's essay, which opens this section, provides a logical transition from Krebs's, since both introduce senior-level students to theoretical interpretation. However, whereas Krebs starts with theory and ends with the novel, Anger begins with the novel and moves into theory. She first helps students identify their "perspective-free" positions ("everyone has his or her own opinion") and then, after calling these positions into question, she raises a variety of theories for students to explore, including New Criticism, psychoanalysis, Marxism, and poststructuralism. She asks students to consider whether "theory creates the text or makes apparent something that is already there." As in Krebs's case, concentrating on one book offers students a number of reading strategies and a rich theoretical vocabulary.

Anger's essay lays the groundwork for the next four essays in this section by suggesting ways to make theory the primary focus of the class. Hoeveler focuses on psychoanalysis, one of the subjects most requested for examination in this volume. By paying attention to dream analysis, fairy tales, and maturation theories, Hoeveler provides instructors with basic psychoanalytic principles; like Beer, she considers the importance of biography, although she reads it from a psychoanalytic perspective. Hoeveler's essay contains an appendix of Web sources on psychoanalysis.

Leilani D. Riehle looks at narrative structure, another subject heavily requested by teachers. Her essay addresses the complexity of the narrative—with its repetitions and circularity. Similarly, she considers ways in which the reliability of the narrators, the uncertainty of the relation between the real and the unreal, and the complexity of the character development make Emily Brontë's novel a struggle for most readers. Her essay includes a detailed diagram for studying the narrative structure in relation to the larger plot.

Surridge presents concrete strategies for introducing students to historical analysis; she gives students primary historical and legal texts and sends them out to do research. Through this method she covers a range of issues, including child custody, the Married Women's Property Act, and wife assault. By turning documents over to students, she empowers them as critics. It may be useful to read Newman's and Krebs's articles in conjunction with Surridge's. Like Newman, Surridge considers the importance of the historical moment to the text; however, like Krebs, she speaks of the disciplinary imperatives that must underlie students' introduction to new historicism.

Patsy Stoneman's essay moves away from the canon to provide a student- and teacher-friendly approach to deconstruction and its application to film, media, and other visual representations of *Wuthering Heights.* Just under half the teacher survey respondents said that they use film or film clips at some point in their discussion; Stoneman (and, later, Elliott) offers useful strategies for these instructors. Stoneman helps students question their assumptions that film adaptations are more or less the same as the book and that authorial intent is key. Using the moors as an example, she reveals that only two scenes in the novel are set there; in contrast, visual and media images of the elder Cathy and Heathcliff on the moors have proliferated. Her deconstructionist reading suggests the sources of the discrepancy.

The fourth section, "Imagining and Reimagining *Wuthering Heights*," considers a wide range of intertextual responses, from film and television adaptations to audio recordings to novels inspired by the original text. Novels emerge out of a sociohistorical and literary context, and, similarly, they provide fuel to spark other fires—new texts that rewrite the original. Contemporary literature and film are rife with reimaginings of the Brontës' work, Charlotte's as well as Emily's. The three essays in this section highlight the subtleties of the "originary" text that emerge when it is paired with auditory, visual, and narrative versions and revisions. Kamilla Elliott's essay on film and television adaptations provides a good transition from Stoneman's. Elliott considers adaptation as a form of literary revision and criticism; she does so by analyzing a range of cinematic texts, from William Wyler's 1939 version through Jane Campion's *The Piano*. She also looks at questions of authenticity, at issues of literary criticism in adaptation, and at intertextuality and representation in different time periods and cultural locations. The appendix to her essay contains a detailed filmography of television and cinematic versions of *Wuthering Heights*.

Dean de la Motte's essay on language and social class uses audio recordings of *Wuthering Heights* to consider how hearing the words aloud makes the issue of class clearer. As de la Motte notes, contemporaries of Emily Brontë would have understood the subtleties of dialect and social class that emerge in speech patterns, whereas for many students and teachers, those subtleties are often lost. Language, the essay reveals, functions as a marker of class, age, gender, and emotional and social conditions. Listening to the text also highlights elements that might be skimmed over or invisible in reading—for example, servants who appear are generally forgotten or dismissed. This form of imagining the text helps center what had been marginal; it also keeps the focus on language and speech, a major concern for both teacher and student survey participants. In response to complaints about the difficulty of understanding Joseph's dialect, Newman suggests that students and teachers should "concentrate less on what he says than on the effects" of what he says on others. It might be useful to read de la Motte's essay in conjunction with Newman's (on reading aloud) and Mardorossian's (on Heathcliff's childhood language as gibberish).

The third essay in this section, by Reddy, focuses on the literary reimaginings of *Wuthering Heights*, primarily Alice Hoffman's *Here on Earth*. Although not all instructors would choose to teach Hoffman with Brontë's novel, they will find in Reddy's essay suggestions for other texts to read with *Wuthering Heights*, as well as strategies for dealing with intertextuality—including attention to plot similarities between two works, to the difference between a third-person and a first-person narrator, to race issues, and to students' more likely identification with contemporary texts. Reddy notes that an intertextual approach encourages students to view *Wuthering Heights* with increased enthusiasm because of its strengths in comparison with later versions. At the same time, this approach helps students pinpoint what may be missing in the original text.

The final section, "Building Skills through Teaching *Wuthering Heights*," examines several techniques instructors can apply in the classroom and in writing assignments. More than 90% of our survey respondents give written assignments, mostly brief reactions but also critical and research papers. About 28% do some form of group work, and between 22% and 26% use presentations, Internet sources, quizzes, or photos or drawings. While the previous essays rely on a variety of these strategies to motivate students, the essays in this section focus on methodology—on composition assignments, close reading exercises, and collaborative work. Tricia Lootens's essay on ballads and composition studies offers an effective transition from the section on imaginings of *Wuthering Heights* because ballads function as another kind of reimagining or literary-critical approach to the text. This essay is particularly important not only for its attention to critical writing practices, narration, and authorship but also for its focus on Brontë's poetic writings.

Paul Vita discusses close reading in the framework of New Critical perspectives. In contrast to other contributors' emphasis on particular theories, he argues that New Criticism teaches students how to interpret rather than how to identify or apply specific interpretations. However, he locates close reading within a rich critical tradition—stressing diction, metaphor, irony, and figures of speech. In an appendix, Vita includes a student's writing sample, which illustrates the student's developing powers of analysis.

Laraine Fergenson presents collaborative learning exercises as a way to start group discussion while she thematically focuses on the question of education and dispossession in the text. As Fergenson observes, her students' educational position mirrors many of the concerns in the novel, and *Wuthering Heights* becomes a means of discussing their own desire to gain an education.

Fergenson's claim that the cessation of education represents severer punishment than any beating contrasts directly with Hancock's position and thus provides another example of competing yet viable approaches to the novel. In addition, the three concluding essays equip teachers with a range of methods they might use to start discussion or to focus student writing on *Wuthering Heights*.

Alternative Groupings

Beyond these categories, we offer alternative groupings that respond to specific instructor questions and concerns. One concern was the difficulty of maintaining student interest in the second part of the novel, since the story of young Cathy and Hareton is not as compelling as that of Catherine and Heathcliff. To help students see the importance of the second part, turn to Hancock (on positive displays of violence between Cathy and Hareton), Heller (on the gothic convention of mothers and daughters), de la Motte (on language and education), Qualls (on the domesticated order of the second part and ambivalent responses to that order), Riehle (on methods to encourage discussion), and Fergenson (on Hareton's education and dispossession). Also turn to Elliott for discussion of cinematic and television versions that present the second part.

Instructors also note, ironically, that even though students express greater interest in Catherine and Heathcliff, they have difficulty sympathizing with them, especially with Catherine. For help with this problem, turn to Hancock, Surridge, Newman, and Reddy. In particular, Newman recommends looking separately at Heathcliff's and Catherine's motivations and emotions, to consider ways in which their relationship might be understood differently through their individual positions. This approach runs counter to the narrative implication that the two are merged as one character, as expressed in the "I *am* Heathcliff" (73) assertion. Reddy also notes that looking at Catherine after reading Hoffman's version of her complicates students' interpretations. Catherine seems less a victim and more passionate, and the comparison also highlights the absence of female friendship and support in her life.

The two most referenced scenes in the essays are, not surprisingly, Catherine's "I *am* Heathcliff" statement and the romp on the moors that results in Catherine's stay at Thrushcross Grange. For further discussion on her statement, see Newman, Mardorossian, Qualls (on smothering gender roles), Heller (on duality in gothic literary texts), Elliott (on video renderings of the scene), and Lootens (on Nelly's narration and role in the scene). For the Thrushcross visit, turn to Stoneman (on discussion of the outside-versus-inside dichotomy), Mardorossian (on racial language), Qualls and de la Motte (on class and gender language), Heller (on gothic violence), and Hoeveler (on psychoanalytic issues of gluttony). Teachers also mentioned students' inclination to discuss the moors—even though, as Stoneman notes, they are the backdrop for only two episodes in the novel. These essays provide varying explanations for reader fascination with this location.

Survey respondents expressed interest in current discussions about gender, class, race, and queer studies in the novel. Although almost every essay addresses gender in some form or another, some essays focus more directly than others. See Qualls (on domestic conduct books), Heller (on the female gothic), Hancock (on women and domestic violence), Mardorossian (on the relationship between gender and race), Hoeveler (on psychoanalysis and female body trauma), Surridge (on legal and historical issues of gender), and Reddy (on teaching the novel in a women's studies course). Social class is also referenced in numerous articles, but readers may wish to turn to the following in particular: Mardorossian (on the nexus of race and class), Newman (on the elder Cathy's social position), Anger (on Marxism), de la Motte (on language as an indicator of class), and Vita (on the merging of ownership and economic issues). Like class and gender, race is a central topic for discussion; instructors can read Reddy, Newman, and especially Mardorossian for a sustained discussion of the topic. Finally, readers may turn to Krebs for an examination of queer studies and student essays.

Most of the essays address contextual issues, such as history, cultural context, and biography. See Newman and Surridge on historical and cultural context. For biography, turn to Beer (on the debates among Brontë biographers), Hoeveler (on pscyhoanalysis and biography), and Fergenson (on education and the Brontës). Of particular interest may be legal issues of the nineteenth century. See Hancock (on domestic abuse and the law), Heller (on the Married Women's Property Act), and Surridge (on legal documents).

Instructors repeatedly indicated that the narrative positions of Nelly Dean and Lockwood represent crucial points of discussion. Riehle addresses this issue at length. Readers might also turn to Anger (on Lockwood and his narrative position), de la Motte (on Nelly and Lockwood), Lootens (on narrative position in the ballads as they illuminate narrative roles in *Wuthering Heights*), and Reddy (a brief but useful reference to the diminishing narrative roles in the second part). Dreams provide another narrative perspective and become an important way of telling the tale. Turn to Anger (on Lockwood's dream), Heller (on the gothic elements of dreams), and Hoeveler (on Freudian dream analysis). Similarly, authorial intent and biography are important to a discussion of narrative perspective. Look to Anger, Stoneman, Krebs, and Elliott for a discussion of authorial intent and then to Beer, Hoeveler, and Lootens for biographical issues.

Finally, the essays are part of a rich exploration of disciplinary issues. It would be interesting to read Surridge and Krebs together as they politicize student positions in relation to the text and the canon. Then, turn to Stoneman's, Anger's, and Vita's examinations of New Criticism, bearing in mind that close reading is also a politicized position that can engender elitism, as noted in Krebs. Vita also compellingly argues that the best theoretical approaches engage in close reading, and the essays in this volume substantiate that claim. Theoretical approaches in competition with one another can introduce students to the lively debates in the discipline of English studies.

The essays in this volume speak to one another in multiple ways, and all are concerned with the complexity of *Wuthering Heights*. The groupings we have cited are not the only ones that might be made, nor do we list all the essays that might fit these alternative groupings; still, we have tried to suggest the immensely varied ways in which the novel can be read and the multiple issues it raises.

In the end, *Wuthering Heights* remains a challenging text to teach. When we were soliciting essays for this volume, a colleague recommended that we include an essay on the topic "why I hate teaching *Wuthering Heights*." The laughter that followed the suggestion ended in a shared sigh. From personal experience, I know that when I am putting together my syllabus for a course on British gothic literature (where I most often teach *Wuthering Heights*), *Wuthering Heights* is often the last book I pull down off the shelf, although it is usually the first book on my mind. I fear that I, like Lockwood, am sometimes a poor reader of the complexity of the characters and narrative before me. The pleasure of working on this volume has been to see how other instructors also struggle with this text and yet provide fascinating and compelling strategies to motivate student learning. One surprise from the student surveys is the degree to which students respond positively to the text. The essays in this volume challenge us to return to the text with a renewed sense of its relevance, its vitality, and its pleasure.

HISTORICAL AND SOCIAL CONTEXTS

Wuthering Heights in Its Context(s)

Beth Newman

Students are quick to embrace as self-evident the claim that a literary text should be interpreted in the light of history. Not surprisingly, they are less able to specify what the assertion means in practical terms and often less aware still of problematic assumptions they make about the meaning of terms like *history* and *context*. The latter may seem like something lying in wait, whose relation to a literary text, once it is known, needs no elaboration; and at least among many of my students, *history* is all too often reduced to an amorphous—and generally benighted—"back then."

Teaching *Wuthering Heights* can provide a good opportunity to dispel some of this cognitive and epistemological haze, although it does so for reasons that may seem counterintuitive. First of all, the novel does not permit readers to draw casual inferences about its relation to its time. The story it tells is set back half to three-quarters of a century before the composition of the book. The novel rarely intimates the existence of a world outside the small, spare, isolated but intense one into which it absorbs us. Even though the novel's first word is a year—the "1801" that makes it possible to date much of the represented action precisely (see Daley)—the narrative never refers to the kinds of events, whether regional, national, or of wider compass, with which the term *history* is most readily associated. Readers seeking obvious historical markers may feel a bit like Lockwood contemplating the blankness of a snow-covered moor, uncertain where the road lies.

Moreover, Emily Brontë's operatic representations of passion have encouraged critics to describe her novel as mythological and cosmic or timeless and metaphysical. (Significantly, Terry Eagleton's project in *Myths of Power* is not to correct this perception but to explain why Brontë turned to myth in exploring the tensions she probed.) The story of two houses nearly destroyed by unconsummated desire and virulent hatred has widespread appeal in our time, and its archetypal plots of an outsider wreaking havoc on a community and of calculated, protracted revenge lend themselves to adaptations in many different cultural milieus. Filmmakers have retold the story of the first generation of Earnshaws and Lintons in settings as removed from the remote Yorkshire moors as medieval Japan, a Mexican chaparral, and upper-caste India. Students respond to the mythic quality of *Wuthering Heights*, and they should be encouraged to recognize and enjoy it. But we can and should help them understand the novel as a fictive engagement with a specific social world. We can demonstrate that Brontë's novel grapples with the conflicts and contradictions of mid-Victorian England—that rather than stand aloof from nineteenth-century discursive currents or tendencies, it participates in them and contributed to them.

I like to open classroom discussion by asking about the changes that took place in England between 1801, the date of the framing story provided by Lockwood's diary, and 1847, the year of the novel's publication. This approach invites the class to ponder the many possible contexts while fleshing out some of the defining features of life in the early nineteenth century. My students can usually point to the spread of industrialization or, if they have taken our British literature survey, to the Reform Act of 1832. I develop such references into a broad socioeconomic context by bringing up the political challenge that new urban and industrial interests posed to the traditional authority of landed proprietors like the Lintons, whose power the Reform Act worked to strengthen (Thompson 20–21). It is also useful to make clear that Haworth was by no means immune to the social and material pressures produced by industrialism: Juliet Barker reports in *The Brontës* (1994) that by the time Patrick Brontë arrived at Haworth with his family in 1820, there were already thirteen woolen mills (92); and more than once during Emily's lifetime, Haworth and neighboring Keighley experienced severe unemployment, industrial poverty, and Chartist agitation.

My goals in providing such information for my students are to foreground the contending social forces produced by the spread of industrialism and to set up the novel's representation of domestic life as a microcosm of the changing relations of class and power in English society as a whole. A little reflection on the technological advances that made industrialization possible may lead students to think about the age of steam and the building of the railroads—and therefore about the accelerated pace of travel and the consequent sense of England as a much smaller place by mid-century than at its beginning, when Lockwood makes his journey to the north of England, or for that matter in the 1770s, when Mr. Earnshaw traverses the sixty miles to Liverpool on foot. These were not academic matters to Emily Brontë. Her brother, Branwell, held a small administrative post on the new Leeds and Manchester

Railway in the early 1840s (Barker, *Brontës* 346), and the boom years of railway construction, 1844–49 (Newsome 30), coincide with the writing and publication of the novel. The making of a fairly homogeneous national culture by mid-century and the consequent weakening of regional differences serve as my second context.

I make it clear that other contexts are possible and that they can illuminate *Wuthering Heights* in different ways. As I solicit the class's input about changes between 1801 and 1847, students frequently mention Liverpool, the city to which Mr. Earnshaw travels. They may be able to link this thriving port with the global commerce of a growing empire and perhaps even with the transatlantic slave trade. According to Maja-Lisa Von Sneidern, Liverpool's role in the slave trade, already significant at the time of Mr. Earnshaw's journey there, had surpassed that of other English ports by the early nineteenth century. The trade and then slavery itself were abolished in the British Empire in 1807 and 1833, respectively. Framing *Wuthering Heights* in this context, Von Sneidern offers a compelling reading that posits African origins for Heathcliff and interprets the novel's depiction of romantic love as an eroticized master-slave dialectic, which she links to early nineteenth-century discourse about slavery. In introductory classes, I am more apt to mention this context than to develop it in detail, in part because I think it important to keep the question of Heathcliff's otherness as open as the text does itself. One way of doing so, however, is to entertain the possibility that Heathcliff has African origins.

In advanced classes, in which I expect direct engagement with literary criticism, I follow our reading of the novel with a pair of contextualizing studies, choosing either von Sneidern's article or Eagleton's chapter from *Myths of Power* and reading the work alongside Nancy Armstrong's "Emily's Ghost."[1] This exercise allows us to explore how scholars construct historical contexts; how contexts influence the interpretations we draw and the aspects of the text that emerge as meaningful; and the different ways in which we can conceive the text-context relationship. Both Eagleton and von Sneidern, for example, treat the literary text as an artifact produced within a social or discursive background with which it imaginatively engages. Armstrong demonstrates the alternative of treating the novel not as a response to a context that precedes it but as an artifact that shapes the social world into which it enters. She places the novel beside nineteenth-century cultural practices of touring the countryside, photographing its people, and collecting and publishing folklore. These activities often constructed the inhabitants of England's geographical periphery as rude, strange, and premodern. Armstrong draws parallels between these practices and the reception of *Wuthering Heights*, especially after Charlotte described it in the preface to the 1850 edition as "a rude and strange production" which, like its author, was the nursling of the wild, remote moors ("Preface" 324–25). Once cast in these terms, Emily Brontë's novel contributed to the process by which English identity was forged at the expense of those living in its provincial regions.

A consideration of the way critics conceive the relationship of text to context is most appropriate for advanced students who have already benefited from a full discussion of the text. I begin this discussion by reading aloud from the opening paragraphs, to bring to life the humor my undergraduates are apt to miss. Hearing Lockwood's elaborate self-introduction together with Heathcliff's gruff reply makes immediately clear that Lockwood is not the "reserved" person he claims to be (1) and leads handily to an examination of the differences, both psychological and cultural (here, regional), implied by his verbose politeness and Heathcliff's taciturnity. As students trace Lockwood's efforts to make sense of his new landlord, they can discover the social incongruities Heathcliff presents: "a dark-skinned gypsy in aspect," he is "in dress and manners a gentleman"; yet he lives in a house befitting "a homely, northern farmer" clad in knee breeches and gaiters (3). More baffling still, he presides over a house full of sullen inmates whose puzzling relationships to one another and ambiguous social status (Hareton's especially) lead Lockwood to a series of comic gaffes.

The novel's evocations of everyday life at Wuthering Heights reveal the unfolding of social change in both its temporal and geopolitical aspects, but readers not schooled in thinking about the sociohistorical contexts of fiction are likely to overlook the relevant details. Sandra M. Gilbert and Susan Gubar have observed that when Hindley returns from college after Mr. Earnshaw's death, he has acquired not only a wife but also new ways of dressing and speaking; in addition, he banishes the servants to the "back-kitchen" and contemplates converting a spare room into a wallpapered, carpeted parlor (*Wuthering Heights* 39). It's useful to draw attention to these details and to ask students to consider their social significance. "College" takes Hindley south, whether to Oxford or Cambridge; there he presumably learns to speak the received Midlands standard and to dress in a more genteel fashion. By segregating the servants, Hindley makes their labor less visible and creates a sharper distinction in everyday life between kin and other members of the household. This change makes it easy for him to reclassify Heathcliff as a servant and to impose the illusion of racial as well as class homogeneity onto the relatively heterogeneous social reality that undergirds both his household and the developing national consciousness.

More concretely, Hindley has reorganized life in his farmhouse so that it more closely resembles the domestic space of the evolving middle-class family, a space that by Emily Brontë's day had become the idealized, sentimentalized Victorian home. I remind students that contrary to the *Flintstones'* portrayal of a Stone Age bourgeois family in a cave, normative middle-class family structure is not timeless. It emerged between the earliest events in *Wuthering Heights* and Emily Brontë's childhood, that is, in the later eighteenth and early nineteenth centuries; it evolved as the manufacture of commodities moved out of and away from the home and as income-generating work became, among the middling ranks, almost the exclusive province of men. By 1847 this arrangement stood as the dominant family form, but in rural England of the 1770s it was only beginning to emerge.

Certainly for American students it helps to sort out the social distinction between the Earnshaws and the Lintons, especially because the houses are presented in such stark opposition that students may underestimate the Earnshaws' position. Nelly observes that Wuthering Heights is the "next best [house] in the neighborhood" after Thrushcross Grange (181); Eagleton identifies the Earnshaws with the yeomanry (*Myths* 112), a class of independent, often prosperous farmers who owned their land and were their own masters. Their ways of life and values differed from those of gentry like the Lintons, as suggested by the contrasting interiors of the houses and the presence on the Linton estate of a park—that is, land given over to leisure rather than to agriculture (see Levy 82–85.) Moreover, as Nelly tells Lockwood, Edgar "had a sweet, low manner of speaking, and pronounced his words as you do" (62). With the significance of these differences clarified, students can recognize the importance of Hindley's self-fashioning: he seeks to reduce the superficial signs of social distinction between himself and the gentry.

This is a good time to raise the question of Cathy's choice of Edgar over Heathcliff and to look closely at Nelly's "catechism" (69) of her in chapter 9. Many of my students are critical of Cathy's choice, pointing out the glibness of her answers to Nelly's question about why she loves Edgar (69–70), her acknowledgment that she is wrong to marry him (71), and what her language reveals about how fully she has bought into the project of upward mobility: "It would degrade me to marry Heathcliff, now" (71)—now that Hindley has brought him so low and now that she has been transformed from a "wild, hatless little savage" to a "dignified person" with higher prospects (46). One can complicate this critical view (or encourage others to do so) by emphasizing Cathy's reasonable fear of being reduced to poverty and by invoking the incestuous status of the fierce attachment between Heathcliff and Cathy. Nelly's objection that Cathy might meet another handsome, rich man is worth considering, too (69). In theory, she might, but her situation makes it unlikely: Cathy has no mother or other dutiful family member to make the necessary social connections. Furthermore, in terms of the companionate marriage that lies at the heart of the developing domestic ideal, Cathy no longer has much in common with Heathcliff: "And should I always be sitting with you. . . . What good do I get—What do you talk about? . . . It is no company at all, when people know nothing and say nothing" (61). Edgar, at least, is "pleasant to be with" (69). Nevertheless, Cathy's dissatisfaction in becoming the "lady of Thrushcross Grange" (111) and her self-alienation in her new identity account not only for her unwonted "seasons of gloom" after her marriage (81) but also for her fervid distraction during her second illness.

The persistent bond between Cathy and Heathcliff dominates most cinematic adaptations and prompts critics to invoke the term *myth*. Eagleton suggests that what originally draws the two together is that neither can expect to inherit property, unlike Hindley (*Myths*); but the fierce, adversarial, grave-defying attachment that the novel imagines seems to defeat any effort to account for it solely or primarily in social and material terms. Both Pauline Nestor and Patsy Stoneman (Introduction) have explored the novel's representation of Cathy and Heathcliff from a psychoanalytic perspective, as a fantasy about dissolving the boundary between self and other and thus returning to a time before ego and identity come into being. I find this reading not only illuminating in itself but also relevant to the social considerations I have been emphasizing here: it points to the nexus of the psychical and the social, which are necessarily intertwined in subjective experience. Cathy's "I *am* Heathcliff" (73) may be understood as an attempt to annul the distinctions of gender, race, and class that Hindley (standing in for the social world more generally) has enforced and from which identities are produced. Some members of the class may choose to regard Cathy's "mental illness" (136) as no more than the self-imposed fit of a spoiled young woman, but others will take more seriously the social and psychical factors that have produced her condition.

This point is important because students are sometimes hard-pressed to sympathize with either the elder Cathy or Heathcliff as individuals—a different matter from sympathizing with their longing to be together. A complex grasp of the novel simultaneously demands such sympathy and makes it difficult, not only because Nelly, by her own admission, is fond of neither but also because Heathcliff is brutal and Cathy is profoundly self-centered. Her "I *am* Heathcliff" may challenge "conventional notions of selfhood," as Nestor argues (xiv), but it does so by appropriating Heathcliff's self, as Von Sneidern's reading of his "complete submission to her will" suggests (178). One way of awakening some sympathy for Heathcliff is to ask whether, and how, his account of the bond between him and Cathy might differ from the one Cathy presents to Nelly. Even Nelly is moved to take his part when Cathy tries to persuade herself that Heathcliff "does not know what being in love is" (72).

Another way of getting students to sympathize with both characters is to consider the way their social situations, born of specific historical pressures, have contributed to their peculiar psychologies and their ways of coping with adversity. Among my students, a minority or working-class student often undertakes Heathcliff's defense on social grounds, speaking passionately about his status as an outsider and laying the charge of his brutality against his own brutal treatment. At such a point in the discussion, I link Heathcliff's remaking of himself during his absence to new possibilities for upward mobility, represented here as an opportunity for the oppressed to become the oppressor. Eagleton suggestively reads Heathcliff as the "indirect symbol of the aggressive industrial bourgeoisie of Emily Brontë's own time" (*Myths* 116). As for Cathy, Heathcliff's arrival in the guise of a (self-made) gentleman perhaps makes her regret what originally seemed the only reasonable choice; at the same time, his presence returns Cathy to the terrifying yet desirable prospect of the effacement of the self's boundaries and tears from its psychical moorings her acquired social identity as the "lady of Thrushcross Grange."

Inevitably my students express frustration with the incomprehensibility of Joseph's Yorkshire dialect. I encourage them to concentrate less on what he says than on the effects of Emily Brontë's representation of his speech and the meanings of those effects. I offer another reference to television cartoon sitcoms (this one more contemporary): Mike Judge's *King of the Hill*. Joseph's speech functions as the mumbling-drawling character Boomhauer's does: its near-incomprehensibility is the joke, the pleasure, and the point. This analogy takes us further into matters of place and audience, because the representation of Joseph's speech would likely seem comic to a literate, novel-reading audience, whether from inside or outside the region. It would be more comprehensible (and therefore more of an in-joke) to readers from the vicinity, but either way it would register as a deviation from the received standard. Joseph's dialogue therefore functions as a sign of Emily Brontë's consciousness of audience and of regional difference. In providing her striking transcription of Yorkshire speech, which the well-educated Brontës did not use but heard all around them, including at home, from the servants, Emily was playing off regional stereotypes that she knew her readers would bring with them to a novel about the north.

In fact, she was playing off what an early twentieth-century folklorist and historian called the "West Riding Dialect movement," a local phenomenon of the late 1830s (Moorman xxix). Like the collecting of ballads beginning in the late eighteenth century and the interest in folklore more generally throughout the nineteenth, the movement was a response to the homogenizing of national society among the educated, literate classes as wider segments of the geographic periphery became integrated into the core. By producing collections of poems, jokes, and stories written partially or entirely in dialect, participants in the movement expressed an ambivalent mixture of nostalgia for, condescension toward, and pride in the moribund local culture, which was depicted as surviving in backward rustics and was enjoyed by others who regarded themselves as being *among* but not quite *of* them, as Charlotte Brontë said of Emily in the preface to the 1850 edition. Emily's representation of the late eighteenth-century rural North for her Victorian readers is complemented and complicated by her comic portrait of the prissy, hypercultivated Lockwood, her surrogate for the urbane reader. Between the poles represented by these two characters lies her own ambivalent identity as a well-educated native of Yorkshire and the daughter of an upwardly mobile Irishman. She resisted the pressure to become more fashionably modern and bourgeois when, at the Pensionnat Heger in Brussels, she defiantly dressed in the out-of-date leg-of-mutton sleeves of the 1820s despite the ridicule of her classmates (Barker, *Brontës* [1994] 393).

The ending of the novel, with young Catherine poised to marry the newly "civilized" Hareton and move back to Thrushcross Grange, works neatly into the related contexts of a changing social structure and the homogenizing of regional differences. Instructors can usefully put to students the questions that criticism has taken up in a variety of ways: Is the picture of cozy, genteel domesticity to be welcomed or regretted? Is the devastation of Joseph's productive currant and gooseberry bushes for an ornamental bed of Grange flowers (284) a positive sign or an ominous one? Is the shutting up of Wuthering Heights and the planned removal to Thrushcross Grange a symbol of the disappearance of the yeomanry and the triumph of a more socially homogenized gentility? Or has the restoration of the old house to its "ancient stock" (298), along with the Earnshaw appropriation of the Grange and its lands, reinvigorated a world ravaged by the rapacity of the "aggressive industrial bourgeoisie" in its new social alliance with land (the spiritual vacuity of which is suggested by Linton Heathcliff, the offspring of a Heathcliff and a Linton)? To frame the questions this way is to emphasize the novel's largely symbolic representation of social forces over the subjective dynamics of Heathcliff's obsession with the elder Cathy and his hope of becoming one with her, finally, in death. Their longing for each other is the recalcitrant mythic remainder of *Wuthering Heights*, which resists being rationalized away in terms of contending social forces. Helping our students understand these forces should not prevent us from acknowledging the novel's enduring mythic power.

NOTE

[1]A shorter version of the Armstrong essay appears in Peterson's 1992 and 2003 editions of the novel.

Geometries of Race, Class, and Gender: Identity Crossing in *Wuthering Heights*

Carine M. Mardorossian

My undergraduate students tend to be extremely adept at identifying the transgressions of class and gender identities in *Wuthering Heights*. Like generations of readers before them, they are struck by the elder Cathy's and Heathcliff's uncanny ability to cross boundaries of class and gender. I usually spend several sessions highlighting the relentless challenges to social norms and conventions these two and other characters in the text embody. What is much less obvious to students and what my subsequent discussion of the novel's racial logic seeks to reveal is, first, the way class and gender dynamics in the narrative are inextricably articulated with racial meanings throughout (race itself inversely acquires its meaning through its articulation with the other categories of social identity), and, second, the fact that racial identity as a social category of belonging is no more stable and coherent than class and gender are. Because race, too, functions as a site of crossing, we need to detect and explain its patterns in relation to other identities.

What I seek to accomplish through my reading of race in *Wuthering Heights* is to help my students rethink their understanding of race as a fixed, unified, and visible identity. As Robyn Wiegman points out, race is

> rendered "real" (and therefore justifiable) through the naturalizing discourses of the body, those discourses that locate difference in a precultural realm where corporeal significations supposedly speak a truth which the body inherently means. (4)

Ever since the nineteenth-century pseudo-sciences of anatomy and craniometry circumscribed its meanings, race has been understood as what can be read from bodily features such as skin color, nose size, shape of the eyes, breast or penis size, and so on. In what is ultimately a legacy of such racist discourses, students tend to visualize race as a biological site of difference. As a result, they see race as preceding and transcending the patterns of meaning created through narrative and literary form. A character is "black" or not, and it is only after his or her racial identity has thus been ascertained that students examine the character's role in the narrative. That "blackness" is not a pregiven identity but a crucial aspect of the workings of narrative itself does not cross their minds because they have, like many of us, been conditioned to think of race as an enduring trait.

Wuthering Heights's representation of race shakes students' investment in "regimes of corporeal visibility" (Wiegman 4)—that is, regimes that anchor race in signs of corporeal difference. Instead, I argue that Emily Brontë's novel exposes racial identity as a site of crossing that functions as a figuration for the characters' violation of class and gender boundaries. The sessions I devote to race are meant to show students that interpretations of her characters as either black or not fail to do justice to the fluctuating meanings of race in Victorian fiction. *Wuthering Heights* stages a tale of interracial encounter in which race, always already internally hybridized, crosses with other categories such as gender and class. What is more, the logic of crossing affects not just racially marked characters like Heathcliff but also white ones, including the Anglo-Saxon elder Catherine; their relations to a particular race change as they are "blackened" or "whitened" according to their shifting relation to class and gender. This reading of race reminds students of something they are wont to forget—namely, that whiteness too is an element of race; thus it should not come as a surprise, as it often does, when "white" and "nonwhite" characters are subjected to the same logic of racial crossing. Indeed, in *Wuthering Heights*, race crossing becomes a figuration for class and gender crossing, so much so that what matters is no longer whether but when characters are "black" or "white."

To make students aware of the complex workings of race in the novel, I ask them to identify each protagonist's race. Usually the elder Catherine is quickly categorized as "white," and Heathcliff's racial identity leads to debate. Students are struck by the many references to Heathcliff's dark complexion but cannot ascertain whether the characterizations indicate that he is "nonwhite." Is he a Gypsy? Are Gypsies nonwhite? Soon the fluctuating and hence disorienting descriptions of Heathcliff's dark coloring become the focus of our discussion. "Is Heathcliff 'black'?" is a question whose answer, students realize, cannot simply be read from his features or skin color. What Wiegman refers to as "regimes of corporeal visibility" are thus exposed as arbitrary modes of identification.

Indeed, far from functioning as a fixed trait, Heathcliff's racial identity remains ambiguous throughout the narrative. When the patriarch Earnshaw brings the little orphan boy back to the Heights, he describes him as "as dark almost as if it came from the devil" (31). Heathcliff wishes he had Edgar Linton's "light hair and a fair skin, . . . [his] great blue eyes and even forehead" (50). Years later, Nelly remembers him as "a gipsy brat" who "repeated over and over again some gibberish that nobody could understand" (31). Lockwood echoes the sentiment by referring to him as a "dark-skinned gypsy in aspect" (3), and Mr. Linton describes him as a "little Lascar, or an American or Spanish castaway" (44). When Heathcliff is supplanted in Catherine's affections, Nelly comforts him through a fairy-tale suggestion that his father might be "Emperor of China, and [his] mother an Indian queen" (50), thus implying that he is of mixed blood. Each of these depictions evokes a different visual image of "darkness" or skin color and introduces a gap between the materiality of race and its representation. Indeed, rather than search for a definitive racial denomination in the text, we should capitalize on the instability of the language used to describe Heathcliff.

After our discussion has highlighted the indeterminacy of Heathcliff's race, I hand out excerpts from recent essays to show students that professional critics have also been grappling with the difficulties surrounding the dynamics of race in *Wuthering Heights*. Emily Brontë criticism is split between scholars who interpret Heathcliff's dark complexion as a metaphor for his moral depravity and postcolonial critics who see it as evidence of a somatic racial difference.[1] Maja-Lisa Von Sneidern and Susan L. Meyer, for instance, argue that Heathcliff's appearance—as well as his provenance from "the streets of Liverpool" (*Wuthering Heights* 31)—evokes slavery. Liverpool was the first slaving port in Britain in the mid-1770s, the time when the events related in the novel begin. Heathcliff's status as slave and commodity, these critics argue, is confirmed when Earnshaw brings not "him" but "it" (31) back to Cathy and Hindley in replacement for the whip and the fiddle they had, respectively, requested as a gift.

Neither interpretation, whether it is of the lactifying or racializing kind, succeeds in doing justice to the novel's complex operations of difference. On the one hand, the "lightening" of Heathcliff's "blackness" is problematic because it reproduces the myth of ethnic purity that the dominant ideology promoted and that Heathcliff's presence at home (hearth and nation) challenges. On the other hand, postcolonial readings that racialize Heathcliff prove, paradoxically, to be as unsatisfactory as those that fail to do so. In emphasizing Heathcliff's "blackness," these progressive readings fix the meanings of race in a way that does not account for the temporalities of narrative. They interpret the tropes of race as a reflection of nineteenth-century theories of the subject and as a contribution to a sociology of race relations, subsuming, in the process, the contradictory ways in which racial imagery is deployed through narrative form.

I suggest to students that rather than try to resolve Heathcliff's racial indeterminacy, we take its implications seriously. I assign homework that asks them to locate the passages in the novel in which Heathcliff's "blackness," or racial distinctiveness, is highlighted. During the following class period, I divide students into small groups and invite them to use the passages they found and to discuss what is happening when Heathcliff is racialized. Who is doing the racializing and designating the racial attributes? In what context? And is the text distancing itself or us from the dominant imperial gaze that is constructing Heathcliff's racial or ethnic difference?

Whereas Rochester in *Jane Eyre* is described as "dark" when he is in a position of class and gender dominance, material references to Heathcliff's black countenance occur mainly when he is an oppressed "ploughboy" (85) at Wuthering Heights and, more specifically, through his association with the elder Cathy. In fact, throughout the narrative, the fluctuations in Heathcliff's racial identity are intricately linked to the tropes of otherness that define the "white" Cathy's identity. For instance, when Heathcliff and Cathy are caught spying at Thrushcross Grange (a scene I discuss in detail once students have identified the racial epithets deployed in it), the Lintons' disproportionate response to the two children's trespass demonstrates the force of this racial economy. The Lintons epitomize the dominant cultural gaze insofar as they explicitly deploy discourses of sexual and racial alterity in an effort to establish an economy of differentiation and exclusion. They construct Heathcliff as an outsider by referring to him as a "gipsy . . . a little Lascar, or an American or Spanish castaway," thus fixing race as a category of difference. The "civilized" world of the Grange, into which, ironically, Heathcliff will eventually gain entry, is indeed based on a powerful system of exclusion that subjects him "to the potent gaze of a racial arrogance deriving from British imperialism" (Meyer, *Imperialism* 97).

The Lintons' effort to construct Heathcliff as an outsider through racial interpellation reproduces the binary posited by the dominant symbolic structures between self and other, human and animal, black and white. Yet the novel also resists the very hegemonic inscription it stages, since it denaturalizes the process through which racial otherness is produced and fixed in discourse to guarantee the normative self. The Lintons (and Lockwood) generate familiar racial tropes that are defamiliarized in the narrative because the ground for these characters' moral and social authority is consistently derided. From the outset, Brontë exposes the Grange's refinement as artificial, its values as conventional, and its inhabitants as pompous.

Once our discussion has encouraged students to denaturalize the racial naming to which the superficial Lintons subject Heathcliff, we explore the processes by which racial alterity is constructed in the narrative. Characters' racial attributes emerge not through their anchoring in "natural" difference but through their association with tropes such as animality, dirt, and linguistic incompetence. In keeping with dominant and stereotypical discourses of race, the characters' attempts to fix Heathcliff's racial difference slip repeatedly into references to his slovenly appearance and incomprehensible speech. The Lintons fall back on comments about his language once they are unable to pinpoint his race with certitude: "A wicked boy, at all events . . . and quite unfit for a decent house! Did you notice his language, Linton?" (44). The unintelligibility of his speech is also what distinguished Heathcliff on his first appearance in the text when he was described as "repeat[ing] over and over again some gibberish that nobody could understand." The "growling" and "snarling" boy is, tellingly, equated with dirt as well as with animality, characteristics that, as students are quick to note, inevitably evoke stereotypes of class as well as of racial difference. Significantly, in response to Heathcliff's lament that he does not and will never have his rival's "light hair and a fair skin," Nelly suggests that he wash and dress nicely. Her emphasis on ablutions as a means of redressing a visible identity that is supposedly fixed highlights yet again the idea that categories such as race, class, and gender are generated through their interrelatedness rather than through real or natural differences.

Heathcliff himself confirms the inextricable, sometimes unexpected entanglement of identities by linking race and class in his statement to Nelly: "I wish I had light hair and a fair skin, and was dressed and behaved as well, and had a chance of being as rich as [Edgar] will be" (50). Later, when he tells his son, Linton Heathcliff, "Now, don't wince and colour up! Though it *is* something to see you have not white blood" (183), he establishes an equivalence between racial difference and his puny, effeminate son's passionate temper that introduces yet again a gap between racial traits and the materiality of the body. Far from being stable, essentialized attributes, class, gender, and race are revealed as inseparable complexes of social meanings that expose the symbolic nature of race. Race, in other words, is shown to be a product of language rather than of visible otherness.

This symbolic economy replaces the facile separatism of an identitarian approach, by which I mean the tendency to analyze social categories of identity such as race, class, and gender in isolation from one another. It also helps elucidate passages in the novel, which—although they occur at turning points in the book—have yet to be commented on, let alone analyzed by Victorian or postcolonial critics of the Brontës. One such puzzling moment—which I single out for discussion in class—occurs when Heathcliff returns from exile and when the representations of race, sex, and class are incongruously linked in the narrative. Despite her husband's obvious displeasure at receiving Heathcliff at the Grange, an excited Cathy wakes a wary (and weary) Nelly in the middle of the night to share her happiness at being reunited with her soul mate and childhood love. Far from partaking of her joy, Nelly Dean advises Cathy not to sing Heathcliff's praises to the jealous Edgar: "What use is it praising Heathcliff to him? . . . Let Mr. Linton alone about him, unless you would like an open quarrel between them." Cathy impatiently retorts, "But does it not show great weakness? . . . I'm not envious—I never feel hurt at the brightness of Isabella's yellow hair, and the whiteness of her skin; at her dainty elegance, and the fondness all the family exhibit for her" (86). Cathy contemptuously wonders how Edgar could possibly envy Heathcliff, since she has never been jealous of Isabella's "whiteness." She uses the contrast between her dark complexion and Isabella's "whiteness" to deride her husband's jealousy. What can her darker hue possibly have to do with her two lovers' sexual rivalry? How could Edgar shed his unseemly feelings by taking as a model her lack of enviousness when it comes to Isabella's fair skin? What does sexual rivalry between the two men have to do with the difference in skin color of the two women? Students are deeply perplexed by the incongruity of the juxtaposition and soon realize that making sense of this passage requires a reconceptualization of race and sexuality in relation to each other.

Cathy's reaction is all the more confusing because Edgar's jealousy springs from anything but Heathcliff's darkened appearance. In fact, it is Heathcliff who, in the past, had reasons to envy Edgar's "light hair" and "fair skin." The parallelism is jarring until students are willing to revise their understanding of race and its workings in narrative. The analogy between the two forms of jealousies makes sense only if they take seriously the contention that tropes of racial, sexual, and class difference are constantly informed by one another. Furthermore, that the incongruity in this passage has never been noted in Emily Brontë scholarship points to the degree to which the imbrications of sex, race, and class have been naturalized in post-Enlightenment discourses on race, at the same time as, paradoxically, criticism persists in presenting identities as discrete categories of analysis. Yet the separation of the three categories serves only to reproduce exclusionary configurations of difference that cannot account for passages such as the one mentioned above.

Cathy's peculiar and unexpected focus on physical traits at this point in the narrative emphasizes the importance of reading the metaphoric operation of race in relation to the text's gender dynamics. It is significant that, separated from each other, Cathy and Heathcliff no longer function as transgressors of norms and become "lightened" instruments of racial and patriarchal oppression. Without Cathy, Heathcliff becomes an abusive husband and father; without Heathcliff, Cathy turns into a spoiled upper-class Linton. In other words, even as explicit references to Heathcliff's darker physiognomy are linked to his relationship with Cathy, she too is darkened in the context of her tumultuous relationship to Heathcliff.

After our discussion of the fluctuating meanings of race that Heathcliff embodies, the passage depicting the effects of his return from exile helps students identify a similar logic at work in Cathy's characterization. Indeed, throughout the novel, Cathy's identity is configured through tropes of racial alterity—as evidenced, for instance, by the repeated references to her "half-savage" nature. Just as I did with Heathcliff, I ask students (in groups and in class this time) to find the passages in which Cathy is darkened or lightened. Students are quick to point to her transformation into a fair-skinned "lady" on her return from the Grange. Her change in social status has literally lightened her as her hands become "wonderfully whitened with doing nothing, and staying in doors," in stark contrast to Heathcliff's "dusky fingers" (47). Significantly, she undergoes a reverse racialization when she adopts a "proper" gender and class position by joining the gentrified world of the Lintons. Her whitening occurs by virtue of her crossing class and gender boundaries, a process reflected in the shifting racial signifiers that define Heathcliff's character as well.

Our discussion of race in *Wuthering Heights* thus reveals that the changing meanings of race occur in a pattern that affects Cathy and Heathcliff in relation to each other. In other words, both "white" and "nonwhite" characters are subjected to a process of racialization as they cross boundaries of class, gender, or national belonging. I conclude our analysis of this racial logic by situating it in a wider cultural context and lecturing about the Victorians' obsession with comparative anatomy. Using Wiegman's work, for instance, I outline the ways in which this pseudo-science too produced a series of analogies between blackness and other visible traits to justify social hierarchies. As Wiegman explains, "comparative anatomy read the African's difference through the twin registers of sexual difference: as both a stereotypically feminized category and the preeminently sexual" (44). Such context helps students see that the crossing patterns of identity we just traced in the fictional narrative do not occur in a vacuum but have to be understood in, and help elucidate, a broader cultural and historical context.

From the reconceptualization of race such an interpretation of *Wuthering Heights* offers, students are encouraged to rethink their facile comprehension of race as a black-white binary. Crisscrossing categories (gender, class, race, nationality) extend the notion of hybridity away from a mixture of races or cultures toward a structural interdefinition of racial, national, class, and gender identities. Rather than view characters as "black" or "white," students look at the mobile relation among race, class, and gender as it develops in the narrative. The reconceptualization illustrates how racial meanings are entangled with gender and class dynamics, to such a degree that interpreting race as a discrete category leads to a flawed and incomplete understanding of its workings. Through this approach to the novel, students can also challenge the epistemology of visibility in which their conventional understanding of race is usually moored.

NOTES

A version of this chapter appears in my book *Reclaiming Difference: Caribbean Women Rewrite Postcolonialism* (Virginia UP, 2005).

[1]For critics who see Heathcliff as the "dark" embodiment of amoral cosmic forces, see Cecil, "Emily Brontë"; and Van Ghent, "Dark 'Otherness.' " In most traditional interpretations, it is because he is "the greatest villain in fiction" (Allott, *Casebook* 88) that Heathcliff is darkened. For critics who discuss Heathcliff's dark skin in relation to race and racial discourse, see Meyer, *Imperialism*; Von Sneidern; and Michie (according to her, Heathcliff is Irish).

Victorian Border Crossings: Thinking about Gender in *Wuthering Heights*

Barry V. Qualls

> No *woman* could write *Wuthering Heights*.
>
> —1848 review, *Union Magazine*

> What, then, I would ask again, is love in its highest, holiest character? It is woman's all—her wealth, her power, her very being. Man, let him love as he may, has ever an existence distinct from that of his affections. He has his worldly interests, his public character, his ambition, his competition with other men—but woman centers all in that one feeling, and "In that *she* lives, or else *she* has no life."
>
> —Sarah Ellis, *The Daughters of England*, 1842

> Woman peculiarly represents the private life of the race. Her ascendancy in literature must mean the ascendancy of domestic ideas, and the assertion of the individual, not as a hero, but as a family man—not as a heroine, but an angel in the house. The individual as a great public character withers. The individual as a member of society in all his private relations grows in importance.
>
> —E. S. Dallas, *The Gay Science*, 1866

Gender is a subject inherent in the domestic realism of nineteenth-century British fiction. Yet when *Wuthering Heights* is the focus, gender tends to be one of the last things that students think about, discuss. They cannot locate a voice discussing the dangers of gender prescriptions as they can in *Jane Eyre*. Charlotte Brontë is certain about the gender ideas that constitute, and confine, ideals of feminine and masculine. For her characters, as for those of most major writers of the period, male and female roles are clearly defined and require strict adherence to divinely ordained rules. Transgressing these rules comes at enormous peril. The woman is the moral guide, her realm the domestic interior; the male, controlled by the domestic fire of the hearth, is the preserver, defender, and—if necessary, in other realms—the creator-enforcer of the settled order. But Emily Brontë? In a course in which gender and social class are primary issues in discussions of authors and novels, *Wuthering Heights* continues to defeat our categories of analysis, as it defeated the ways of reading of its original critics.

Yet in Emily Brontë's story gender and class are connected in ways more troubling and paradoxical than in any other novel we read. When I teach

Wuthering Heights (in an upper-level survey course of nineteenth-century British fiction that runs from *Frankenstein* or *Oliver Twist* to *Dr. Jekyll and Mr. Hyde* or *Tess of the d'Urbervilles* or *The Odd Women*), I usually place it at the end of term. For me, no other nineteenth-century novelist offers so critical a reading of traditions of narration, representation, and thus of gender issues as Emily Brontë does. By 1847, as *Jane Eyre* illustrates, the patterns that shaped the century's novels were clearly established. The marriage plot reproduced the march toward domestic order and tranquillity guided by good women who served as patrollers of the moral territories that men left behind when they set out to make an imperial world. Of course no novel actually does all this (though many of Dickens's come close), but the example of *Jane Eyre* is a potent model for a critique of the domestic order and for an example of its constitution. Indeed, students of George Eliot's *The Mill on the Floss* often find Maggie Tulliver's drowning the result of her failure to fit the requirements of the pattern commandeered by Jane Eyre.

To place students in a Victorian environment of gender discussion, I provide them at the outset of the course with examples of gender formation from conduct books like Sarah Ellis's *The Women of England* (1839), *The Daughters of England* (1842), and *The Wives of England* (1843); from *Mrs. Beeton's Book of Household Management* (1861); from George Henry Lewes on the function of women as novelists; and from paintings of Queen Victoria.[1]

These texts together give students a sense of what the novels will at once illustrate and complicate: how pervasive gender distinctions are in these works (as powerful in *Frankenstein* as they are in *The Mill on the Floss*) and how inextricably connected they are to issues of social class. Ellis offers an ideal example of the codification of gender issues. In her preface to *The Women of England*, which she wrote "to show how intimate is the connexion which exists between the women of England, and the moral character maintained by their country in the scale of nations" (38), she declared that "one of the noblest features in England's national character . . . is the domestic character of England—the home comforts, and fireside virtues for which she is so justly celebrated" (9–10). Lewes was equally certain that the "domestic experiences which form the bulk of woman's knowledge find an appropriate form in novels. . . . Love is the staple of fiction, for it 'forms the story of a woman's life' " ("Lady Novelists" 43). Thomas Barker's 1861 painting of Queen Victoria presenting a Bible to a kneeling African chief, generally titled *The Secret of England's Greatness*, perhaps makes the point best of all.[2] Here the queen, in white, brings the foundation of English life to someone not English. The painting is a perfect emblem for the work of home building and cultural construction that is the task of the younger Catherine in *Wuthering Heights*.[3]

Students encountering these texts and the painting, as well as novels by Charles Dickens, Charlotte Brontë, and George Eliot, should be ready for the challenges that a novel like *Wuthering Heights* presents. They have come to understand the supervisory power that the doctrine of separate spheres obtained over middle-class women as characters and as writers of character. They have witnessed Dickens's good woman gazing toward heaven: Rose Maylie arrives in *Oliver Twist* "made for Home; for fireside peace and happiness" (227; ch. 29); her presence beside the incorruptible Oliver concludes the novel. Maggie Tulliver, even as she longs for a world "outside of loving," still desires the "sanctuary" of home (413, 479). Jane Eyre herself is providentially blessed with an English home when her pilgrim's progress concludes. Yet her insistence that "women feel just as men feel" marks her individualism as unfeminine, even masculine. That she connects her discontent to the "silent revolt" (178) of millions like her, in a novel being read during the 1840s, at a time of the Chartist rebellions at home and revolution in France, indicates the novel's implications for gender boundaries and for social ones. But these implications exist in tension with the novel's desire to feminize and domesticate masculine individualism and with its refusal "to purchase liberty at the price of caste" (82). Jane knows, from the first page of her narrative, that home and hearth require the stabilities of economic life marked as middle class. She may assert a woman's right to feel as men feel, but she does finally live in love that is amazingly near the boundaries that Ellis specifies for "the daughters of England."

The education of Catherine Earnshaw and Heathcliff into comprehending, and for Catherine ambivalently incorporating, what Thrushcross Grange represents illuminates the tensions in *Wuthering Heights* and exposes its radical questioning of the gendered dimensions of domestic realism. It is not simply that the domestic economies of Thrushcross Grange differ from those of Wuthering Heights. It is that the exposure of Catherine *and* Heathcliff to the world of the Grange introduces the gender and class issues that will kill both of them by novel's end.

This exposure begins, before Catherine and Heathcliff go to the Grange, when Hindley Earnshaw returns to the Heights with his new bride, Frances. They bring with them an alteration in the domestic arrangements of the Heights (the separation of servants and family, the exile of Heathcliff to the servants' quarters) that provokes Catherine's notes of rebellion that Lockwood will later read: "H. and I are going to rebel" (16). The rebellious excursion of Catherine and Heathcliff to the Grange produces one of Emily Brontë's most brilliant narrative choices, the introduction of the Grange through Heathcliff's narrative to Nelly. He notes the "petted" children (42) that he and Catherine spy through the window; but in his remarkable "ah! it was beautiful" response to the material splendor of the room where the Linton children fight (41), he also introduces into the novel the seductiveness of the Grange. That seductiveness is inseparable from the class-defined gender issues that are at the heart of the novel.

Students immediately see the meaning of Catherine's experience of the Grange. Her return to the Heights, "look[ing] like a lady now" (46), is perceived by Heathcliff, according to Nelly, as the return of someone "converted into a stranger by her grand dress." Her return provokes Heathcliff's desire to be made "decent" (49); and it provokes Catherine's fatal schizophrenia between desire for Heathcliff and affection for Edgar Linton and the protection of class that the Grange offers. At the same time, her stay at the Grange introduces her to a world of gender discriminations, all powerfully clear when, married to Edgar, she and Heathcliff damn him in gendered terms during their confrontation scene. Catherine sees Edgar as part of "a colony of mice" and "a sucking leveret." Heathcliff calls him a "lamb [that] threatens like a bull" and a "milk-blooded coward" (102).

Catherine's confusions and madness, students see, are the result of the inculcation of gender and class distinctions at the Grange that Catherine cannot resist, even as she recognizes their demands and their falseness for her. She knows that "if Heathcliff and I married, we should be beggars" (72). Nelly agrees, characteristically noting that marrying Edgar will allow Catherine to "escape from a disorderly, comfortless home into a wealthy respectable one" (70). The mad scene summarizes the gender and class issues:

> But supposing at twelve years old I had been wrenched from the Heights, and every early association, and my all in all, as Heathcliff was at that time, and been converted at a stroke into Mrs. Linton, the lady of Thrushcross Grange, and the wife of a stranger; an exile, an outcast, thenceforth, from what had been my world—You may fancy a glimpse of the abyss where I grovelled! . . . Why am I so changed? (111)

Catherine has seen, in her madness, that the social and financial comfort that being a lady requires "is also a bondage; it encloses her in the oppressive security of the family," in the words of Leo Bersani (222).[4] Yet even before her marriage, Catherine has recognized its madness. In telling Nelly her dream of going to heaven, she notes that "heaven did not seem to be my home; and I broke my heart with weeping to come back to earth; and the angels were so angry that they flung me out, into the middle of the heath on the top of Wuthering Heights; where I woke sobbing for joy" (71). Home is always out there, not in a house or in heaven. It is a vision of, and a necessity for, existing outside the social, cultural, religious, gender, and narrative conventions that make the world of the Grange a death to her.

Catherine's "I *am* Heathcliff" (73) is thus not the speech of a Jane Eyre or a Maggie Tulliver, who need to secure themselves, not dissolve into another. It is the proclamation of a woman for whom gender discriminations smother and whose choice of smothering leads to her death. Her weariness of "being enclosed here" in "this shattered prison" (141) is a profoundly antidomestic gesture. Her life in love is a cri de coeur against all that Ellis promotes when she proclaims love as "woman's all—her wealth, her power, her very being" (*Daughters* 224). Catherine is not a character conceived to survive the requirements of Nelly Dean's conduct books or of Victorian domestic realism. Her mad scene and death in childbirth are the result of a confinement at once physical and profoundly metaphysical.

Nor can Heathcliff survive (in) the world of domestic realism. As he begins his expropriation of the Earnshaw property and his brutalization of Hareton, of his son, and of Catherine Linton, he becomes the conventional villain of Victorian melodrama, acquiring capital and property at the expense of all family values.[5] Students inevitably know the first part of the novel in detail and often, as with the Laurence Olivier film (Wyler), give the second half only cursory attention. Though their sense of Heathcliff must come from both parts and though many see, and abhor, the villainy and meanness in the second half of the novel, they tend not to register its serious role in Brontë's overall narrative scheme. They do not easily assimilate the idea of Heathcliff as villain to the love story that many of them admire. No more bothered by the atheism of Heathcliff than they are by Catherine's, they cite his great speech—"The entire world is a dreadful collection of memoranda that she did exist, and that I have lost her!" (288)—as something they have not found in other Victorian novels, not even *Jane Eyre*. Here the world of feeling seems more real to them, even if it is closer to the madness of Bertha Mason than to the passion of Jane Eyre. Yet it is not mad, even if Nelly finds it so. We understand again the social implications of the move from the Heights to the Grange and the implications of this move for narrative representation. (The alignment of class issues with those of narrative representation is important in talking about a novel that is contemporary with Elizabeth Gaskell's *Mary Barton* and other "condition of England" novels, where the struggle to represent the impoverishment and alienation of class is foregrounded.) But why that movement from the Heights to the Grange produces this story is for students more elusive.

Wuthering Heights of course also concludes at the Grange, in Nelly's ending, with a vision of a happy middle-class home. But because the novel has two main narrators, one female and one male, one a housekeeper and the other a London tourist seeking repose from the busy-ness of town life, and because it seems to "tell the same story twice" (Bersani 222), with carefully worked out replications of names and events, it submits gender issues, class issues, and novelistic conventions to intense questioning. Indeed, the gendered foundations of domestic realism are implicit in the narrative work of Nelly Dean and Lockwood.

The novel's heroine and hero—and students insist on seeing Catherine and Heathcliff in these terms, even though many may not like the two characters—do not belong to the worlds of Nelly's Thrushcross Grange and Lockwood's London. And yet the story is told from the Grange; it is the home of narration, and it is the home of clearly understood and clearly articulated gender distinctions. Nelly Dean's delight in the approaching marriage of Catherine

Linton and Hareton Earnshaw is a delight in the assertion of the domestic Englishness and hierarchical order that are being restored to the Grange. The blonde heroine of Nelly's narrative, the daughter of the heroine of students' reading, has taught the rightful heir how to read *and* how to apprehend her value as "angel in the house." Hareton's desire to touch young Cathy's blonde curls and to hear her read (262–63) and his desire to be clean so that he can participate in these blessings (192) provide some of the most moving scenes in the novel, all the more so because they recall Heathcliff's "Make me decent" speech to Nelly (49). But Heathcliff instinctively knows he cannot be a Linton. He may say, "I wish I had light hair and a fair skin, and was dressed and behaved as well, and had a chance of being as rich as he will be!" (50); he may become as rich as Linton, but he also sees that achieving this status entails the extinction of himself and Catherine as unified beings who find life only outside the Grange and its conventions, outside all middle-class understanding of familial bonds. Hareton Earnshaw, on the other hand, requires the Grange and what it means—its education, its central woman figure, its clear boundaries and definitions—for life, as it were.

To clarify the elusiveness of *Wuthering Heights* as it moves toward a new generation and a newly reconstituted family, I ask students to think about the ways Nelly Dean and Lockwood look at their world and how they construct it through language. To help students see that their generally sympathetic response to Catherine and Heathcliff results from a narrator who is anything but sympathetic to them is important indeed if the gender foundations of Nelly's narrative perspective are to be realized. The elder Catherine resists until her death being an angel in the house; Heathcliff rails against the story he inhabits. Yet in Nelly Dean and Lockwood, and in Catherine Linton and Hareton Earnshaw, Brontë constructs narrators and characters who use, and live by, the design for living that characterizes the conventional Victorian novel. Nelly Dean belongs to Thrushcross Grange by sympathies of class and culture and by modes of storytelling. In her desire for household and social order (she is, after all, a housekeeper) and for narrative order, she expresses Brontë's genius for representing characters who escape the order of fiction so seemingly necessary to Victorian life. In *A Future for Astyanax*, Bersani has said that Brontë, in telling the love stories of two generations united by family ties and by the two women named Catherine, presents in the second story "a conventionalized replay" of the first:

> Until Catherine's death, the voices of Lockwood and of Nelly Dean have had to obey rhythms and tones with which they are deeply out of sympathy; indeed, they seem to be in the wrong novel, they are ludicrous vehicles for the story they tell. But gradually the story begins to obey them. . . . It's as if Emily Brontë were telling the same story twice, and eliminating its originality the second time. (222)

I want students to discover that much of Brontë's originality resides in her representations of the gender boundaries of nineteenth-century England and their inextricable connection to the conventions of domestic realism.

Brontë does tell the same story twice, and when its strangeness, its originality, is exiled from the novel, Nelly can live happily ever after at Thrushcross Grange and Lockwood can tour the moors. Together they can construct a Victorian novel. These narrators often sound like characters created by Sarah Ellis and the conduct books of the period. Meeting Catherine Linton Heathcliff at the Heights, Lockwood labels her a "beneficent fairy" (10) and repeatedly gazes on her golden curls and imagines her as a potential bride in "something more romantic than a fairy tale" (270); he assumes her pretty face means she's "good-hearted" (12), though later he finds in her lack of politeness indications that she's "not an angel" (265). The paragraph with which Lockwood ends his story and the novel, with its balanced sentences, expels all wayward human energies he has heard and narrated and in the process buries again the demonic, nightmarish elements of himself that his visit has provoked. He needs the conventions of class and gender to preserve his shallowness.

Students without exception find him "effeminate," his language out of place in this novel, his perceptions unreliable, even as his reading and his nightmare allow Catherine Earnshaw to enter the novel. Indeed, I've had students just starting the book insist that the narrative voice of its opening chapter is a woman's—a telling illustration of the gender issues confused, or codified, by their reading of *Wuthering Heights*. The gender labeling by students originates apparently in his prissy Latinate language and his fears about the woman he has fled. No more than Edgar Linton, whom some students have called a wimp (he is almost never liked by students), does Lockwood seem adequate for the romance he discovers. Clearly, the gender and class distinctions that he and Linton appear so facilely to illustrate retain their power, just as some romantic longing to topple them still appeals—and produces misreadings, in Lockwood and in us. There's something more profound in the contrasts that Brontë makes between uncontrolled nature and well-structured nurture. The confinements of gender and class transform Heathcliff into a villain and kill him, as surely as they do the elder Catherine, and yet, paradoxically, these confinements construct Lockwood and his perceptions.

But if Lockwood's gender perceptions are as predictable as his nightmare is not, Nelly Dean is consistently herself, consistently the voice of domestic order, or of the desire for domestic order, and its representation in narrative, the happy ending in marriage. It is she, looking on at Catherine's death scene, who says of Heathcliff, "I did not feel as if I were in the company of a creature of my own species" (141). It is she who celebrates the respectability of a good family and a good home and tries to remove Heathcliff when he first arrives at the Heights, as a replacement for the whip Catherine asked her father to bring her from Liverpool. It is she who tells the dying Edgar Linton that "people who do their duty are always finally rewarded" (227). Despite the stories she has been telling throughout, she knows that good people live happily ever after, rewarded by Providence. It is she who tells us repeatedly that Edgar Linton is "too soft" (100) and who says of him, in one of the most remarkable metaphors in the novel that students may easily read as one more gender cliché: "The soft thing . . . possessed the power to depart, as much as a cat possesses the power to leave a mouse half killed, or a bird half eaten" (64). Here students may discover Brontë's singular genius in constructing the ambiguities of gender and their potential for violence. It is not surprising to hear Edgar called a "soft thing"; but to think of Edgar as preying on Catherine and to confront the idea that she is already "half killed" (64) (as she has been since she went to the Grange) is to encounter a finely civilized man as a natural predator.[6] This gender delineation is even more difficult for students than "I *am* Heathcliff" because it challenges their world, our world. The novel insists that all readers are a part of the Grange world, are Lockwoods and Edgars who take refuge in books. We are the children of the people of the book, the readers who seek the patterns for living that the Victorian novel offers so generously.

Because Nelly knows who's good and who's bad, who should marry and who should not, and because she knows who should rule and who should patrol the moral territories of our lives, she is the perfect storyteller for Lockwood. Exiling Catherine and Heathcliff from her story of emotional violence and domestic love—of us versus other—she is the perfect narrator and Lockwood the perfect publisher of a good nineteenth-century English novel. Narrative, the providential plot, and middle-class order centered on a good woman are inextricably connected in the alliance of teller and publisher. It is, then, no surprise that at the end of the story Lockwood "wondered how any one could ever imagine unquiet slumbers for the sleepers in that quiet earth" (300). In this story only ghosts refuse to live inside respectable English homes.

"No *woman* could write *Wuthering Heights*." This comment summarizes the sense of many reviewers during the nineteenth century. The gender issues that are central to the novel continue to intrigue students. They come to understand why Charlotte Brontë and George Eliot challenge the conventions of the novel, even as the two authors finally uphold them; and they see how much these women writers focus their challenge around the cultural work of gender. They see the same operation in sensation novels: Mary Elizabeth Braddon's Lady Audley must be exiled to a foreign madhouse to remove the pollution she brought on an English home by playing the role of angel. But even as *Wuthering Heights* manages to secure the same ending, it eludes the celebrations of that finale. Neither Nelly's delight in the forthcoming marriage nor Lockwood's pleasure in hearing a good story accounts for the power of the novel or the dismay it causes some readers. Most paradoxically, what interests students is that the sister of Charlotte Brontë has constructed a narrative in which the woman housekeeper who loves the order of class and gender inclusions and exclusions tells the story of another woman who was fatally seduced by them and who yet, always, longed to escape them: "What were the use of my creation if I were entirely contained here?" (72). In Catherine's question, Emily Brontë challenges students to read against the orders, cultural and narrative, that shape the Victorian novel and their lives.

NOTES

[1]I also place on library reserve, and frequently cite, Murray; Showalter; Gilbert and Gubar; David; Boone; and Poovey. The Broadview edition of *Jane Eyre* is particularly useful for issues of gender.

[2]This painting is on display at the National Portrait Gallery in London. Also, see Lambourne.

[3]Ellis dedicated *The Wives of England* to Queen Victoria, "in whose exalted station the social virtues of domestic life present the brightest example to her countrywomen, and the surest presage of her empire's glory."

[4]Joseph Boone sees in Brontë's handling of the marriage plot an insistence on "the harrowing effects of wedlock on female identity" (158).

[5]For a discussion of Heathcliff and of gender negotiations in *Wuthering Heights*, see Nancy Armstrong's *Desire and Domestic Fiction*.

[6]Q. D. Leavis offers a brilliant discussion of this passage (115–18).

Teaching the Language of Domestic Violence in *Wuthering Heights*

Catherine R. Hancock

Because Emily Brontë's *Wuthering Heights* is replete with characters who both fantasize about and commit violence, it is surely one of the most violent novels in the English language. For this reason, *Wuthering Heights* can be a challenging novel to teach; although students are fascinated with the highly charged atmosphere of the novel, they are often overwhelmed by its unrelenting violence, especially between family members. Some students perceive the climate of hostility in the novel as an impenetrable barrier, one that prevents them from identifying with and understanding the characters. To motivate students to appreciate the full humanity of the novel's characters, I emphasize that violent words, desires, and deeds function as a language of sorts that Heathcliff, Hindley, and the elder Cathy use in expressing a range of emotions, from love and passion to hate and even indifference.

In the classroom I implement assignments that encourage students to translate this language so that they are better able to analyze the feelings and behavior of the volatile characters who populate the tempestuous world of *Wuthering Heights*. The language of domestic violence in Brontë's novel is unorthodox because it consists of both verbal and nonverbal elements. To fathom the novel's complex characters, students must interpret their physical actions (the slaps and hair pulling that can signal emotions from affection to hatred) as well as their words (the violent threats and fantasies that can communicate feelings from apathy to devotion). Characters' violent words and actions, even their reactions to the violence of others, all speak of their feelings. To make sense of the novel, students need to become versed in this unconventional tongue.

I usually spend about six class periods on *Wuthering Heights*. On the first day, I provide social and historical context that helps students understand why there is such an emphasis on domestic violence in *Wuthering Heights*.[1] I often begin class by asking students what they associate with the word "Victorian"; invariably, they conjure up stereotypical images of large, happy families gathered round the hearth. It is helpful to explain that in nineteenth-century England the family was a complex cultural construct. The Victorians revered the home as a sacred space and viewed the family as the bedrock of their civilization; at the same time, they were acutely aware of social evils that threatened its stability, such as infanticide, child abuse, and wife beating. Victorian novels reflect the era's conflicted attitudes toward the family. Although many Victorian narratives celebrate the strength of the family and idealize family life as a state of blissful domesticity, others portray the home as a site where families are decimated by domestic violence.

Wuthering Heights seems less alien to students when they realize that it belongs to a rich tradition of Victorian novels, such as George Eliot's *Adam Bede* (1859) and Wilkie Collins's *Man and Wife* (1870), in which domestic violence plays a prominent role. These authors depict kin-on-kin violence to expose the inauthenticity of the Victorians' ideal of the home as a paradise and to highlight aspects of family life that were ripe for legislative reform. Much of *Wuthering Heights* is a critique of the Victorians' patriarchal family structure, which legally granted the lion's share of economic and social power in the home to husbands and fathers, who could use this power to abuse and exploit wives and children. When students recognize that Brontë's focus on domestic violence often constitutes a form of protest against male-dominated Victorian culture, they become more interested in analyzing the violent threats, fantasies, and actions by the novel's characters.

Once I have established the prevalence and significance of intrafamilial abuse as a theme in Victorian fiction, we begin our reading of *Wuthering Heights* by exploring the violence between the foster siblings Heathcliff and Hindley. One scene early in the novel captures the essence of the power struggle between these surrogate brothers, when Heathcliff uses Hindley's violence against him to his personal advantage. By threatening to tell old Earnshaw of Hindley's violence toward him, Heathcliff acquires Hindley's splendid colt. Heathcliff insists to Hindley, "You must exchange horses with me; I don't like mine, and if you won't I shall tell your father of the three thrashings you've given me this week, and show him my arm, which is black to the shoulder" (33). Although Hindley responds to the blackmail by calling Heathcliff a "dog" and injuring him with an iron weight, he quickly realizes that he has been thoroughly beaten in this battle of wits and capitulates to Heathcliff's extortion, but not before cursing him: "Take my colt, gipsy, then! . . . And I pray that he may break your neck; take him, and be damned, you beggarly interloper!" (34).

This passage illustrates the basis of the animosity between the two boys; Hindley's references to Heathcliff as a "gipsy" and a "dog" underscore the ethnic and class prejudices that fuel his hatred for the orphaned boy, and his calling Heathcliff a "beggarly interloper" reveals Hindley's fear that Heathcliff will usurp his place in the hierarchy of the Heights. Although Heathcliff's bruises are a visible manifestation of Hindley's dominion, Heathcliff transforms these marks of humiliation into a weapon he uses against Hindley and thus diminishes Hindley's power within the Earnshaw family.

I ask students to reconsider this scene when halfway through the novel we encounter Hindley's attempted murder of Heathcliff. Throughout *Wuthering Heights*, Brontë defines characters by showing how their attitudes toward violence evolve or fail to evolve. When Hindley and Heathcliff struggle for control of Hindley's gun, "[t]he charge exploded, and the knife, in springing back, closed into its owner's wrist" (157). Asked to compare the two episodes and interpret Hindley's actions, students notice the parallels: in both assaults,

Hindley's violence recoils upon itself. It is Hindley, not Heathcliff, who is seriously wounded, literally in the attempted murder scene and figuratively in the colt scene. Once students examine the pattern of Hindley's fraternal violence throughout the novel—behavior that invariably proves self-destructive—they perceive Hindley to be a static character, incapable of growth or change and thus destined to be defeated by his nemesis, Heathcliff, who is always able to adapt to achieve his goals.

After Hindley's death, Heathcliff turns his attention from sibling to paternal violence. In the second half of the novel, he is obsessed with fatherhood: he becomes Hareton's surrogate father, brings his biological son, Linton, to live with him after Isabella's death, and forces young Cathy to marry Linton so that she can be his daughter-in-law. Hareton, Linton, and Cathy are not so much the objects of Heathcliff's rage as they are surrogates, stand-ins for their parents, whom Heathcliff wishes to punish. He acquires the mantle of fatherhood solely for the authority it confers on him to abuse and control others; in this way, Heathcliff dismantles the Victorian ideal of domesticity because he assumes familial relationships not to express love but to give vent to his hatred.

The brother-against-brother aggression between Heathcliff and Hindley engenders a discord in the Heights that is not diminished by time or even death. After Hindley's demise, Heathcliff perpetuates his campaign of revenge against his inveterate enemy by unofficially adopting his son, Hareton, and relegating the former heir to the Heights to the status of an illiterate, degraded servant, the mirror image of himself at Hareton's age after Hindley deprived him of learning and cultivation. Students often question why Heathcliff abuses Hareton psychologically but not physically. In class discussions, we usually conclude that Heathcliff identifies too closely with Hareton to beat him and that Heathcliff seeks a more devastating, permanent revenge against Hindley by depriving his son of education, cultivation, and his rightful inheritance of the Heights.

Heathcliff's preference for psychological torture is also evident in his relationship with his biological son, Linton. Students may initially misread the nature of Heathcliff's abuse of Linton, insisting that he beats the boy to express his loathing of Isabella. To clear up this misconception, I draw their attention to one passage in which Heathcliff takes great pains to point out that he does not lay a finger on his effeminate, sickly son. When Linton angers Heathcliff by helping young Cathy escape from the Heights to visit her dying father at the Grange, Heathcliff boasts to Cathy of his ability to torment his child with his mere proximity:

> I was embarrassed how to punish him. . . . he's such a cobweb, a pinch would annihilate him—but you'll see by his look that he has received his due! I brought him down one evening . . . and just set him in a chair, and never touched him afterwards. I sent Hareton out, and we had the

> room to ourselves. In two hours, I called Joseph to carry him up again; and, since then, my presence is as potent on his nerves as a ghost. . . . Hareton says he wakes and shrieks in the night by the hour together. (253–54)

I often use this quotation for an in-class exercise that requires students to analyze characters' violent speech. I separate students into small groups and assign each group a passage to interpret. I then ask students to respond to the following questions: What is this character trying to communicate? Why does he or she use violent language to convey these feelings? How is this character defined by this statement? In examining the passage quoted here, students usually respond to the first question by observing that Heathcliff expresses complete indifference toward his son; the sneering remark that "a pinch would annihilate him" suggests that Linton is so weak and insignificant that Heathcliff is unwilling to exert even the minimal effort it would take to strike him. Instead of beating Linton into submission, he capitalizes on his son's morbid, fearful temperament and inflicts a form of psychological torture that Heathcliff finds both enjoyable and effective.

While Heathcliff spares the rod for Linton and Hareton, he reserves his most explicit paternal violence for his daughter-in-law. Although he becomes young Cathy's father-in-law to gain control of Thrushcross Grange, his motives are not purely mercenary. Equally important to Heathcliff is acquiring the status of Cathy's guardian so that he can exercise his legal right to discipline her by force should he see fit. Students often have difficulty understanding Heathcliff's brutalization of Cathy; some comment that they expected Heathcliff to be more lenient with her because she is the daughter of the woman he so passionately loved. I emphasize that Heathcliff exhibits such rage toward young Cathy because she is a living symbol of the union of elder Cathy and his rival Edgar Linton. This idea is apparent in the scene in which he assaults her and destroys her most treasured possession, the locket containing pictures of her parents. When Cathy desperately tries to preserve her father's miniature portrait, young Linton relates, Heathcliff "struck her down, and wrenched it off the chain, and crushed it with his foot" (248). In this scene, Heathcliff communicates his feelings not through words but through his behavior. When Heathcliff lashes out at young Cathy, he is really doing violence to the marriage she represents.

Heathcliff's financial and physical subjection of Cathy as his surrogate daughter provides many parallels to his brutality toward his wife, Isabella, earlier in the novel. In both cases, Heathcliff's actual target is not the woman he abuses but her male relative. Students often remark on Heathcliff's propensity to abuse women physically rather than just psychologically, as he does with male characters such as Linton and Hareton. I usually respond to students' questions about the role gender plays in Heathcliff's violence by citing Maggie Berg's explanation. According to Berg, Heathcliff "literally inscribes [women] with and as signs of his ownership, and therefore of his victory over his male rivals" (57). Since wives and daughters were legally considered the property of husbands and fathers, Heathcliff deliberately humiliates his enemy Edgar Linton by establishing possession of Edgar's daughter, Catherine, and his sister, Isabella, by inflicting visible wounds. In a sense, Heathcliff brands young Cathy and Isabella to signal the transfer of ownership from Linton to himself. In this way, Heathcliff decreases the value of the property and transforms Edgar's female relatives into, quite literally, damaged goods. Once Heathcliff's violent gestures toward young Cathy and Isabella are decoded, it becomes apparent that Heathcliff views violence against women as the most potent way of declaring his contempt for male characters such as Edgar Linton.

Heathcliff desires to gain access to and control over Isabella's body through the institution of marriage and to revenge himself on Edgar through his sister, whom he insists will be Edgar's "proxy in suffering" (128). Although Heathcliff boasts to Nelly that he avoids inflicting severe or life-threatening injuries on Isabella so that she has no recourse to a legal separation, he often manhandles her, and their brief cohabitation as husband and wife ends after he attempts to kill Isabella by throwing a knife at her head. I often ask students to interpret this scene carefully because it reveals the startling differences between male and female marital violence in the novel. After Isabella taunts Heathcliff, telling him that Cathy would have eventually come to loathe him had she "assumed the ridiculous, contemptible, degrading title of Mrs. Heathcliff," her husband perpetrates his most explicit assault on her body:

> [H]e snatched a dinner knife from the table and flung it at my head. It struck beneath my ear, and stopped the sentence I was uttering; but, pulling it out, I sprang to the door and delivered another which I hope went a little deeper than his missile. (160)

Students notice the clear distinction here between male and female aggression. They recognize that, like Heathcliff, Isabella has murderous desires, but her gender prohibits her from expressing these fantasies in a physical form. As a woman living at a time when middle-class female behavior was rigidly circumscribed, Isabella cannot fight back physically against her husband; instead, she uses her tart tongue, her verbal missiles, to injure her enemy. In the hellish universe of Brontë's novel, marriage is a state of perpetual combat, and wives have vastly fewer resources to use on the battlefield than their husbands do. Wives' violent tendencies are thus confined to the realm of fantasy, and wives such as Isabella and the elder Cathy are often defined by the words they use to express their animosity toward their husbands.

In stark contrast to Hindley, whose attitude toward fraternal abuse remains essentially the same from childhood to adulthood, Isabella's view of marital violence undergoes a distinct metamorphosis. Brontë develops Isabella's character by showing how this pampered, docile young woman is transformed as a result of Heathcliff's emotional and physical violence into a bitter, vengeful wife who harbors homicidal fantasies of her own. In an in-class writing assignment, I provide students with three quotations in which Isabella expresses her hostility toward Heathcliff and ask them to chart the progress of her evolving perspectives toward spousal violence. When she first speaks to Nelly after her marriage, Isabella describes her abject misery and imagines that the only way to end her suffering is through death: "I pray that he may forget his diabolical prudence, and kill me! The single pleasure I can imagine is to die, or to see him dead!" (134). In translating the language of violence in this scene, students frequently notice the passive, self-destructive nature of Isabella's words. Feeling helpless and demoralized as a result of her abusive marriage, Isabella is willing to die to escape it. At this point in the novel, she clearly envisions herself as a victim.

Later, however, after she runs away from the Heights and her marriage, a different Isabella emerges. Her words to Nelly after her escape reveal a far more assertive, aggressive personality: "I've recovered from my first desire to be killed by him. I'd rather he'd killed himself!" (152). Isabella's intense desire for self-preservation smothers her earlier wish for a swift, merciful death at her husband's hands. Now she actively longs for Heathcliff to perpetrate deadly violence against himself, not her. For the first time in the novel, Isabella herself becomes physically violent: she smashes her wedding ring with the poker and throws it into the fire (151). Students frequently assert that these scenes reflect that Isabella has absorbed some of her husband's brutality. Her words and actions reveal that Heathcliff's contemptuous attitudes toward marriage are, to a certain degree, contagious.

As with Isabella, the elder Cathy's ability to express her wifely anger is limited by her gender. Her hostility toward Edgar is articulated through her words, not her actions. Her verbal abuse is especially apparent during the crucial confrontation between Edgar and Heathcliff in chapter 11 of volume 1 and in its immediate aftermath. Enraged because Edgar orders her to end her friendship with Heathcliff, Cathy strikes back at her husband the only way she knows how; she exclaims, "I wish Heathcliff may flog you sick, for daring to think an evil thought of me!" (102). When I ask students to decipher Cathy's violent fantasy, they often observe that Cathy commits a form of symbolic violence against her husband through the agency of Heathcliff. But when Heathcliff refuses to strike Edgar because he deems him to be an unworthy opponent, Cathy tries a new tactic: self-directed violence. She decides that the only way to injure Edgar is to injure herself, and so she attempts to starve herself. Cathy's intentions are evident when she confides to Nelly, "If I were only sure it would kill him, . . . I'd kill myself directly!" (107). Because in the cultural context of *Wuthering Heights* it is socially unacceptable for women to act out their hostility toward their husbands, Cathy turns her violence inward.

But Cathy does not simply use cruel words to express her malignity toward Edgar; the vocabulary of violence also enables her to communicate feelings of love and affection for her husband. She describes the extent of Edgar's love for her when she tells Nelly, "I have such faith in Linton's love that I believe I might kill him, and he wouldn't wish to retaliate" (87). Because violence is the principal means of understanding reality in the passionate world of *Wuthering Heights*, the only way Cathy can articulate Edgar's unconditional love is through a violent imaginary act. Similarly, when Cathy pulls out clumps of Heathcliff's hair and Heathcliff leaves bruises on her arm during their last, passionate embrace before her death (140), these gestures signify their desire, not their antipathy, for each other. These passages help students understand that brutality does not simply perform a negative function in the novel.

The capacity of violence to express love is particularly evident in the relationship between young Cathy and Hareton, the cousins who eventually become lovers. Like Isabella, Hareton is depicted as a character whose attitude toward domestic violence evolves. While Cathy's initial mockery of Hareton's illiteracy results in retribution from Hareton in the form of "a manual check given to her saucy tongue" (268), Hareton expresses his growing affection for his cousin when he later protects her from Heathcliff's paternal abuse. When an irate Heathcliff grabs Cathy by the hair, Hareton "attempt[s] to release the locks, entreating him not to hurt her that once" (285). Hareton's reaction to Heathcliff's brutality speaks volumes about his feelings for Cathy. His chivalrous defense of her heralds the transition of their relationship from acrimonious cousins to affectionate lovers. The cycle of violence comes full circle when, after Heathcliff's death, Lockwood witnesses a stunning scene: Hareton cheerfully tolerates the "smart slap on the cheek" Cathy dispenses after he becomes distracted during their reading lesson (273). Hareton willingly becomes the recipient of a violent gesture that communicates affection instead of aggression. Cathy's love-taps are a signal that violence has been domesticated and civilized within the world of the Heights.

Whether it communicates love and desire or the deepest hostility, domestic violence is an essential component of *Wuthering Heights*. Once students overcome their repulsion at the novel's graphic intrafamilial abuse, they come to understand that domestic violence is the primary vehicle through which characters are developed in Emily Brontë's novel. In the classroom, a close reading of the vocabulary of violence that permeates *Wuthering Heights* can function as the interpretive key that helps students unlock the novel's mysterious, enigmatic characters.

NOTE

[1]The designation "domestic violence" is a twentieth-century invention. Victorians themselves used other terminology to describe familial abuse, such as "wife-beating" and "wife-torture," an expression made famous by Frances Power Cobbe in her seminal article "Wife-Torture in England," published in 1878.

Haunted Bodies: The Female Gothic of *Wuthering Heights*

Tamar Heller

> . . . my fingers closed on the fingers of a little, ice-cold hand!
>
> The intense horror of nightmare came over me; I tried to draw back my arm, but the hand clung to it, and a most melancholy voice sobbed,
>
> "Let me in—let me in!"
>
> —*Wuthering Heights*

Haunting Lockwood at the beginning of *Wuthering Heights*, Catherine Earnshaw Linton's ghost sets the *unheimlich* tone of one of the most gothic of canonical British novels. In the past several decades there has been a strong renewal of interest in the gothic, formerly a marginal genre locked out of the house of classic literature just as the spectral Catherine is barred from Wuthering Heights. Indeed, it seems fitting to envision the gothic as a feminine ghost, because a major force driving the critical revaluation of the genre has been the rise of feminist criticism and its focus on female gothic, the depiction, in the work of women writers, of female confinement within, and rebellion against, domesticity.[1] In this essay, I discuss classroom strategies for situating *Wuthering Heights* in the tradition of female gothic in ways that illuminate for students the gender issues raised by the novel's representation of marriage and sexuality. I argue that, just as the spectral Catherine's exile from the house symbolizes women's conflicted relation to domestic ideology, her transgressive desire for Heathcliff suggests that the female body, with its potentially dangerous passions, is the ghost haunting Emily Brontë's text.

Before analyzing *Wuthering Heights* as female gothic, I introduce students to the larger category of the gothic, a genre that many have never examined in a classroom setting. I place on reserve several concise, accessible introductions to the gothic, such as Fred Botting's *Gothic* and Markman Ellis's *The History of Gothic Fiction*. Before directing students to these critical sources, however, I ask them to do an exercise that demonstrates how much they already know—even if unwittingly—about the gothic, one of the most influential and resilient literary genres of the last few centuries. In class, students compile a definition of gothic, culled either from their knowledge of classic eighteenth- and nineteenth-century works (with which not all are familiar) or (this always evokes more responses) of contemporary popular-culture sources such as stories, movies, comics, and music. We then compare the list of gothic conventions students come up with to a definition of the genre prepared by Ann Merrill Ingram that I received in response to a survey of instructors when Diane Hoeveler and I coedited the MLA volume on approaches to teaching gothic fiction. Ingram's definition, which I give to students as a handout, brings together a number of the genre's important themes:

> Conventions of gothic: haunted or decayed structures (castles, abbeys, mansions, etc.), obsession with the past, the supernatural, entrapment and confinement (especially of the gothic heroine), terror, horror, family lineage, curses.
>
> Additional gothic elements and concerns: unreliable or compulsive narrators, displaced cultural or social anxiety, concerns with "bad parenting" and "bad education" practices, nightmare or inverted domesticity, embedded texts and embedded narratives (including frame narratives), fascination with liminal states (often signaled by a literal threshold), boundary transgression. (qtd. in Heller, "Materials" 4)

Asking students to identify the items on this list relevant to *Wuthering Heights* elicits a rich exploration of the novel's gothic elements. For instance, to note how the prejudices of Lockwood, a classic gothic unreliable narrator, ironize his frame narrative allows us to recognize the genre's typical disruption of linguistic authority and of a stable worldview. Heathcliff's status as resident other (whether we see him, as various critics have done, as a member of the working class or Irish or black) helps us trace the novel's thematics of "boundary transgression"—in this case, the threat posed to English domesticity by the dark outsider. The gothic "fascination with liminal states" is evident from the first image of the novel—Lockwood's crossing the threshold of Wuthering Heights—as well as from his sighting of the ghostly Catherine at a window (DeLamotte 127–32). Discussion of Catherine's liminal state in Lockwood's dream (outside, yet begging to be let in) leads naturally to an examination of the gender issues raised by her ambiguous position between nature and culture.

The discussion of the spectral Catherine draws our attention from the gothic in general to the female gothic in particular and its representation (as Ingram puts it) of "nightmare or inverted domesticity" and the "entrapment . . . of the gothic heroine." To introduce students to these themes, I tell them briefly about the tradition of Radcliffean gothic and its permutations in such works as Mary Wollstonecraft's *Maria* and Mary Shelley's *Frankenstein*. In addition, I ask students to draw on their knowledge of beleaguered heroines in popular gothic romances, Hitchcock movies, and other sources. After we discuss students' examples of female gothic, concentrating on images of women imprisoned in castles, houses, and threatening marital or familial situations, we consider to what extent "nightmare . . . domesticity" and trapped heroines appear in Emily Brontë's text. Although Wuthering Heights is not the medieval castle in which the heroine is imprisoned in Radcliffean gothic, it is an antique structure with "crumbling griffins" (2) over the lintel that bears the Earnshaw name, emphasizing what Ingram identifies as the gothic preoccupation with "family lineage." In this case, the preoccupation with family history underscores the experience of the women who inhabit the Heights across generations.

For at least two of the novel's women, Isabella Linton Heathcliff and young Cathy, Wuthering Heights is a carceral site associated with marital trauma. I describe for students the plot of that quintessential female gothic, *The Mysteries of Udolpho* (1794), in which the villainous Montoni imprisons the heroine, Emily, and tries to force her to marry so that he can gain control of her inheritance—a plot that feminist critics have read as a critique of women's disadvantaged legal and economic position before the passage, in the late nineteenth century, of the Married Women's Property Acts of 1870 and 1882. (To familiarize students with nineteenth-century married women's lack of power, I assign the excerpt from Caroline Norton's *Letter to the Queen on Lord Chancellor Cranworth's Marriage and Divorce Bill* [1855] that appears in Peterson's edition of *Wuthering Heights*.) Once students have in mind the Radcliffean plot of male theft of female property, I ask them to identify the similarities between Ann Radcliffe's *The Mysteries of Udolpho* and *Wuthering Heights*. After Catherine's marriage to his rival, Heathcliff turns into a Montoni-like tyrant who seeks ownership of the Linton fortune through marriage—his marriage to Isabella Linton and the forced marriage of young Cathy to his son, Linton. In class we discuss the gothic elements in Isabella's nightmarish homecoming as Heathcliff's despised bride (119–28), as well as in his incarceration of young Cathy when he compels her to marry Linton (234–45). In her version of female gothic, Emily Brontë emphasizes women's vulnerability to domestic violence: Heathcliff strikes young Cathy and even attempts to murder Isabella by flinging a knife at her head. One is reminded of Joanna

Russ's essay on gothic romance, "Somebody's Trying to Kill Me and I Think It's My Husband."

It is important, however, to draw students' attention not only to Brontë's use of female gothic conventions but also to her innovative melding of these conventions with traditional narratives of courtship and romantic love. The figure most clearly associated with the intersection of courtship narratives and female gothic (both genres traditionally linked with women writers) is Catherine Earnshaw Linton. Initially, Catherine's experience seems less clearly gothic than Isabella's and young Cathy's. Despite being associated with the drunken tyrannies of her brother, Hindley, Wuthering Heights is not the site of the "feminine carceral" (D. A. Miller 120) for Catherine but rather a space from which she escapes to be "half savage and hardy, and free" (111) in nature. Nor does her marriage evoke the female gothic as obviously as Isabella's loveless union with Heathcliff or young Cathy's forced marriage to a dying boy. Edgar Linton is not a brutal villain but the gentle, cultivated, even feminine lover idealized in late eighteenth- and early nineteenth-century domestic fiction. The very reference, however, to domestic fiction indicates the extent to which Brontë transforms it into gothic. I assign Lyn Pykett's essay "Changing the Names: The Two Catherines," which places *Wuthering Heights* in the context of the domestic novel by exploring Brontë's revision of the "fictional paradigm which structures a woman's life as a choice between two men." While the elder Catherine's marriage to "the sensible, educated man of property and standing in the community" (469) rather than to the penniless Heathcliff would be the correct choice in an Austen novel, it is problematic in Brontë's text, where Catherine claims to Nelly that both her soul and her heart tell her it is wrong to marry Linton (70). Split between the part of her that values class status and stability and the part that claims "I *am* Heathcliff" (73) and hence outside convention, Catherine is doomed, as Nelly puts it, to "adopt a double character" (59), a type of duality and inner conflict frequently found in gothic texts.

In reading Catherine's marriage to Linton as a version of female gothic, I ask students to analyze the scene (recounted by Heathcliff) in which she is first taken in by the Lintons. Peering with Heathcliff in the window at Thrushcross Grange, Catherine is in the liminal state—at once identifying herself with the natural world and being drawn to the cultivated one—that typifies her ambivalent relation to domesticity. When Edgar and Isabella notice the interlopers and call for help, Catherine attempts to remain in her "half savage and hardy, and free" world with Heathcliff, only to be dragged back by the Lintons' guard dog. I direct students' attention to the gothic violence of this scene, where Catherine's foot is injured seriously enough that Mrs. Linton fears she will be lamed, and how this wounding initiates the taming of her unruly body that will result in the transformation of a "hatless little savage" into the "very dignified," fashionably dressed young woman who returns to the Heights following her stay with the Lintons (46). Catherine's marriage to

Edgar Linton will only lock her more securely into this properly socialized feminine persona and its attempted containment of her passionate nature.[2]

Addressing Catherine's passion and the extent to which it can be controlled leads class discussion to one of the novel's more daring aspects: its treatment of the plot of adulterous desire. In the depiction of Catherine's unquenchable love for Heathcliff, Brontë revises earlier female gothic in a particularly innovative way. In Romantic-era female gothics such as *The Mysteries of Udolpho* or Charlotte Dacre's *Zofloya; or, The Moor*, the virtuous woman is typically distinguished from the fallen one.[3] In *Udolpho* the chaste heroine, Emily, and the fallen woman, Madame Laurentini, are not the same character, and in *Zofloya*—a precursor to *Wuthering Heights* with its prominent figure of a demonized racial other—the female lead murders her virtuous rival. In Charlotte Brontë's *Jane Eyre,* the gothic figure of Rochester's incarcerated first wife may be, as Sandra M. Gilbert and Susan Gubar famously put it, the "truest and darkest double" (*Madwoman* 360) who embodies Jane's latent anger and rebellion; yet these qualities are obscured in Jane even as they are externalized, and punished, in Bertha.[4] In *Wuthering Heights*, however, the elder Catherine is simultaneously heroine and antiheroine, an "angel" (88) who acts according to the script of appropriate feminine behavior and a married woman who loves another man. Indeed, one amusing thing about Catherine is her apparent ignorance of, or indifference to, the awkwardness of bringing into her husband's presence a man with whom she is obviously close. In class we examine the scene in which, following Heathcliff's return after her marriage, Catherine invites him into the Grange and ecstatically greets him before the dismayed Linton (83–86).

Students are quick to note, though, that, even while Brontë reworks the traditional gothic split between good and bad girls in some regards, she repeats it in others. Eventually the elder Catherine *is* split into two characters, as Brontë kills off her problematic heroine to replace her, in the novel's second part, with her daughter, a figure who, though not exactly conventional, is not associated with adulterous desire. It is significant, however, that even the elder Catherine apparently never consummates her love for Heathcliff, suggesting that Brontë sensed the limitations of making her heroine a fallen woman.[5] Reflecting the difficulty in representing extramarital love, Catherine's transgressive desire is, finally, associated not so much with embodiment as with disembodiment. To address this tension between embodied and disembodied love in the novel, I spend time in class looking at the scene just before Catherine's death when Heathcliff insists on seeing her. For the first time we see Heathcliff kiss Catherine "with frantic caresses," and the two, according to Nelly, are "locked in an embrace from which I thought my mistress would never be released alive" (142, 141). The ardent physicality of this scene, however, is diluted because it is obviously linked to the impending dissolution of Catherine's body. As we later find when Heathcliff knocks out the side of Catherine's coffin, only as their bodies crumble into dust will he and Catherine experience a kind of gothic sexual union. Catherine's death may be read as a response to the predicament in which she finds herself, in that she escapes into disembodiment. Rather than continue to live in an unbearable tension between convention and her desires, she hastens her end by self-willed anorexia, wasting away so that the form Heathcliff clasps is already incorporeal. In this sense, the gothic realm of the supernatural and Catherine's ghostly haunting of Heathcliff—including his necrophiliac attachment to her dead body—is the only way that Brontë can accommodate her heroine's socially unsanctioned desire.[6]

One can link the female gothic of Catherine's tale to that of the younger Catherine by noting that the mother's death follows immediately on her daughter's birth. Having read Lockwood's frame narrative, students are already aware of the daughter's existence, yet they usually express surprise at the baby's unannounced advent at this point in the story. Capitalizing on their startled reactions, I ask them why we have not been informed of Catherine's pregnancy earlier. What difference does it make to our interpretation of the scene of Catherine and Heathcliff's farewell if we reread it with this information in mind? How does our response to the sexually transgressive woman shift if we think of her as a mother-to-be? Students' answers to these questions lead us to discuss the gothic representation of maternity that allies it with death, emphasizing the persistent tension between female sexuality and domesticity. By dying, Catherine escapes not only the confinement of her marriage to Linton but also an extended experience of motherhood, in nineteenth-century gender ideology associated with a Madonna-like erasure of female sexuality. Instructors can place Catherine's death in childbirth in the context of other nineteenth-century texts that conflate maternity and death, such as *Frankenstein* or Elizabeth Barrett Browning's *Aurora Leigh*, in which we hear of Aurora's mother that "the mother's rapture slew her" (bk. 1, line 35). Of course, given the high maternal and infant mortality rates in the nineteenth century, women's experience of childbirth was often gothic in actuality.

Significantly, the mother-daughter theme introduced through Catherine's death is an important one in female gothic, which often contains the theme that feminist critics have called "matrophobia," or the fear of becoming like the mother (Kahane; Heller, *Dead Secrets* 17–21). At one point the conventional Lockwood, who sees young Cathy as a potential romantic object, fears that she will turn out "a second edition of the mother" (136), betraying his anxiety that she will share her mother's rebellious, sexually transgressive nature. Yet more typically in female gothic, matrophobia is linked to the fear, not of the daughter's inheriting her mother's vices, but of the daughter's being doomed to repeat the mother's experience of oppression. For instance, in Wollstonecraft's feminist gothic *Maria*, the heroine, incarcerated in a lunatic asylum by the husband who seeks to control her fortune, "mourned for her child, lamented she was a daughter, and anticipated the aggravated ills of life that her sex rendered almost inevitable" (8). Indeed, Maria writes her memoirs in the hope that her infant daughter will eventually escape the cycle of female victimization that holds her mother captive.

To introduce students to matrophobia in the female gothic, instructors can prepare a handout with relevant brief excerpts from *Maria*, as well as assign Adrienne Rich's discussion of matrophobia in her chapter on mothers and daughters from *Of Woman Born* (237–40) and, for an application of the concept specifically to female gothic, Claire Kahane's essay "The Gothic Mirror." Once students have become familiar with this material, instructors can ask whether *Wuthering Heights* is a matrophobic text. Does young Cathy repeat her mother's fate—the repression of her sexuality and autonomy within domesticity—or does she evade it?

Discussion of the potential repetition of the mother's fate leads naturally to a class session in which students are asked to respond to the ambiguity of the end of the novel, which, like young Cathy and Hareton's story in general, has been read by a number of critics as a tamer version of Heathcliff's and the elder Cathy's unconventional romance. Giving feminist critics particular reason to criticize *Wuthering Heights*, Brontë achieves closure by resorting, with young Cathy's marriage to the domesticated Hareton, to the traditional happy ending of domestic fiction. So forced, indeed, does Susan Meyer find the "exclusive, walled-in bliss" of the Cathy-Hareton union that she reads it as a satire on the conventions of domestic fiction ("Your Father" 502). Pykett, however, views young Cathy's marriage with Hareton more positively, claiming that Cathy acquires a power denied her mother ("Changing," "Gender"). In her spirited resistance to Heathcliff's domestic tyranny and her free choice of Hareton following her reluctant marriage to Linton, Cathy, according to Pykett, "relinquishes her role as the victim of a gothic plot" ("Changing" 476) to become the heroine of a revisionary romance that grants women an autonomy unavailable either in female gothic or in earlier domestic fiction ("Gender" 83–85).

To foster a careful consideration of the gender politics of the novel's end, I prepare the students by assigning Pykett's "Gender and Genre in *Wuthering Heights*." I ask students to come to our last class on the novel ready to argue either in favor of or in opposition to Pykett's claim that young Cathy's marriage empowers her. In the debate that ensues, students tend to be divided, some agreeing with Pykett and others reading young Cathy's domestic bliss as a closure that can be accomplished only over her mother's dead body and, with it, the extinction of the sexually transgressive power associated with the elder Catherine. Since we have also seen Hareton striking Cathy during the tumultuous early stage of their relationship, the gothic shadow of domestic violence is not entirely dispelled by the truce between them at the novel's end (and, of course, Hareton, as Cathy's husband, will gain control of her estates).

In this debate, as throughout our discussion of the novel, I encourage students to observe how Emily Brontë's appropriation of the gothic tradition expresses her ambivalent response both to the radical feminine autonomy represented by the elder Catherine and to the orthodox domesticity embodied in her daughter. The ambiguous fate of the female gothic, and of feminine independence, is underscored by the novel's final image, Lockwood's incredulity, on seeing Catherine's, Linton's, and Heathcliff's graves, that "any one could ever imagine unquiet slumbers for the sleepers in that quiet earth" (300). By reminding us of Nelly's claim that there have been sightings of the dead Catherine and Heathcliff, Lockwood's attempt to dispel the novel's transgressive ghosts conjures up the very specters it would deny, suggesting that the gothic cycle of female victimization and rebellion cannot be easily exorcised.

NOTES

[1]For a bibliography of feminist criticism of female gothic, see Heller, "Materials" 15–17.

[2]Hoeveler, in *Gothic Feminism*, usefully discusses Catherine's "conversion to bourgeois values" (192–93).

[3]One female gothic that draws attention to the parallels between virtuous and fallen women is Wollstonecraft's *Maria*.

[4]See Heller, "*Jane Eyre*," for more on teaching Charlotte Brontë's version of female gothic.

[5]Some critics have read Catherine and Heathcliff's relationship as asexual, like that between brother and sister in Romantic literature. Sexuality and brother-sister love are not incompatible in Romanticism, however; incest is, in fact, a prominent theme. I argue that the degree to which physical contact between Catherine and Heathcliff is minimized is a sign not of the absence of sexual desire but, rather, of the difficulty in representing that desire in the context of adultery.

[6]In my introduction to *Cometh Up as a Flower*, I discuss a similar pattern of what I call "disembodied embodiment" in the sensation novels of Rhoda Broughton.

Biographical Keys to the *Heights*

Frances Beer

As mine is a two-semester graduate course dealing with all four Brontës, I am fortunate in being able to employ a number of approaches in teaching *Wuthering Heights*. There's not room here to discuss them all, and many are dealt with elsewhere in this volume. However, one that I've found effective and that I believe can help students at many levels is a consideration of a range of biographical materials—not only biographies of the Brontë family but also writings by Emily: her diary papers, the Belgian essays, and some of the Gondal poems.[1]

It goes without saying that *Wuthering Heights* is an utterly engrossing novel, but as students begin their reading, they may nonetheless be troubled and confused, as indeed Lockwood is when he first visits the Heights. They are intrigued by the paradoxical image of a Victorian spinster—Emily Brontë, daughter of an Anglican minister—who is yet capable of unflinchingly describing such violence and cruelty, such passionate love. A comparison of several biographies may shed light both on the famously private Emily Brontë and on her enigmatic novel. The barest outline of the story (of four shy, bereaved children, their home overlooking a graveyard, playing alone on the moors, reading their way through their father's library, creating extravagant fantasy worlds, carrying the fatal seeds of consumption) in itself rouses even the most reluctant student; the details of the family's life and the origins of the novels are perhaps even more irresistible.

The biographers' approaches are varied, to say the least. May Sinclair takes an exalted view of Emily Brontë, comparing her with Blake: she is the solitary, fierce, virgin, pagan, mystic (175). Phyllis Bentley's romantic Emily Brontë is akin to Wordsworth, "a pantheist [who] saw the universe as a whole" (88). Winifred Gérin discusses Emily's artistic evolution, including such literary influences as *Blackwood's* magazine, Byron, both Shelleys, Scott,[2] and James Hogg's *Confessions of a Justified Sinner.* Edward Chitham considers the ways in which Brontë's upbringing influences the themes and style of her novel, and Stevie Davies, through an examination of her writings, reads her as a skeptic, a heretic, and a revolutionary: "*Wuthering Heights*," Davies argues, "is a sublime act of filial and religious disobedience" (*Heretic* 18).

Of particular pedagogical interest is the contrast between the views presented by Elizabeth Gaskell and Juliet Barker. No doubt because Gaskell wished to valorize Charlotte Brontë, she makes scant reference to Emily; yet through this biographer we have Ellen Nussey's description of the young Emily—"a tall, long-armed girl more fully grown than her elder sister; extremely reserved in manner" (although she enjoyed playing with tadpoles) (147); to Gaskell we owe Charlotte's accounts of Emily's love of the moors—"out of a sullen hollow in a livid hill-side, her mind could make an Eden"—

and of her soul-destroying homesickness at Roe Head (159); of Emily reading on the parsonage rug with her arm around "her rough bull-dog's neck"; of her courage in self-cauterizing the bite of a rabid dog with a red-hot iron (268). Gaskell tells of the two sisters clinging to each other while in Brussels, "full of the exile's sick yearning" (230), but also of Emily's anger when she discovered that Charlotte had been reading her private poems and of her solitary strength in the face of death (285, 357).

Barker seems at times to be driven by an impulse opposite to that of Gaskell, peppering her descriptions of Charlotte with such adjectives as "truculent," "envious," "scornful," "snobbish," "unjust," "ungrateful," and "ruthless" (*Brontës* [1994] 353, 354, 363). She sees earlier biographies as distorted, since the family members are looked at in isolation; Barker thus offers a useful contrast to Gaskell, for whom Charlotte, the dutiful Victorian heroine, is always in the spotlight (see Shelston). Barker painstakingly weaves the family portraits together to show how the members influenced one another; the sisters' solidarity is evident in the splendid story of how they defied their aunt by going on a hunger strike, forcing her to let them care for their servant Tabby, who had broken her leg (259). She gives us detailed descriptions of life at the parsonage and Emily's close collaborations with her "play partner," Anne, as well as her times away at Roe Head and Brussels, when her bond with Charlotte was predominant (224–25; 383–95); yet in insisting on Branwell's creative preeminence, Barker perhaps gives short shrift to the sisters: by her account, Angria was basically his creation; Charlotte just tagged along, and Emily and Anne formed their Gondal writings after their brother's pattern (272).

All biographers have their own agendas and thus present what must be partial truths: a salutary reminder to student and professor alike that there is really no such thing (perhaps especially for the Brontës) as a single, unambiguous truth. Still, taken together they may give us something approaching a reliable image. In class, students seem to value the process of trying to assemble a composite portrait, by comparing the biographies, of the elusive Emily Brontë—courageous, proud, brilliant, more at home with nature than with society—and then relating it to the novel, which can be seen as a kind of mirror of its author.

Some apparently relevant factors emerging from the family profile may also help address problems encountered by students in their reading of *Wuthering Heights*. The Reverend Brontë's inclination for solitude, to the point of eating alone; the absence of a mother and the delegation of her responsibilities to Aunt Branwell, who seems to have possessed a rather narrow Methodistical mindset and a preference for keeping to her room: such circumstances fostered the emotional isolation and resultant interdependence of the four surviving children, as they sought to come to terms with the deaths of their mother and their two older sisters, Maria and Elizabeth. Unquestionably, the theme of loss threads through the Brontës' works, and students are struck by the pall of death that shadows Emily's novel: Heathcliff is parentless (unless perhaps he is Mr. Earnshaw's illegitimate son; still, when we pick up the narrative, he effectively has no mother); Frances dies, leaving Hareton motherless; both senior Lintons die, leaving Edgar and Isabella parentless; the elder Catherine dies, leaving young Cathy motherless; and Isabella's death leaves Linton motherless: the centrality of this trope may be at least partly explained by the successive bereavements suffered by the Brontë children.

Also perplexing is the cruelty that pervades *Wuthering Heights*. Despite the nobility of Laurence Olivier's film portrayal of Heathcliff (dir. Wyler), which is many students' first exposure to Emily Brontë's hero, the character reveals himself, in the novel, to be capable of extraordinary sadism—far more than is necessary to gain control of the Heights and the Grange. Perhaps most painful is Isabella's letter about the "honeymoon," more ghastly as the details of the abuse are left to our imagination. Brontë seeks to excuse neither Heathcliff's cruelty nor the evident satisfaction it inspires.

Where does this preoccupation with cruelty, pervasive in the works of all four Brontës, originate? Can the father in any way be fairly implicated? Here biography may be a useful teaching tool, as students consider the possible role he might have played: some condemn, some defend. Gaskell tells us of the reverend's temper and his tendency to violence: burning the children's colorful boots, cutting up his wife's dress, sawing the backs off chairs, firing his guns out the back door (89). Barker, in turn, systematically tries to discredit these views as the lies of a disgruntled servant (107). Aiming to dramatize the lives of the children by drawing them as lonely and fearful, Gaskell may exaggerate. Where she paints the reverend as capable of "volcanic wrath," as "wild," "eccentric . . . and almost misanthropical" (89, 90), Barker may err in the other direction, presenting him as a near saint: it was "Patrick and Patrick alone who nursed his beloved sufferer [Mrs. Brontë]," and it was by "mistake" that a mere three months after her death he proposed to his wife's good friend (she turned him down) (102, 106).

Was their father in fact violent and frightening, or was he tender and devoted, or was he both? Can anything approaching the truth be arrived at from these conflicting views? Surely it is possible that, even as Patrick Brontë cared for his children, some of his behavior may have seemed threatening, his absence perceived as abandonment. The Gaskell-Barker war, in presenting such opposing portraits of the reverend, provides a valuable pedagogical lesson: both biographers appear willing to skew their material for the sake of their agendas; in doing so, they arguably undermine their own work.

As gothicism is center stage these days, the novel's general spookiness is an early hook for engaging students; this approach, of course, relates to the cruelty motif: the appearance of young Catherine's ghost (whose wrist Lockwood rubs against the window's broken glass [21]); Heathcliff's hanging of Isabella's spaniel and Hareton's of the puppies (114, 161); the moor as an otherworldly presence; Catherine's haunting of Heathcliff; and his opening of her grave (255–56). Again, biography pertains. An appetite for the gothic was shared by all the children.[3] The factors that led to their isolation at home also meant an exceptional freedom; they had full access to their father's library, where they became familiar with the works of various gothic adherents. The pages of *Blackwood's* magazine, for example, frequently included serialized tales of horror, imprisonment, torture, mysterious births, dark secrets, treachery, blasphemy, and murder.[4]

The fascination with cruelty can also be linked to Byron and his cult. The Brontë children had read the sensational reports of Byron's cruelty to a string of women and of the scandals that drove him from England; as well, they knew Thomas Moore's adulatory posthumous biography. They seem to have internalized all of this: his brilliance, his sensuality and irresistible sexiness, his haughty beauty, his degeneracy and sadism, and the poignancy of his exile (see Chew; Rutherford). The combination of Byronic traits repeats and varies itself both in the Brontë juvenilia and in the novels, perhaps most dramatically in the gloomy, charismatic, outcast avenger, Heathcliff. Whatever the influence of the family dynamics may have been, the power of the gothic and the Byronic influence must not be overlooked.

The world of her father's traditional library was important to Emily Brontë, if not as vital as her famous love of the moors or her devotion to the world of her imagination. But though she admired such literary antecedents as Wordsworth, Byron, and Scott, she was not bound by them; she declined to be cowed by the canon. A consideration of her literary autonomy leads naturally to a discussion of the novel's stunning radicalism, its wholesale repudiation of convention—the pregnant wife passionately in love with another man of unknown pedigree; the denigration of respectability; the valorization of the outlaw, of revenge in the name of extramarital passion; and the posthumous union of the lovers' spirits on the moor.[5]

Many such themes can be traced back to the Gondal poems, which arguably "represent a kind of foreshadowing" of *Wuthering Heights* (Visick 310). Frustrating as it is to have none of the prose Gondal writings, I find that discussing scholars' hypotheses about the cycle can be fruitful. First, I introduce students to Fannie E. Ratchford's putative reconstruction, in her view, of "the life story of A.G.A., from dramatic birth, through tempestuous life, to tragic death" (27, 41–45). Although she takes many liberties in filling in the blanks, Ratchford convincingly speaks of the "compact unity . . . and intense conviction of the Gondal world," arguing that "Emily was working out an over-all design comparable to the clear-cut blueprint of *Wuthering Heights*" (24, 23). Mary Visick similarly argues that "the story that [the Gondal poems] can be shown to tell is the story of *Wuthering Heights*" (309); for the most part, she agrees with Ratchford's interpretation, "in which the heroine first loves Julius, then abandons him for various lovers the last of whom is Lord Alfred, and finally leaves Alfred and returns to him." According to Visick, this reading "seems justified . . . because it is a sketch of the relations between Catherine, Heathcliff and Edgar in the first part of *Wuthering Heights*" (324).

Janet Gezari's analysis of Ratchford's reconstruction—"the first and still the most comprehensive attempt to reconstruct a narrative of Gondal" (xvi–xviii)—is tactful. Yet as Gezari gives credit to Ratchford's work, she also shows its limitations:

> A reading of the poems themselves does not easily sustain Ratchford's first hypothesis . . . [which] requires the conflation of three important female characters . . . and the idea that Julius . . . is involved with only one woman. (xxx–xxxi)

As in the case of Gaskell versus Barker, a classroom discussion of this dialogue can be of value: here we have two intensely committed Emily Brontë scholars from different generations who do not arrive at precisely the same conclusions. Yet by respecting Ratchford's contribution, Gezari offers students a positive paradigm: engaging in the business of literary criticism does not require the repudiation of earlier scholarly work.

There are two generations of Gondal characters, as there are two generations in *Wuthering Heights*. The first is dominated by the fiery heroine, Augusta Geraldine Almeda, queen of Gondal—who, as she evidently has a succession of lovers, is rather less constrained by convention than her counterpart Catherine Earnshaw—and the second by "a dark boy and a fair girl," evidently the precursors of Hareton and young Cathy (Sale 377; Visick 313–15). Visick notes the equation between Alfred and Edgar, Julius and Heathcliff (311), as does Gérin, who remarks that Augusta is divided in her "dissimilar" tastes in men: "[their] strongly marked traits could be said to prefigure the gentle Edgar Linton and the ruthless Heathcliff" (144).

I have no problem interesting students in the melodramatic outlines of the Gondal saga, with its plethora of intrigue, infidelity, imprisonment, suicide, and murder. However, there is a technical question about how to introduce them to specific poems, since there are so many—forty-four in the *Gondal Poems* notebook alone (Gezari 200–01). One solution is to select a few representative poems and make transparencies that can be projected on a screen, so that all the students in a class can see them at once. Two that I would suggest are "Song by Julius Brenzaida" (1838) and "Remembrance" (1845). The eight-year spread between these two works effectively shows Emily Brontë's poetic development. They are a natural pair, as well, Julius showing his longing for Geraldine and R. Alcona her love and grief for her lover, who has been dead for fifteen years.

Students can be asked to read these relatively short poems aloud, giving them an immediate appreciation of Brontë's range of voice. An in-class analysis of the two poems and of the ways in which they prefigure the novel could ensue. For instance, Julius's "Song," addressed to his absent beloved, may be seen to foreshadow Heathcliff's longing for Catherine. It also exemplifies the familiar identification with nature, the theme of enduring love and longing, the pain of separation, and the importance of memory. "Remembrance" presents many of the same subjects, although in a more sophisticated verse form. It is similarly fraught with themes of hopeless longing, loss, and fidelity after death, but also, "when the days of golden dreams had perished," of the subsequent bitter triumph of will, "without the aid of joy" (Gezari 8, lines 21–24); here, the bereaved woman could be linked to Heathcliff and to Emily Brontë herself.

Other important examples of Brontë's voice can be found in the diary papers and her Belgian essays, or *devoirs*; because they are so distinctive, providing a revealing complement to the Gondal material, I've found it valuable to consider them along with the poems. The diary papers reveal how intertwined Emily's imaginary world was with the everyday life of the Brontës, and in their touching mundanity they also provide a striking contrast:

> [1845] The Gondals still flo[u]rish bright as ever I am at present writing a work on the First Wars—Anne has been writing some articles on this . . . —We intend sticking firm by the rascals as long as they delight us. . . . Tabby has just been teasing me to turn as formerly to "pilloputate" [peel a potato] . . . —I must hurry off now to my turning and ironing . . . and writing and am altogether full of business with best wishes for the whole house . . . and as much longer as may be I conclude EJ Brontë. (qtd. in Barker, [1994] 453–54, 456)[6]

A radically different voice can be heard in her 1842 *devoir* "The Cat."[7] Emily speaks of the cat's duplicitous, cruel, ungrateful nature, arguing that because of these qualities it more closely resembles human beings than does any other creature. In fact, her essay is not about cats but about the fallen nature of humanity. So she ends:

> The ingratitude of cats is another name for penetration. They know how to value our favors at their true price . . . undoubtedly they remember always that they owe all their misery and all their evil qualities to the great ancestor of humankind. For assuredly, the cat was not wicked in Paradise. (Lonoff 56–58, no. 6)

As they are moved by the vulnerability of the diary papers, so students are awed by the revelation of this bitterly satirical side of Emily Brontë's nature. If "The Cat" were the only record we had, it would be an invaluable entrée to the ethos that governs the world of the Heights and the Grange. Heathcliff is certainly no cat,[8] and it is part of his torment to see his beloved Catherine becoming one. In this *devoir*, as Sue Lonoff says, "Emily's views emerge with startling clarity. She makes no attempt to mouth traditional pieties. . . . She argues through examples that display her scorn of orthodoxies, social as well as pietistic" (61).

The combination of Gondal poems, diary papers, and Belgian *devoirs* is a good way to conclude; there is a haunting authenticity to Emily Brontë's words that puts the insights of even the best biographer into perspective. Yet all the biographical bits, Brontë's and others', work effectively in interface to provide useful keys to the *Heights*.

NOTES

[1]I'm aware that using Emily Brontë's poems autobiographically will raise some eyebrows and perhaps a few hackles. But I defend my decision on the grounds that the Gondal material was an integral part of the Brontë children's life and that Emily Brontë identified intensely with both A.G.A., the heroine of Gondal, and her lover, Julius.

[2]Gérin, noting that Scott was the chief man to "inhabit [Emily Brontë's] dream island [of Arran]," argues that "Scott gave her the yardstick by which to measure the truth of her creations" (212, 214).

[3]See Gilbert and Gubar; Hoeveler, *Gothic Feminism*. In "Tales of the Islanders" (1829–30), Charlotte Brontë describes a satisfyingly gothic dungeon, where naughty children are incarcerated and tortured; luckily she and Emily (who are characters in the story) have the keys, so they can intervene to prevent "the most unjust torturing" (Ratchford 21).

[4]Gérin notes a parallel between *Wuthering Heights* and Batholomew Simmons's "Bridegroom of Barna," in which the hero finds his entombed beloved, embraces her, is betrayed and buried with her (218).

[5]These elements were what the Victorians found profoundly subversive and caused reviewers to write of the novel's "singleness of malignity," to describe it as "odiously and abominably pagan" (see Allott, *The Brontës*, for a complete listing of critical reviews).

[6]See also Barker (1994) 271–72; 357–58.

[7]Again, as with the poems and diary papers, it's possible to make transparencies that can be shown in class so the students can read collectively.

[8]Although Edgar is compared to one: "he possessed the power to depart, as much as a cat possesses the power to leave a mouse half killed, or a bird half eaten" (64).

Wuthering Heights in the Culture of the English Department

Paula M. Krebs

Few English majors in United States universities and colleges are organized around traditional period and genre models anymore. Many, like mine, include film, creative writing, and cultural studies, along with their Old English, Shakespeare, and postcolonial courses. In a curriculum so diverse, taught by faculty members with widely varying approaches to the field and to their material, it is challenging to organize a gateway course that serves the needs of all.

The one that I teach, Approaches to Literature and Culture (Eng 290), must prepare students to enter the debates that characterize English studies today. To that end, I introduce students to many different positions about what the study of English is or should be as well as many perspectives on the texts we study. *Wuthering Heights* plays an important role in the class because of its place in literary history and popular culture as well as its value as a complex and rich narrative. In a field increasingly diverse, with less and less agreement about notions that used to be taken for granted (the definition of literature, criteria of literary quality, the value of complexity in texts, the notion of what constitutes a text at all), the novel works as a solid center, pulling together the competing interests of a class of many kinds of English majors. Film students, popular culture students, creative writers, and high aestheticists become a discursive community as they read, discuss, and write about the phenomenon that is *Wuthering Heights.*

My course takes Gerald Graff's "teach the conflicts" approach to introduce students not to templates for literary interpretation but to the theoretical debates that shape our discipline—for example, What is the proper material for study in an English department? Should we abandon or expand the notion of the canon? What do we mean by reading? *Wuthering Heights* can bring these conflicts and changes into focus. Many students have heard of Emily Brontë's novel and some have read it in high school, so they are resigned to studying it, although they might not necessarily have chosen the book on their own. Even majors who want to concentrate in film or popular culture understand that an English degree requires training in reading canonical texts. What they don't realize until we take up the text, though, is that their particular interests can be reflected in the work we do on the novel. They don't anticipate that they can study a canonical text using the tools of cultural studies analysis or that the film theory concept of the gaze can be applied fruitfully to a narrative such as *Wuthering Heights*. I enjoy making English majors aware that although we have widely different methodologies, we all study cultural texts, we all engage with narrative and image, and we all must come to terms with the role of literary history in our discipline and in our culture at large.

Wuthering Heights rewards close reading, has inspired fascinating films, has engendered much critical controversy, and has produced a broad range of popular culture, from the preservation of Haworth village to the plethora of Brontë Web sites. The novel allows me to complicate the notion of the canon as I teach a canonical text; it is an infinitely malleable document with an infinitely expanding context.

In the course, I first set up key debates for the field of English studies, using and supplementing David Richter's *Falling into Theory*. Students come to grips with questions of canonization, authorship, and the definitions of the English major in the twenty-first century. They read Roland Barthes, Harold Bloom, Judith Fetterley, Michel Foucault, Jane Tompkins, and others, and they write their own case studies of critical reception of a particular author or text. Compiling reception studies enables the students to test their assumptions about when and how particular works or authors achieved canonized status or to speculate about what factors may have facilitated or prevented critical attention to a work.

Although I don't ask the students to read Emily Brontë until later in the semester, some of them choose Brontë-related topics for this first essay. One student was curious about the relative reputations of *Shirley*, *Jane Eyre*, and *Wuthering Heights* and speculated about the reasons why *Shirley* captured so much less critical attention than the other two: were critics more attracted to the romance of the violent Heathcliff and the brooding Rochester than to Charlotte Brontë's Caroline and Shirley, who are caught up in economics? (O'Brien).[1] Because a reception study does not necessarily demand a thorough knowledge of a text, students can trace *Wuthering Heights* criticism before they have examined the text in class and so get a sense of the trajectories of critical opinion about the work. On what issues did reviewers focus when the book was first published? What did scholars see in the 1920s? the 1980s? What do they see today? What might be the significance of the changes?

This assignment introduces majors to the notion that the discipline has never been constant in its evaluation or analysis of a text or an author. As Tompkins explains, classic texts "have certainly been written and rewritten by the generations of professors and critics who make their living by them. They are the mirrors of culture as culture is interpreted by those who control the literary establishment" (127). New English majors who are drawn to popular-culture genres or to film nevertheless understand that they need to know the history of their field, especially of canonization debates. And students who come to English because of a love of literature benefit from being confronted with the idea that the canonization process has always involved real people making real choices. Likewise creative writers: seeing reputations change in ways more complicated than the simple "he wasn't appreciated until after his death" model helps students understand the interdependence of critics and authors and the influence of the literary marketplace.

When students trace the reception of a text or an author, they get a sense of what values our field seems to hold constant (if any) and how trends in criticism may affect the place of a particular text or author in the canon. A study of a canonical author can help students see fashions in criticism—when psychoanalytic approaches began to take hold or which journals first published queer criticism of a particular author. Students begin to perceive the evolution of their discipline and of the debates that shape it. Later in the semester, when we read *Wuthering Heights* together and write essays on it, using secondary sources, the work on reception helps the students to contextualize the Emily Brontë criticism they find. They understand, for example, that the "Was Heathcliff black?" question did not arise from thin air and that Nelly Dean was not always considered an unreliable narrator. Because my goal is to unite a classroom composed of different types of English majors, I try not to privilege traditional literary analysis by assigning an edition of *Wuthering Heights* that offers various schools of literary criticism. I do teach the schools, but to do so I use a student guide (most recently Lois Tyson's *Critical Theory Today*, which is keyed to *The Great Gatsby*, although I've also had good luck with Peter Barry's *Beginning Theory*, which is not keyed to a text), making clear to the class that what we learn from the guide is simply the baby-steps preparation for the real work with *Wuthering Heights*. They can practice with Tyson and *Gatsby*, but then they will go out on their own with Brontë.

One risk of starting students on a schools approach is that they'll simply choose the label they like best. For instance, they may call themselves feminist critics just because gender issues interest them. Critical editions divided by schools may reinforce this simplification. Nevertheless, it's useful for students to be able to identify the techniques they encounter. So once we've run through the schools, we revisit the works we read earlier in the class to determine which techniques the critics have used and which tools from the critical toolbox I provide. Students recognize that Laura Mulvey's "Visual Pleasure and Narrative Cinema" employs psychoanalytic concepts as a base within its feminism. They see that Henry Louis Gates, Jr., and Toni Morrison can hardly be tagged with the same label, as their approaches to race and American literature are so different. They learn the uses of reader-response criticism and the differences between the methods applied by Fetterley and, say, by David Bleich, and they learn ways to examine their reading in terms of their interpretive communities, à la Stanley Fish. By the time we get to *Wuthering Heights*, students have such a complex understanding of critical approaches to literature that they cannot demand, "Which one do you want me to use for my essay?"

For the paper on *Wuthering Heights*, then, I ask students to build a theoretically informed essay that draws on their strengths and interests and on the theorists and critics we've read during the semester. They are taking on a complicated Victorian novel, albeit one that may be familiar to many of them, without the kind of context they are used to having; the novel comes at the end of a course on literary and cultural theory rather than in the middle of a literature course. Class time is devoted to discussion, to be sure, and student surveys reveal that they learn more from class discussion than from any other aspect of the course's treatment of *Wuthering Heights*. But in class discussion I highlight the ways we are using the critical tools and addressing the theoretical questions they learned earlier in the course.

Students are able to suggest, on their own, which of the critical issues or approaches they have encountered (canonization, authorship, semiotics, etc.) might be most helpful in relation to particular topics on *Wuthering Heights*. Recently, for example, students immediately invoked psychoanalytic and feminist criticism to help them make sense of the elder Cathy's death. They suggested, in class, that she brought her death on herself as a hysterical reaction to feeling trapped by a patriarchal system into making a choice she didn't want to have made. Because the course addresses popular-culture issues throughout, even students for whom other genres are more important than the novel find themselves engaged in the *Wuthering Heights* debates. For example, this class addressed contemporary culture's apparent acceptance of melodramatic violence like Heathcliff's in various mainstream genres such as television programs. More important than the discussion of television culture was the fact that the discussion was intelligent and respectful, marked by none of the scorn or condescension I have occasionally seen in faculty debates on the topic.

Because we read John Guillory and John Fiske on television culture, along with Robert Scholes and even Stanley Fish on the importance of broadening our definition of text and of the texts we study, popular culture became for many of my students as rich a source as *Wuthering Heights* itself. Having read Bloom's "elegiac conclusion" to *The Western Canon*, they had also been forced to decide where they stood on the issue of whether the difficult pleasures of the Brontë novel were more rewarding or more important than their readings of television's brooding, violent heroes. Allowing them to consider such characters as Angel and Spike (from *Buffy the Vampire Slayer* and its spinoff, *Angel*) in relation to Heathcliff brings the debates about canonization to life: Does our training on the complicated narrative structure of *Wuthering Heights* help with or distract from our analysis of a television vampire? Is there room in the English major for both?

I tell the class about Monty Python's semaphore *Wuthering Heights* (they've seen *Monty Python and the Holy Grail*, but not many have watched the television series) and about the hilarious show I saw at an alternative-theater venue in London in the late 1980s, called *Withering Looks*. In it, the depressed Brontë sisters frequently burst into melancholy song, such as "It's No Life Being a Ghost," in which they complain about all the posthumous attention ("all my life I was repressed / and now I'm dead I get no rest"). Some students choose to write about film versions of the novel, but I found that the students who were concentrating in film studies actually preferred not to write about the films, perhaps because they were not much interested in questions of literary adaptation into film. They have learned how to write about other kinds of narrative in ways that are informed by their facility with film theory. They did not default to film as a topic but instead understood that much of the theory we'd been reading allowed them to ask interesting questions of a variety of genres.

By the time students approach their final essay on *Wuthering Heights*, they are acquainted with some pretty big issues in English studies—canonization, authorship, and so on—as well as with the methods associated with various schools of criticism. When they choose a topic to explore through *Wuthering Heights*, then, I expect them to demonstrate that they are members of the discursive community of English studies. They must pick topics that acknowledge the issues with which we've been wrestling all semester. I tell them that they have to write an essay that would have been impossible for them before they took the class.

They must acknowledge not only the community of scholars who have written about *Wuthering Heights* but also the theorists who have asked us to consider why and in what context we have chosen to write on a text like *Wuthering Heights*. So, for example, one student examined *Wuthering Heights*'s influence on the twentieth-century gothic romance, fully acknowledging the implications not only of the gender politics of the gothic tradition but also of the class politics involved in writing about mass-market fiction. (They read Janice Radway, too.)

Some of the best essays I received were queer readings of the text, including a sophisticated analysis that took off from Bonnie Burns's queer reading and Beth Newman's focus on the gaze. This student located queerness in the novel in "the narrative frame," which "forces" us to read the novel's romantic relationships in terms of alternate possibilities of gender and sexuality (Gavett). Another student, who examined Brontë Web sites, took a Foucauldian approach, noting, "With technological advances, the authorship function is changing. Students no longer read the novel by itself, but they bring popular culture and what they have learned in that environment to their reading of literature" (Crowley). She cited various interactive Brontë Web sites, including one that invites visitors to "enter the world of the Brontës by taking part in one of our drama workshops. Find out what life was like for the Brontës." She noted that Brontë Web sites bring together literature and popular culture, all the while reinforcing the status of canonized literature. Although she had had little confidence in her abilities to work with canonized literature, she found a way to engage directly with *Wuthering Heights* as a novel at the same time that she worked with it as a cultural phenomenon. She was not somewhere else in the department, investigating popular culture while most of the majors worked on literature. She was contributing to what all of us were learning about *Wuthering Heights*'s place in the major and in Anglo-American culture.

As much as students were able to discuss popular culture, romance fiction, film, and abstract questions of authorship in relation to the novel, they were all also working with a canonized work of fiction. Many students became obsessed with the novel's structure. The best paper in the class examined every transition in narrative voice in the novel and located moments in which paragraphing or quotation marks result in a lack of clarity about who is speaking. The student discussed the narrative function of such blurring, and his speculations about truth in the novel in relation to those moments of narration were stunning (Asancheyev).

Despite their interest in cultural context, most of the fifty-three students in the class loved the ways in which the novel repaid close reading. Peter Rabinowitz notes that the kind of close reading most of my students ended up doing "implicitly favor[s] figurative writing over realistic writing, indirect expression over direct expression, deep meaning over surface meaning, form over content, and the elite over the popular" (219). But my students seemed genuinely able to combine what they learned about literary and cultural theory with the close reading skills they were honing. The methods proved compatible. They realized that a focus on aesthetics is not at odds with attention to history, ideology, or reception.

Wuthering Heights is a "difficult pleasure," a novel that repays close reading and that rewards students in proportion to the effort they invest in it. My students demonstrated that such difficult pleasures do not have to be enjoyed on Parnassus with Bloom. *Wuthering Heights* can be understood, examined, and savored in a context that allows for its place in popular culture as well as in the literary canon. The students who took the most traditional approaches to the novel nevertheless learned from the course, especially from other students, the importance of not removing a novel from its historical or cultural context. They learned that historical context can include the culture in which they are reading the novel as well as that in which the novel was written. They bring to the text a fuller understanding of English studies as a field that includes film, media studies, and history as well as literary criticism. In the Approaches to Literature and Culture course, the students came to see *Wuthering Heights* as part of a number of larger cultures—not only of Victorian Britain and the contemporary United States but also of the English department and of English studies today.

NOTE

[1]All student writing in this essay used with permission.

"The Writing on the Wall": Interpreting *Wuthering Heights* in a Class on Theories of Interpretations

Suzy Anger

It is fitting that a course introducing students to contemporary theories of interpretation should anchor itself in a text that is notoriously difficult to interpret and has given rise to an almost bewildering range of interpretations. *Wuthering Heights* calls attention to the problems of interpretation in many ways, from its shifting first-person points of view to its emphasis within the narrative on hermeneutic difficulties—for instance, in Lockwood's misreadings of the Height's inhabitants. The novel also creates dramatic situations that demand interpretive work of its readers—for example, in the exegesis of Lockwood's dream (itself about exegesis) and in its refusal to decide between contending views on the presence of spirits.

This essay discusses the teaching of Emily Brontë's narrative in a senior-level class on contemporary literary theory in which *Wuthering Heights* is the single literary work read. I begin the course by asking students what they do when they interpret a literary text; the discussion serves as an occasion to tease out some of their tacitly held assumptions about interpretation. Often students have not given much thought to the question, and when they do, two types of vaguely formulated, commonsense positions typically emerge. The first is a fuzzy subjectivist view that everyone has his or her own opinion. The second is a loose objectivist view that we read the text to understand what the author wanted us to get from it; this view is often connected to students' claims that they also write creative works and want people to understand their words as they mean them.

This preliminary discussion allows me to introduce basic ideas about the locus and status of meaning. We consider a series of questions: Is meaning determinate? Is it found in the author's intentions? If so, how do we discover those intentions? Is meaning discovered or created? Will interpretations necessarily vary from interpreter to interpreter? Will they vary over time? Can principles that guide interpretation be established? What, if any, contextual information is necessary in interpretation? When should constraints on interpretation enter in and of what should they consist? Are preconceptions escapable? Is interpretation connected to authority? Can subjective bias be eliminated in interpretation? I emphasize that the theories we will discuss in the class are difficult, that we move through them rather quickly, that there are no easy answers to the questions posed, as our study of *Wuthering Heights* will underscore, and that a central goal for the course is for students to become more aware of what they think the interpretation of literary works involves.

We then examine formalist and New Critical accounts of meaning (Wimsatt and Beardsley, "Intentional Fallacy"; Brooks) before considering E. D. Hirsch's intentionalist views.[1] These first critical readings help us begin thinking in more precise ways about the positions we have formulated in discussion. A look at the New Criticism and Hirsch, for instance, leads to debate over whether semantic features and the conventions of language are enough to provide determinacy. I ask students to consider two questions about each of the theories they encounter: Does the critic believe that meaning inheres in the author, in the text, or in the reader (or in some combination of those positions)? Does the critic believe that the meaning is objectively there or subjectively constructed (or something in between)?

The class next moves to a reading of *Wuthering Heights*. I want our discussion of the novel to take the form of what students sometimes describe as a perspective-free reading: "This is just my response." I do not, therefore, begin by offering background information on the novel and its author, as I would be likely to do in other courses. Instead, we plunge into discussion, and I wait for students to remark on material that they think would be helpful to them in interpreting the novel. As we consider the novel, I draw attention to the sorts of critical assumptions that are implied by their comments. Typically their initial comments are primarily about characters and relationships. Students frequently remark that they don't like any of the characters. They find the narrative hard to follow, cannot keep the names straight because of the repetition of initial letters or names across generations, and are confused by the genealogies. They are as well always struck by the novel's violence. Because students quickly become curious about the author's biography, we can examine how knowledge of Emily Brontë's life affects our reading of the novel.

I ask, Does it change your reading of the text to know about Emily Brontë's religious background, her brother Branwell, or the numerous deaths in her family? Why might we think that this information is (or is not) necessary for interpreting the novel? Some students pose questions about the historical and cultural context, and we can similarly ask what that knowledge does for our interpretation of the novel.

I sometimes give students a couple of pages from Dorothy Van Ghent's essay on the symbolism of windows in the novel, as an example of the New Criticism and of the sort of close reading and attention to symbols that many students take to be the sine qua non of literary studies. Mark Schorer's reading of the novel's imagery in "Fiction and the Analogical Matrix" is another possibility here. We note that such an approach does not ask us to go (much) beyond what is found in the words of the text itself. Can close reading alone tell us everything we need to know to interpret the text? The specific and practical discussion of these theoretical issues helps students get a clearer sense of what is at stake in the abstract critical works we've examined thus far.

Because it is a course on interpretation, I take opportunities to steer the discussion to aspects of the novel that underscore hermeneutics. For instance, when discussing Lockwood's role as a first-person narrator, I ask students to consider what sort of values he holds, whether he seems to be a good judge of character and an accurate observer, and whether they trust his construction of the events. We also examine the proposition that his interpretive difficulties are analogous to the ones that students have been describing in their attempts to make sense of the novel's world. Lockwood's initial narrative, as has often been noted, represents a series of his own interpretive blunders; it culminates in the description of his dreams, one of which is based on a biblical text that is interpreted and responded to in the form of a dream. Students notice that Brontë gives detailed accounts of the dreams, which they believe invite interpretation. (Dream interpretation is a familiar idea among students, I find. Invariably a student brings in a popular guide to the subject.) After some general discussion, I hand out a copy of the biblical text on which Jabes Branderham's dream sermon "Seventy Times Seven and First of the Seventy-First" (*Wuthering Heights* 18–20) is based:

> Then came Peter to him, and said, Lord, how oft shall my brother sin against me, and I forgive him? Till seven times?
>
> Jesus said unto him, I say not unto thee, Until seven times: but, Until seventy times seven. (Matt. 18.21–22)

We talk about the ways in which knowing the biblical text offers new possibilities of interpretation. (This topic provides an opportunity to talk about intertextuality as well.) Students notice that Lockwood's dreams take up the themes of sin and forgiveness (or, here, a refusal to forgive, directed at the preacher as sinner, then turned back by preacher onto Lockwood with a violence equal to Heathcliff's). The connection between the biblical text and the dream also opens the way to a discussion about the ways in which interpretation, the central activity of current literary studies, was secularized in the nineteenth century as the Bible came to be understood as a historical document. I invite students to think about whether literary interpretation continues to reveal its roots in biblical exegesis.

As we continue our discussion of the novel, we ask whether it is possible to know what the novel sanctions, given the series of first-person narrators with which we are presented. About halfway through our reading of Nelly's narrative, I introduce the first page from a 1958 article, "The Villain in *Wuthering Heights*," in which James Hafley states his thesis that Nelly is not merely an unreliable storyteller or the representative of a conventional morality the narrative may reject; she is in fact a reprehensible, manipulative character responsible for many of the novel's miseries. Hafley's text evokes a lively response, and although many students take the argument to be hyperbolic, most begin to read suspiciously, seeking aspects of the narrative that seem to undermine Nelly's credibility. A few continue to defend her as the voice of reason.

After we have finished our initial discussion of the novel (to which we devote about two weeks), we turn to Charlotte Brontë's "Biographical Notice of Ellis and Acton Bell" and her "Editor's Preface to the New [1850] Edition of *Wuthering Heights.*" I like to look closely at Charlotte's response, in the "Biographical Notice," to the reviews of Emily's novel, because the older sister's remarks are deeply concerned with interpretation. In defending Emily and praising one reviewer of the novel, Charlotte writes:

> Too often do reviewers remind us of the mob of Astrologers, Chaldeans, and Soothsayers gathered before the "writing on the wall," and unable to read the characters or make known the interpretation. We have a right to rejoice when a true seer comes at last, some man in whom is an excellent spirit, to whom has been given light, wisdom, and understanding; who can accurately read the "Mene, Mene, Tekel, Upharsin" of an original mind (however unripe, however inefficiently cultured and partially expanded that mind may be); and who can say with confidence, "This is the interpretation thereof." (322)

I ask students to think about Charlotte Brontë's model of interpretation in this passage. Some recognize that when she speaks of "the interpretation" of the novel, she takes for granted that there is one "accurate" reading and that the ability to discern that right interpretation is tied to sagacity, intelligence, and the possession of a particular sort of "spirit." As we discuss the common

Victorian idea that a good interpreter has particular characteristics (Matthew Arnold's "tact" [276], George Eliot's sympathy, Benjamin Jowett's "finer perception" [520]), we draw out the implications of such a view.

When students point out that Charlotte's words make reference to a biblical story, we examine the passage in which Daniel interprets the spectral finger's "writing on the wall":

> The king cried aloud to bring in the astrologers, the Chaldeans, and the soothsayers. And the king spake, and said to the wise men of Babylon, Whosoever shall read this writing, and shew me the interpretation thereof, shall be clothed with scarlet, and have a chain of gold about his neck, and shall be the third ruler in the kingdom.
>
> Then came in all the king's wise men: but they could not read the writing, nor make known to the king the interpretation thereof. . . .
>
> Forasmuch as an excellent spirit, and knowledge, and understanding, interpreting of dreams, and shewing of hard sentences, and dissolving of doubts, were found in the same Daniel, whom the king named Belteshazzar: now let Daniel be called, and he will shew the interpretation. (Dan. 5.7–8, 5.12)

After examining Daniel's detailed (and apparently correct, given the immediate consequences for the king) interpretation of the writing, I tell students that the Aramaic words on the wall could literally be translated as "It has been counted and counted, weighed and divided." How does one move from those few words to Daniel's lengthy interpretation? I ask. As if to set us up for our study of the theories to come, the novel sends us back to other texts, themselves both demanding and preoccupied with interpretation.

I next have students look at the review that Charlotte Brontë commends, Sydney Dobell's *Palladium* review of September 1850, and we compare his analysis with her remarks on the novel in the "Editor's Preface." Do we agree with her judgments? Because many students are by this time convinced of Nelly's unreliability, they take issue with Charlotte's views: "For a specimen of true benevolence and homely fidelity, look at the character of Nelly Dean." How persuasive is Charlotte's claim that Emily "held that mercy and forgiveness are the divinest attribute of the Great Being" (326), when it is applied to this novel? And is Charlotte right about the "perverted" and "infernal" (327) nature of the elder Cathy and Heathcliff? Her view of the two characters is a reading that more students are likely to agree with, since the traditional Hollywood interpretation of a surpassing love has given way to many students' current assessment of the relationship as dysfunctional. We wonder about Charlotte's apologetic perspective, her representation of Emily as immature and unschooled, and her oblique reference to herself as "the auditor" who "shuddered" on hearing her sister's manuscript (326). I hope students will see that we can ask much the same questions about Charlotte's claims in the

"Preface" that we ask about Lockwood's framing narrative. What were Charlotte Brontë's motives in construing the novel as she does? What conditions her interpretation? Wouldn't being Emily's sister give her special insight into the correct meaning of the text? Is Charlotte standing as interpreter to her sister's world? I ask, recalling that in the "Biographical Notice" she writes, "an interpreter ought always to have stood between [Emily] and the world" (324). If Charlotte is playing that role, does her "Preface" offer the loving, sympathetic understanding of one who knows the intentions of another? Or is she, rather, more like Nelly as interpreter to Cathy's and Heathcliff's world? Does Charlotte's interpretation stand as that of "a true seer" or an appropriator? By probing Charlotte's perspective on the novel, we begin to anticipate some of the theories of interpretation that we turn to next in the course.

For the remainder of the course, we move through a series of contemporary critical approaches: reader response, poststructuralism, Marxism, feminism, postcolonial criticism, and cultural studies. My selection of theorists and texts changes a bit each time I teach the course. In every unit, after examining the theoretical texts, we return to *Wuthering Heights*, reading an essay that approaches the novel from the theoretical viewpoint we are studying. This strategy gives us a concrete site for understanding abstract theories. Furthermore, students often cannot see why the issues matter until they are applied in actual readings.

There is a wealth of critical material on the novel. One option is to use the essays in Linda Peterson's edition of *Wuthering Heights*, perhaps supplemented with additional essays.[2] Two benefits of using this text are that the introductory material on schools of criticism is presented in terms that students find more accessible than the theory itself and that some of the essays are themselves written or revised for undergraduate students.

I mention here some sample clusters of readings that I have used; there are, of course, many other possibilities, and one must limit the readings, since it is crucial that students spend time with the theory. For Marxist criticism, we look at selections from Karl Marx and Friedrich Engels, *The German Ideology*. We might next read Walter Benjamin, "The Work of Art in the Age of Mechanical Reproduction," followed by Louis Althusser, from "Ideology and Ideological State Apparatuses." We end the unit by returning to the novel, with an examination of Terry Eagleton's analysis in *Myths of Power: A Marxist Study of the Brontës*.[3] Although students find Eagleton's essay difficult, Marxist criticism of the novel is largely well received, given that students have themselves recognized that issues of class are crucial to the narrative. Students also point out that Althusser's theories on interpellation into ideology are useful for understanding the elder Cathy's transformation from Earnshaw to Linton. The unit on Marxist criticism opens the way as well to a general discussion of current views on the Victorian novel's relation to nineteenth-century bourgeois ideology.

For a unit on poststructuralism and deconstruction, we discuss excerpts from Friedrich Nietzsche's "On Truth and Lies in a Nonmoral Sense" and *The Will to Power*, followed by a selection from Ferdinand de Saussure's *Course in General Linguistics*. We might then read Roland Barthes's "The Death of the Author," followed by a piece by Jacques Derrida. His "Structure, Sign, and Play in the Discourse of the Human Sciences" works well, because it allows us to discuss the move from structuralism to poststructuralism; additionally, it is somewhat more accessible than his later works. (Not surprisingly, students find Derrida's work the most difficult to understand.) We return to the novel with a reading either of J. Hillis Miller's "*Wuthering Heights*: Repetition and the 'Uncanny' " or of Carol Jacobs's "*Wuthering Heights*: At the Threshold of Interpretation" (a textbook deconstruction of the novel).[4]

We begin our study of psychoanalytic criticism with readings from Sigmund Freud's *Interpretation of Dreams*. Freud's theories afford a perspective on interpreting Lockwood's dreams that differs from the scriptural comparison. Armed with the concepts "latent" and "manifest" and steeped in Freud's sexual analyses, students point out the recurrent images of staffs in Lockwood's dreams, connecting those images to the nocturnal visitation of the female ghost and his fear of romance. I have not yet seen students develop such an interpretation before reading Freud, so this is a good moment to take up the question of whether the theory creates the text or makes apparent something that is already there. At this time I also briefly introduce Victorian theories on dreams, asking if those theories seem to capture the way in which Emily Brontë uses the dreams in the novel. The discussion opens the way to deliberation on the validity of using later theories to explore works written before the theories had been formulated. Students (who often take Emily Brontë to be somewhat neurotic) also eagerly read the book as her manifest content, which needs interpretation to reveal the author's psyche (latent content).

As we return to the treatment of the novel in the critical readings, we ask whether the theoretical analyses encourage us to modify our earlier interpretations. Some students have strong opinions about which readings illuminate the novel and which do not, and the class engages in arguments over whether the interpretations are really about the novel or whether the novel has been bent to fit the theories. Or whether, to use Oscar Wilde's words, "to the critic the work of art is simply a suggestion for a new work of his own, that need not necessarily bear any obvious resemblance to the thing it criticizes" (1030). I have noticed that late in the term, students can anticipate the features of the novel to which, say, a postcolonial or a feminist reading is likely to attend.

By the end of the course, students have lived with a single novel to a greater extent than is possible in a course that covers a variety of literary works, while having gained appreciation for the rich interpretive possibilities that the text affords. That at least is the positive view of the course, and at best students feel that the introduction to a range of views on a single novel has changed their understanding of the interpretive process. Others, however, feel that they have had more than enough of one text, and a few note with frustration that there cannot possibly be anything left for them to say about *Wuthering Heights* or any other literary work, given the existing heaps of criticism. Still others express bewilderment that we have not finally figured out what the text means. I remind them that when the king in Daniel's story was given "the interpretation" that he demanded, he also received death. Theory, I suggest, perhaps shows us that we do not want a Daniel to deliver the final interpretation of the writing on the wall.

NOTES

[1]I use the anthology edited by Julie Rivkin and Michael Ryan or *The Norton Anthology of Theory and Criticism,* edited by Vincent Leitch et al. These fine compilations contain excellent introductory materials and many of the theoretical essays mentioned in this article.

[2]I have used the 1992 edition of the Peterson text but not yet the 2003 revised edition, which replaces a number of the essays that appear in the earlier work.

[3]Eagleton's work is included in Peterson's first edition.

[4]Miller's essay is reprinted in Dunn (2002).

Teaching *Wuthering Heights* as Fantasy, Trauma, and Dream Work

Diane Long Hoeveler

I have taught literature through the methodologies of psychoanalysis for many years, and in this essay I sketch, first, how an instructor can use some basic psychological concepts to teach *Wuthering Heights*.[1] In defense of such a method, I would argue that by learning to read *Wuthering Heights* psychoanalytically, students can understand how life cycles tend to have a narrative pattern of their own: a nursery drama (food, gluttony, and starvation anxieties), then childhood traumas (loss, abandonment, body issues), followed by adolescent angst (identity concerns), and then the challenges of adulthood and maturation (reconciling love and work). As psychoanalysis is based on explaining the coping mechanisms that the psyche uses throughout life, it is crucial for students to see that all stages of life are characterized by particular traumas and fantasies. Second, this essay outlines how to use basic psychoanalytical theories to teach the novel, as well as to introduce students to the most important, or most accessible, psychological approaches to critical reading. I recognize that teachers may be hesitant to use psychoanalysis in the classroom, fearing that they are not adequately trained in psychology or that its introduction will force them to address issues that could become inappropriately personal or awkward. But with a basic background in what I would call student-friendly Freud, most teachers should feel comfortable with raising and discussing some of the deeply resonant psychological issues that *Wuthering Heights* raises. A listing of Internet sources for the definitions of the psychological terms used is provided in the appendix at the conclusion of the essay.

To my surprise, students enjoy studying fairy tales; not only do the tales contain blatant use of literary devices, but they also provide miniature case studies that allow students to use the psychoanalytic concepts that literary critics employ: fantasy, trauma, repression, condensation, displacement, repetition, the death wish, the uncanny, mourning and melancholia, and transference and projection. I begin my teaching of *Wuthering Heights*, then, with the introduction of a few core fairy tales, to demonstrate the basic structure of narrative, while at the same time making the point that the simplest texts exist to accomplish psychological work for their readers (not to mention their writers). Fairy tales mediate nursery anxieties, and there is no better way to illustrate this idea than to teach "Hansel and Gretel" and to talk about the earliest food and body issues (bread crumbs as the means to survival, starvation versus gluttony, the gingerbread house as symbol of the mother's body, and mother as ambivalent—both feared and loved—source of nourishment).

Early childhood issues are also developed in *Wuthering Heights*, in the oral imagery that suffuses the text, as well as in the early abandonment of Heathcliff and his continual uncertainty about his parentage—remember Nelly's comforting him with the notion that perhaps he is displaced royalty (50). The concern with childhood gluttony or starvation is played out in the scene in which Heathcliff and the elder Catherine watch Isabel and Edgar quarreling over their tea table, just before Catherine is attacked by the Linton dog. This Linton family tea party is uncannily repeated with variation when Lockwood thinks he is being served tea by young Catherine and mistakenly sits down on a mass of cats and is threatened by a dog. The human and animal anxiously coexist in the worlds of both Wuthering Heights and Thrushcross Grange, suggesting that they are never fully resolved in any of the characters.

We move next to fairy tales that mediate adolescent issues, especially bodily transformations and the need to separate from one's parents before one can seek a suitable mate. The classic text here has been "Sleeping Beauty," a tale that speaks in graphic terms about menstruation (pricking one's finger at a spinning wheel) and the latency period of psychosexual development (the 100 years of sleep). The kiss that awakens Sleeping Beauty also effectively places her in the arms of her new mate, allowing her to survive her parents—and even reject them—without suffering guilt or indeed even observing their demise: they died during the hundred years of sleep. Another fairy tale that explores adolescent issues (anxiety about body changes, control of the emotions, public scenes of shame and embarrassment) that are pertinent to *Wuthering Heights* is "Brother and Sister," in which orphaned siblings flee their wicked stepmother and live in the forest, where the sister retains her human form, marries, and gives birth to the king's son, while her brother is transformed into an animal, a deer, and is never fully civilized. A heterosexualized version of this tale is "Beauty and the Beast," another well-known story in the animal-groom cycle, in which the love of a good and beautiful woman redeems a man whose faults have transformed him into a beast.[2]

By way of introducing my approach to fiction, I explain that Freud never resolved the question of which comes first in the development of a person: traumas or the fantasies that help the person cope with those traumas. In fact, it seems certain that what some people report as physical traumas are sometimes fantasies. To extrapolate from what we know of the slippery slope of the psyche, it appears that literature can be understood as almost always a fantasy formation designed to ward off an experience that writers understand as traumatic. By replaying it imaginatively, they master the trauma. I use Freud's theory that there are three basic fantasies—seduction, castration, and primal scene—and that all of them have the same psychic structures of meaning. Fantasies function as the disguises of real or imagined traumatic events of childhood. By translating those traumas into an imagined scene that veils a memory without obliterating it, the fantasy allows the adult to master the experience in a substitute formation (the poem, the novel). Fantasies mediate between the conscious and the unconscious mind because repression will screen a trauma that can be expressed only after the event and in a distorted fashion. As Jean Laplanche and Bertrand Pontalis have observed, "Fantasy precedes identity."[3] To schematize how I think fantasies operate in conjunction with trauma in literary texts, I provide my students with the following chart:

> *Fantasy of seduction:* Corresponding trauma of betrayal; manifested in literature through the fantasy of desire; oedipal rivalries; incest; solipsism and narcissism; self-loathing; gynophobia; somaphobia; emergence of sexuality; eating disorders.
>
> *Fantasy of castration:* Corresponding trauma of adandonment or desertion; manifested in literature through the fantasies of death and sexual difference; beating fantasies; persecutory fantasies; decapitation; fetishism; sadism and masochism; self-mutilation.
>
> *Fantasy of primal scene:* Corresponding trauma of separation or otherness; manifested in literature through the fantasy of heritage; identity or origins; voyeurism and exhibitionism; family romance scenarios; scopophilia and epistemephilia; gossip; boundary issues.

What is crucial about this chart is that it maps trauma onto fantasy—or, rather, it illustrates the idea that trauma will always manifest itself as a variety of fantasy formations that in turn can be recognized in fairly discernible ways in literary texts.

Following the categories in this chart, I generally start by explaining the fantasy of seduction, which arises as a defense against childhood betrayal (real or imagined). Seduction is perhaps most familiar to my students, as its tropes are highly visible in our culture, dominating the action and meaning of most cinema and popular culture. Seduction operates largely through oedipal configurations, which function throughout *Wuthering Heights* in the sheer proliferation of triangles. The fantasy of seducing a parental figure (or the substitute of a parent) is a powerful denial of a child's actual sense of powerlessness; hence we see Isabella desperately trying to win the love of the sadistic Heathcliff, wallowing in her abjection before finally gaining enough self-esteem or survival instinct to flee him. Psychoanalytic critics have read the elder Cathy as Heathcliff's mother figure, while others have interpreted Heathcliff as the mother figure of the text. Still others see Nelly Dean positioned in the mother's role or young Catherine functioning as mother to Lockwood, Heathcliff, Linton, and Hareton (see Wion; Reed).

Solipsism and narcissism are also key manifestations of seduction and betrayal, defenses that posit love of the self as a safeguard against accepting the otherness of another person. *Wuthering Heights* provides one of the most famous solipsistic statements in the history of literature: "Nelly, I *am* Heathcliff—he's always, always in my mind . . . as my own being" (73). Heathcliff suffers from the same solipsism in regard to Cathy, going so far as to remove the coffin sides so that their remains can mingle as one after their deaths. This absorption of one's self into another is the essence of one type of love

(Narcissus staring into his reflected face in the pool), and perhaps forms the basis of the incestuous pull we discern between Cathy and Heathcliff, but it is not a mature love that values the unique otherness of the beloved. The desire to merge totally with another who looks similar to oneself is a manifestation of the childhood fantasy of having an identical twin, and despite their physical differences (he dark, she light), Heathcliff and Cathy seem never to have outgrown the union they experienced in their childhood bed. Just before her death, Cathy locates the source of all her unhappiness in being shut out of the oak-paneled bed she had shared with Heathcliff, while he is haunted throughout his life by memories of Cathy "resting her darling head on the same pillow as she did when a child" (257).

The fantasy of seduction, so frequently thwarted by society's conventions, often manifests its blockage in a variety of attacks on the body—most typically, eating disorders and fear of emerging sexuality. Certainly such disorders can be seen in the strange eating scenes throughout the novel, in the elder Cathy's anorexia (her identification with the starving lapwings left in the nest), her hysterical rejection of her pregnancy (her failure to recognize herself in the mirror), and in Heathcliff's death by starvation.

The second fantasy, castration, appears most dominant throughout the novel (interesting in a female-authored text). If we see a literary character constantly being beaten, as the child Heathcliff is, then we know that much of the psychic energy of the text can be located in the fantasy of castration and, therefore, in fears of abandonment or desertion. I point out to my students that Emily Brontë's mother died when she was three, while her two oldest sisters died at Cowan Bridge School when she was seven and trying to survive with them in a typhus-infected dumping ground. To lose one's mother and then one's mother substitutes at such an early age would be a difficult trauma for any child to process. In addition, Emily could easily have experienced being sent to Cowan Bridge School, along with her three older siblings, at the age of six, as abandonment by her father, a repetition of her mother's abandonment of her in death. And then to survive when the two older girls died would have produced a level of guilt that we now call the survivor syndrome. Certainly father figures are ambivalent forces throughout the novel, as well as in the poetry Brontë authored during her life.[4] Beatings as well as beating fantasies occur throughout *Wuthering Heights*; some of the most obvious are the dreamed assault by cudgels on Lockwood in the Jabes Branderham dream, the whippings of Heathcliff, the hanging of Isabella's dog, the beatings of Isabella, the persecution of young Catherine, and the beatings of Linton Heathcliff. Masochism and sadism dominate the relationship of Isabella and Heathcliff, but the positions are reversed in the Heathcliff and Cathy relation; Heathcliff identifies Cathy as a torturer and himself as her victim (100).

The third fantasy, primal scene, is always the most awkward and embarrassing for my students to identify and discuss in a class. But a manifestation of primal scene fantasies reveals the underlying trauma of otherness or separation from one's origins. I generally refer to Keats's "Ode to Psyche" as an obvious example of a primal scene fantasy—in which the poet stumbles on Adam and Eve post coitus in the Garden of Eden—but I admit that such a scene does not occur in *Wuthering Heights*. There are, however, curious patterns in the text that suggest a fairly obsessive concern with trying to understand a secret, perhaps a sexual secret, like where babies come from. Isn't it odd that the identity of the orphaned child Heathcliff is the crux of the novel? It is almost as if by solving that mystery—where did the baby Heathcliff come from?—we, as well as the characters, will solve all the conundrums of the novel and of life. And where there are secrets there will be gossips—hence Nelly and her ever-willing listener Lockwood. Like a mother trying to tell a child the facts of life, Nelly just keeps talking to Lockwood; by the end, they both seem as foggy about everything as they were on the night of his arrival. Nelly observes, "But where did he come from, the little dark thing?" (293).

When one uses psychoanalytic theory in the classroom, one is soon dealing with an author's biography or psychobiography. With Emily Brontë we are presented with a particularly tough case. We know nothing about how she processed her adult experiences, since we have no letters, no journals, only the poetry and the novel. Of course, we do know the barest biographical facts, and from those I would suggest that we can locate the origin of her traumas in childhood, where we know all trauma begins. When an adult experiences another rejection, betrayal, or death of a loved one, the original trauma is reactivated, like a wound that has never fully healed. We know only that Emily Brontë left home twice as a student and once to work as a governess; each time she ventured from home, she became so depressed or sick that she had to return to Haworth within months. Clearly her identity was bound up with her status and security in the tight network of family and moors over which she held sway. I often point out to students that Brontë was most alive and most conscious when she was at home; life outside her home environment must have seemed like a bad dream to her—unreal, nightmarish, ghostly.

Thus it is no coincidence that dream work begins *Wuthering Heights* when Lockwood, the interloper, falls asleep in the elder Catherine's oak-paneled bed after reading her childhood diary. That his two dreams are foregrounded in the novel and that Catherine considers her dreams as important, highly charged moments throughout her life cause us to confront the meanings of dreams, as well as the text itself as dream work. Freud locates four main aspects to the dream work, the means by which the hidden wish becomes expressed: condensation, displacement, considerations of representability, and secondary revision.

Condensation is one of the methods by which the repressed (in an author's life or in a literary character's history) returns in hidden ways in the dream. For example, in dreams multiple thoughts are often combined and amalgamated into a single element of the manifest dream (Cathy's dream about being thrown out of heaven and landing on top of Wuthering Heights suggests her fear of marriage to Edgar, as well as her understanding that separation from Heathcliff and her childhood home and bed will destroy her). Cathy herself tells Nelly how important dreams are to her, although clearly she doesn't read the warnings well: "I've dreamt in my life dreams that have stayed with me ever after, and changed my ideas; they've gone through and through me, like wine through water, and altered the colour of my mind" (70).

Displacement is one of the methods by which the repressed returns in hidden ways. For example, in dreams the affect (emotions) associated with threatening impulses is often transferred elsewhere (displaced), so that apparently trivial elements in the manifest dream seem to cause extraordinary distress, while "what was the essence of the dream-thoughts finds only passing and indistinct representation in the dream" (Freud, *Lectures* 22).[5] For example, in Lockwood's first dream, he fixates on Joseph as a guide through a snowy walk home (which home? *Heimleich,* the opposite of the uncanny?). Joseph is equipped with the "heavy-headed cugdel," but Lockwood has no such "weapon" to enter his house (18). However, they are not actually going home; they are going to a chapel where Jabes Branderham is preaching, and much extraneous detail is given about Jabes's salary and the state of the chapel itself (childhood memories of hearing the Reverend Patrick Brontë grouse about his salary and the state of the church and parsonage?). After a long, boring sermon, Lockwood objects, and the entire assembly suddenly arises and starts to beat him; the churchgoers have sticks, but he does not. Castration anxiety and a very blatant beating fantasy begin the novel; I ask my students if it isn't fair to ask if the text itself functions as dream work to resolve the repressed childhood memory of abuse, of being dragged unwillingly to church and then subjected to the demands of social conformity that Emily Brontë understood as a form of psychological abuse.

The third technique exhibited in dream work is representability, or "figurability," the tendency to transform thoughts into visual elements. ("I was stuck in a church and beaten by the congregation" might mean "I am overwhelmed with and angry about the demands to be the pastor's perfect daughter.") Literary critics as well as students who are attuned to psychoanalytic approaches to texts can distinguish between what is known as the manifest content of the dream ("I am in a church") and the latent content (the buried meaning that I am attributing to the dream just described). The two levels combine to form what is known as the dream work (the resolution or release that takes place in the psyche of the dreamer). As Freud notes,

> at bottom dreams are nothing other than a particular form of thinking, made possible by the conditions of the state of sleep. It is the dream-work that creates that form, and it alone is the essence of dreaming—the explanation of its peculiar nature. (*Interpretation* 649–50)[6]

Finally, what Freud called the secondary revision makes something whole and more or less coherent out of the distorted product of the dream work. Consider Lockwood's second dream as an example of how secondary revision functions. In this much shorter dream, Lockwood falls back asleep and dreams that the tree branch is still scratching the windowpane. He gets up to stop the noise, unlocks the window, and suddenly grabs or is grabbed by ice-cold fingers (note the uncertainty about agency here). The horrible cry, "Let me in—let me in!" is followed by a voice that identifies herself as "Catherine Linton. . . . I'm come home, I'd lost my way on the moor!" (20). Lockwood, claiming that terror made him cruel, relates that he pulled the wrist over the broken glass pane until it bled, soaking his bed clothes. When he is given the chance to let go of the hand, he does so, but shuts the pitiable creature out of the house, forcing her to be uncanny, homeless. This particular dream neatly brings together castration anxiety once more (cutting the hand over glass), another beating fantasy (complete with a woman's sacrificial blood), the search for the home of one's origins (primal scene reenactment), and that constantly annoying tree branch (primeval nature struggling continually to uproot and assault what we construct as civilization, a reference to the moors, which are superior to the heaven that will figure later in Cathy's dream). Lockwood's two dreams could be read together, as one extended dream work and as a manifestation of the unresolved residue of Cathy's traumas—losing her childhood home and identity to an artificial one imposed by marriage to a stranger, a man outside her endogamous family.[7]

Students frequently ask how we can understand a phenomenon like dreams, which appear repeatedly and in different ways. My response is always to stress the context in which an action or pattern occurs. Of course, as a teacher I am reminded of what Freud said to his critics about the notorious fuzziness of his concepts—tails I win, heads you lose. It is also necessary to address the primary turf of any psychoanalytic critic, the author's biography. This is contested and controversial ground, and I can understand teachers who do not want to venture into speculating about an author's intentions or the text as a manifestation or "working through" of an event in an author's life. Again, my position is that it is almost impossible to understand literary texts as psychological documents without delving into the author's life history.

Wuthering Heights is a strange novel to read, even stranger perhaps to teach. Clearly, fantasies and traumas swirl through the text, and what is one to make of them? The text is like a cry from the walking wounded. By providing students with at least five literary psychological case studies of how trauma displaces itself into fantasy, as well as a treasure trove of dreams, I help them see how literature expresses both the desires and the nightmares of life.

NOTES

[1]My course syllabi are available at www.marquette.edu/english/faculty/hoeveler .shtml.

[2]See Bettelheim. The most accessible text for the fairy tales is Zipes.

[3]Freud's theories are most succinctly presented in Laplanche and Pontalis 22.

[4]For a collection of Brontë's poetry placed in context with the novel, see my edition of *Wuthering Heights*. In addition to the novel and poems, my essay in that volume, "*Wuthering Heights* and Gothic Feminism," develops more fully my reading of the psychodynamics in the novel.

[5]See also www.sla.purdue.edu/academic/engl/theory/psychoanalysis/definitions/ condensation.

[6]See also John Phillips, at http://courses.nus.edu.sg/course/elljwp/dreamwork.htm.

[7]For a fuller discussion on the theory of the phantom, see Abraham.

APPENDIX
Internet Sources for Definitions of Psychological Terms and Concepts

Durbin, Paul G. 14 Dec. 2005 <http://www.hypnos.co.uk/hypnomag/pdurbin7.htm>.

Felluga, Dino. "Terms Used by Psychoanalysis." *Introductory Guide to Critical Theory*. 17 July 2002. Purdue U. 14 Dec. 2005 <http://www.purdue.edu/guidetotheory/psychoanalysis/psychterms.html>.

"Freud and the Literary Imagination." 14 Dec. 2005 <http://courses.washington.edu/freudlit/Uncanny.Notes.html>.

Kaufmann, Doug. "Psychology Glossary." *Alleydog.com*. 1999. Kaufmann Research and Consulting Group. 8 Sept. 2002. 14 Dec. 2005 <http://www.alleydog.com/glossary/glossary.cfm>.

The Narrative Design of *Wuthering Heights*: Interpreting the Telling of the Tale

Leilani D. Riehle

Wuthering Heights is a wonderfully wild and unwieldy book whose disparate elements famously resist unified, resolved interpretation. My classroom approach to the novel treats this wilderness as a virtue, so as to avoid the pedagogical equivalent of converting the "half-savage and hardy, and free" (111) Catherine and Heathcliff into the tamer, domesticated young Cathy and Hareton. Of greatest importance to me is an interpretive paradigm that is eye-opening and inclusive: a compass, if you will, for navigating the multiplicity (of plots, genres, characters, names) and complexity of Emily Brontë's masterpiece, rather than a carefully mapped tour. That compass is furnished by the novel's complicated narrative structure and by what I see as the ideological implications of such a structure.

First, however, a word on context. My readings of *Wuthering Heights* are greatly indebted to Terry Eagleton (*Myths*) and Nancy Armstrong (*Desire*), among others. In my course, *Wuthering Heights* comes early (just after *Jane Eyre*) in an upper-level majors' survey of the Victorian novel, for which my teaching style may be described as student-centered. I use active student involvement (heavy student participation in discussion-cum-lecture of 50-plus students), lots of literary analysis (e.g., close-reading of details, form, and design), and as much consideration of cultural context as is possible without any required secondary readings or theory. Having used *Jane Eyre* to illustrate how artfully a Victorian novel can naturalize plots of social, moral, and aesthetic progress, I then use *Wuthering Heights* to deconstruct the seeming naturalness of those progressions. Emily Brontë's novel is ideal for this job because its narrative structure is too complicated and contrived to be received, like *Jane Eyre*'s, as innocently mimetic. The contrast between the two novels thus alerts undergraduates to the significance of narrative design and sensitizes them to the representational assumptions they often bring to Victorian realism. To these ends, I take two weeks, less to walk students through a polished interpretation of the novel than to guide them through a series of related questions that revolve around the act of interpretation itself, as deployed in the novel; around the meanings that can be extrapolated from the ways a narrator tells her or his story; and around what the design of the novel reveals about the value judgments assigned (by characters and readers) to the elder Catherine and Heathcliff, especially, and to the progress of culture and social order into the Victorian period.

What follows is designed in the spirit of that approach. This essay is organized around questions that students, in my experience, have found particularly useful and interesting; after each question comes a brief discussion of what might be expected in response (allowing, of course, that lessons and their outcomes vary as much as instructors and their students).

Is Cathy's ghost real or a dream? How do we know, and why does the distinction matter?

I raise this question over a close reading of Lockwood's nightmare, beginning with "the tremendous tumult" caused by the fir-tree branch (20) and ending with Lockwood's tirade to Heathcliff about "the little fiend" (22). By emphasizing Lockwood's contradictory interpretations of the experience (nightmare or visitation?), this question gets students talking about the novel's interest in the distinction between real and unreal, realistic and unrealistic, conventional and nonconventional experiences—as evidenced by the abundance in *Wuthering Heights* of ghosts (and, in the second generation, the ghostly presences of the first), madness, hallucinations, cosmic despair, and vivid rememberings. Why is there so much concern in this novel with the distinction between the actual and the ideal, the imagined, or the supernatural? between the normal and the abnormal? And why are those distinctions viewed differently from different perspectives? I ask students, for example, how Nelly and Lockwood treat such distinctions as compared with Heathcliff and Catherine. Our post-*Matrix* students are galvanized by these distinctions and need little encouragement to apply them to literary analysis. Once they do, they generate outstanding ideas about who in the novel is empowered to name a phenomenon real and by what standards. If I ask them to describe Lockwood's responses to the ghost-nightmare and invite hypotheses about why he responds as he does, they may direct me to his violence and his name-calling of Catherine as a "little fiend," "minx," and "wicked little soul" (22), and extrapolate from these examples some controversial conclusions about his misogyny and his desire to match his masculinity to Heathcliff's. Alternatively, students might talk about Lockwood's investment in empiricism and the violence with which he dispels whatever threatens it—a point of departure for looking at the phenomenological assumptions of literary realism.

An opening question on realness thus prepares students to think critically about the values built into the distinction between realness and its others and draws their attention to Lockwood's participation in shaping the story they are about to hear. These benefits are especially helpful if your students, like mine, must continually fight the urge to discuss Victorian characters as if they were real persons dutifully recorded by reliable narrators. (Be prepared, for example, for the students' initial aversion to the novel's seemingly amoral protagonists.) If you make the realness itself a matter of conflict in *Wuthering Heights*, the class will more eagerly explore the relationship between the storytelling *in* the novel (by Lockwood, Nelly Dean, etc.) and the storytelling *of* the novel (which thus no longer need agree with Lockwood's and Nelly

Dean's). Finally, this line of discussion prepares students for the possibility that, despite the narrators' protestations, not all behaviors or events in the novel are conventionally explicable. The class is then ready to examine how insistently Lockwood and Nelly wrest events into conventional shapes and individuals into conventional roles.

How do Lockwood and Nelly Dean shape their narratives? And why can't Heathcliff and Catherine fit into them?

I find this point in the discussion a good place to shift gears a bit and turn students' attention to the more familiar terrain of character analysis. Citing Lockwood's curiosity about "that pretty girl-widow" who is either "a native of the country, or, as is more probable, an exotic that the surly indigenae will not recognise for kin" (28), I point out that Lockwood is a tourist to Wuthering Heights and Thrushcross Grange. Like a tourist, he exoticizes his destination. He searches for its differences from his home. Through examination of the first three chapters of the novel, we discuss why Wuthering Heights seems so unusual to Lockwood and how he views its occupants. Of special interest here are those moments when the guest compares himself with Heathcliff (1, 3); demonstrates his interest in material possessions, especially the "apartment and furniture" (2–3); discusses women, his "goddess" (3–4), and "Mrs. Heathcliff" (7–8); and worries over the social hierarchy operating in Heathcliff's household. In sum, Lockwood applies prescriptive social classifications and rules of behavior to an environment that resists them. In that resistance to social order and conformity, students begin to perceive Heathcliff's heroism and to distrust the normative, befuddled interventions of the first narrator.

This discussion brings us to Nelly Dean, whose status as a narrator I direct students to analyze. Having destabilized the reliability of one narrator, they are now better prepared to critically approach the savvier and generally more sympathetic one. While ready to allow that Nelly is hard on the elder Catherine and Heathcliff, students can easily overlook her reasons for being so. Thus I ask them to describe Nelly's tools of interpretation: What are her values? What is important to her? What does she look for when she observes an event? How are her acts of interpretation affected by her beliefs and expectations? How is she (dis)empowered by her interventions in the action, especially during Catherine's sickness and death? Students respond with a range of ideas that stimulate analysis of class, gender, and the domestic tableau. They discuss, for example, Nelly's liminality in the family structure; her exile from Wuthering Heights on Heathcliff's arrival (32); her underappreciated social value as a working woman (earned or not?); her thwarted or withheld efforts at more direct participation, especially in chapters 11 and 14; and her manipulativeness or her powerfulness. Although sympathies for Nelly vary widely, the class generally agrees that, while exercising a power that is by necessity covert, Nelly nonetheless (and perhaps inadvertently) exercises it in service of patriarchal authority, social order, and prescriptive behaviors.

Now students can more comfortably explore the epistemological and hermeneutic questions that *Wuthering Heights* raises about its remarkable protagonists. How do Nelly Dean and Lockwood perceive and then interpret the lovers? What *can* Nelly and Lockwood know about them or their experiences, given the earlier ideas the two narrators had about what is real? How does their understanding compare with what we know (or think we know) about Catherine, Heathcliff, Edgar, and the rest? How does our knowledge compare with what Nelly and Lockwood have observed? By coaxing my students to think about the epistemological challenges of the plot's unfolding, I can in turn suggest to them that the novel is about the act of interpretation: not just the power consciously or unconsciously exercised in the effort to interpret and therefore shape a history but also the very instability of interpretation itself (as argued by J. Hillis Miller, "*Wuthering Heights*: Repetition and the 'Uncanny' "). Like Nelly interpreting Catherine and Heathcliff, we can only transform the inexplicable, the strange, the unexpected, or the socially deviant into terms of the explicable, the normal, the expected, or the ordinary.

Arguing about Nelly as an interpreter as well as an observer and thinking about interpretation as an act of participation lead students to address what Brontë's novel reveals about the act of shaping and narrating history—a useful line of inquiry in any class on the Victorian novel that seeks to denaturalize realism as the baseline experience of reality from which modernism and postmodernism departed. At this point, I provide students with a map of the novel's narrative design (see pp. 110–11). This map diagrams the novel's chapters, 1–34, indicating which are narrated by Lockwood and which by Nelly, when Nelly directly addresses Lockwood, and when Lockwood interrupts with present-tense commentary. Visualizing the timing of these interventions against plot events allows students to contrast the narrators' disclosures about themselves and each other with the judgments and values built into and implied in the episodes that follow.

When asked to analyze these moments, students frequently make a case for what Lockwood and Nelly need from these stories even as they construct them. For instance, I ask students what Lockwood and Nelly are trying to demonstrate about themselves when they discuss Nelly's narratorial skills at the end of chapter 7, and why. Or I invite them to reflect on Lockwood's desire to view Catherine as a romantic heroine and Heathcliff as her hero, "come back a gentleman" to live with his beloved happily ever after (80). Why does Nelly want so dearly to justify her decision to deliver Heathcliff's letter to Catherine at the end of chapter 14, and why does she earlier obfuscate Catherine's illness? I lead students here to consider how aggressively the social machine grinds down both Nelly and Catherine for their deviant female energies. As a body, these examples evidence the interpretive effort that Lockwood and Nelly Dean expend to make characters and events conform to conventional values and expectations.

After such exploration, students can approach Catherine's and Heathcliff's unconventional actions and desires with open minds that are, by now, more analytical and less moralizing. My strategy is to withhold a specific interpretation of the two characters and instead simply suggest that Catherine and Heathcliff are Emily Brontë's approximation of energies for which description and narrative are only ever limited approximations, ours as well as hers. Put another way, I discuss these two antiheroes as beyond interpretation: outsiders to the classifications, categories, and trajectories by which the Earnshaws and Lintons (and, of course, Nelly and Lockwood) organize experience. Whether they represent nature, the raw as opposed to the cooked, primal passion unregulated by social order, an unorthodox moral code, or challenges to normative gender identities, Catherine and Heathcliff together pose a threat to the social, sexual, and cultural status quo that must be neutralized (see Eagleton, *Myths*). Heathcliff's social and racial indeterminacy threatens the sexual and social hierarchies around which the household is organized, as Susan Meyer observes; Catherine's famous expression of oneness with Heathcliff signals her defiance of sexual binaries and the cultural normatives built on them. Here, I might discuss marriage, the nuclear family, servanthood, the marriage plot, and the bildungsroman—take your pick.

Of course, the danger that the elder Catherine poses to the cultural order is deactivated by her indoctrination into Thrushcross Grange, marriage, and eventual death in childbirth; and Meyer argues that Heathcliff comes to mimic the very system against which he rebels (116). But students are entranced by the possibility that the conventional happy endings achieved by their more successful offspring are the product of Nelly's wishful thinking, not Emily Brontë's. A look at Lockwood's closing words never fails at this point to generate debate. Lockwood "wondered how any one could ever imagine unquiet slumbers for the sleepers in that quiet earth" (300). Why end with these words? Does "any one" include Nelly? Is that why Nelly can only "imagine" the more conventional happy ending she assigns to young Cathy and Hareton? Or is Lockwood explaining why it is difficult to accept the truth: that Heathcliff and the elder Cathy do not rest in peace—and, what is more disturbing, maybe they don't want to.

Students often remark that the second half of *Wuthering Heights* is duller than the first. Young Cathy and Hareton are less compelling, less dynamic, they say, than the elder Catherine and Heathcliff. To which I say—exactly. Using their reader responses to interpretive advantage, I suggest that the social success of the younger generation exemplifies what socially acceptable behavior gets you: a good marriage, a happy home, traditionally organized household roles, and a comfortably familiar moral system. Boring and conventional, I say with a yawn, a sellout. Students usually take my bait. Some counter, on behalf of a more successfully feminist outcome, that young Cathy is the best of both generations. Or they point out that, quite nontraditionally, Hareton must be educated by Cathy. In any case, the debate itself is the goal: my approach to *Wuthering Heights* aims to generate multiple interpretations of a number of meaty issues that activate students to cite and analyze textual evidence. In questioning the progress of the Earnshaw-Linton history, students investigate the problem of Heathcliff's education (Where did he go? What did he learn? Why is he less likable afterward?); young Cathy's lavish devotion to "papa"; the anemia of Thrushcross Grange (and the Lintons) as opposed to the troubled vitality of Wuthering Heights (and the Earnshaws); the energies of class conflict, rebellion, and authority (Nelly Dean, Zillah, and Joseph; husband and wife; slave and master); and the significance of the elder Catherine's brain fevers and death in childbirth.

According to Nelly, what is the point of history and history telling? What values and beliefs are suggested by the narrative shape of her/history?

By now, students understand that the act of interpretation operates not just to uncover some truth or genuine subtext to the story but also to impose order and values on otherwise mystifying observations and experiences. Here, I flesh out the chapter-by-chapter diagram with the symmetrical patterns observed by C. P. Sanger. The novel is divisible into two equal plots (plot 1 = elder Catherine-Heathcliff-Edgar; plot 2 = young Catherine-Linton-Hareton). Each plot is divisible into inverted sequences of action: Plot 1 = the elder Catherine's movement away from Wuthering Heights and into Thrushcross Grange; plot 2 = young Catherine's movement away from Thrushcross Grange and into Wuthering Heights. As J. Hillis Miller argues, such symmetries abound in *Wuthering Heights* ("*Wuthering Heights*"). Either actions and events repeat with striking frequency (elopements, secret letters, brain fevers, ghosts), or everything that a character accomplishes is later undone (Heathcliff's membership in the Earnshaw family and his disenfranchisement after Earnshaw's death; Heathcliff's efforts to destroy Wuthering Heights and Thrushcross Grange followed by Hareton's repossession; Heathcliff's illiteracy and Hareton's learning to read). I ask students to share what they have observed about the reversals, symmetries, or narrative patterns; in addition to developing our map, the exercise allows them to reintroduce their thematic interests into the discussion.

Finally, I ask the students to describe the narrative movement of the novel as diagrammed. In responding, they have used the terms "circular," "symmetrical," "repetitive," and "history repeats itself." I pick up on the idea of history repeating itself to guide them to questions about the role of individual agency in determining the shape of the narrative. Does history unfold as a narrative of perpetual dialogue (at best) or conflict (at worst) between the opposing forces cited above? Is rebellion against the social order doomed to failure? Does the novel suggest that social forces are always more powerful than and indifferent to individual desire? Does it suggest that change inexorably overtakes everyone, regardless of will, design, or desire? Or does it

NARRATIVE DESIGN OF

NARRATIVE INTERVENTIONS AND KEY DISCLOSURES

a Lockwood (54)
b L (79–80)
c Nelly Dean, aside to Lockwood (96)
d ND to L (98)
e N: "I related the scene in the court" (100)
f N: "I should not have spoken so" (107)
g N: "It is nothing" (112)
h Isabella's letter (119–28)
i N: "I blamed her, as she deserved" (130)
*j *ND to L (135–36)*
k L (136-37)
l Isabella's escape (152–61)
*m *ND to L (163)*

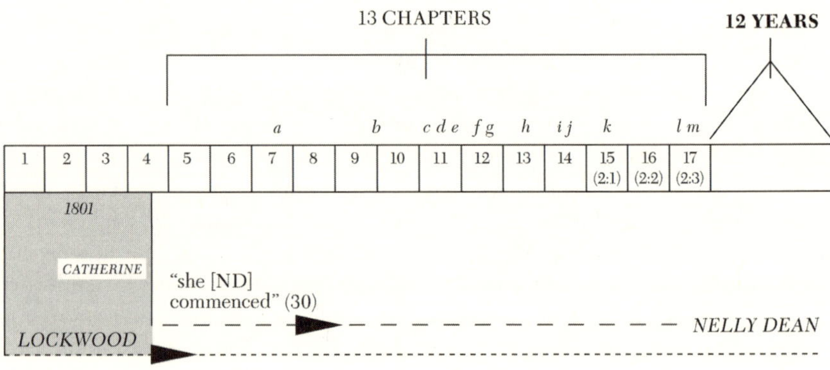

Mirrored

CATHERINE'S

EARNSHAW ——► HEATHCLIFF ——► EDGAR LINTON

WUTHERING HEIGHTS

*n *ND to L (174)*
o the housekeeper of Wuthering Heights (186)
p N: "I determined to take a peep at her mysterious treasures" (198)
q Cathy (217–24)
r ND to L (226)
s L (226)
t Zillah (246)
u Zillah (259–64)

**extranarrative asides*

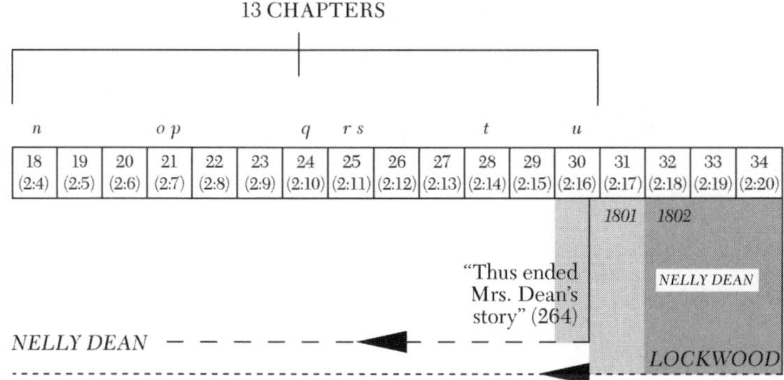

Marriage Plots

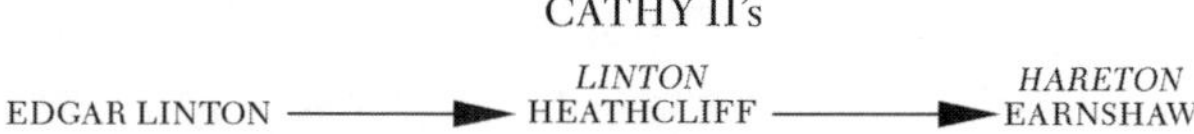

embody a cycle of destruction and renewal that, while less teleological than Charlotte Brontë's myth of progress, is nonetheless as generative? Here, the class reads Charlotte Brontë's disturbed, apologetic preface to *Wuthering Heights*. If history repeats itself (in the form of repetition with variation), then how do students interpret the novel's concluding tableau: Are the likely futures of young Cathy and Hareton an improvement on what was possible for the elder Catherine and Heathcliff? How? Why?

Although as an undergraduate I answered this question with a resounding (and Gilbert-and-Gubar-influenced) affirmative, I have led my students to more troubled waters. The open-ended question of *possibility* haunts them. It is the possibility that lurks beyond nineteenth-century social order, the intelligible shape of history, and Nelly Dean's epistemological-hermeneutic assumptions that has, by now, made them newly sympathetic to Heathcliff and Catherine. The narrative's strangely symmetrical design, likewise, leaves students with a gratifying sense of Emily Brontë's troubled (and troubling) take on the Victorian tale of progress.

Wuthering Heights, Women, and the Law: A Historical Approach

Lisa Surridge

Having taught *Wuthering Heights* every year for over a decade, I find that the novel's scenes of domestic violence and confinement consistently provoke an emotional response from my students. Many find the novel loathsome—"saturated in violence," as one person remarked in class. Others are drawn to Heathcliff as romantic hero and yet are torn because this feeling contradicts their deeply held views on marriage and marital assault. As a result of this potent mixture of attraction and condemnation, the novel's violent scenes produce impassioned and fascinating discussion in my classes. Recently, however, I decided to experiment by challenging students to historicize their analysis of the novel's gender violence.

To this end, I provided my class with an archive of primary texts from the 1840s and 1850s. I chose texts that showed how individual men's and women's lives were situated in the nexus of legal and social forces governing marriage, child custody, and family violence, as well as more general overviews that revealed the way such forces were perceived in the mid-Victorian period. This archive, I hoped, would enable students to view *Wuthering Heights* as part of a broader ideological debate on the legal nonexistence of Victorian women and to focus on issues such as coverture, child custody, married women's property, and wife assault.

It seemed especially important to undertake this historicizing exercise with Emily Brontë, an author traditionally seen as "detached from history and uncontaminated by political concerns" (Armstrong, "Imperialist" 429). The image of Brontë isolated from Victorian society—alone, as it were, on some kind of timeless moor—persists among students even though it has been thoroughly debunked by studies such as Juliet Barker's *The Brontës*, Nancy Armstrong's *Desire and Domestic Fiction*, and Maja-Lisa Von Sneidern's article "*Wuthering Heights* and the Liverpool Slave Trade." For students, the remoteness of the Heights from other habitations in the novel all too readily translates into a sense that the plot is isolated from Victorian cultural and political forces. (Students do not make a similar mistake about Dickens.) I felt, then, that my teaching of *Wuthering Heights* would gain appreciably from an approach that reduces the isolation of literary "masterpieces" and emphasizes their "embeddedness" in "the contingencies of history" (Greenblatt 313, 308).

The archive included the following documents:

Caroline Norton. *A Letter to the Queen on Lord Chancellor Cranworth's Marriage and Divorce Bill*. London: 1855.

Written by a woman whose marriage was physically abusive and who campaigned for maternal custody rights over infant children, Norton's polemical letter on the

Divorce Bill captures the irony of the legal "non-existence" of women in a country governed by a female sovereign. It summarizes married women's property law, the husband's conjugal rights, and the laws relating to separation, marital cruelty, and condoning of cruelty.

Barbara Leigh Smith. *A Brief Summary, in Plain Language, of the Most Important Laws concerning Women*. London: 1854. (See Lacey's *Barbara Leigh Smith Bodichon and the Langham Place Group*.)
Usefully divided into laws covering unmarried and married women, Smith's summary covers much of the same material as Norton's but focuses more on professions and careers for women. She also includes a succinct statement of the principle of coverture—that is, the wife's absorption into the legal "cover" of the husband.

John Stuart Mill and Harriet Taylor. "The Suicide of Sarah Brown" and "The Case of William Burn." London: 1846.
Sarah Brown drowned herself because the father of her illegitimate child had gained partial custody. William Burn savagely beat his horse, but the magistrate reduced his fine because he had a needy family. In 1846, Mill and Taylor featured their cases in polemical leaders for the *Morning Chronicle*, hoping to draw public attention to injustices surrounding child custody as well as to the relation between animal abuse and family violence.

"The Luxury of Assault." *Punch*, 1842.
This satirical article cites contemporary fines for wife abuse and suggests facetiously that the list will enable "the lovers of assault to know what they are about." Its tally of fines (10s for a pair of black eyes, £3 for a dislocated arm, £5 for kicking a woman in the abdomen) uses black humor to suggest their inadequacy.

Re Cochrane (1840) 8 Dowling 633.
This legal decision concerns a husband's right to confine his wife in the home. In 1836, Cecelia Cochrane refused her husband's conjugal rights; when Alexander Cochrane obtained a writ for restitution of these rights, she went abroad with her baby and her mother. In 1840, Alexander lured Cecelia to his rooms and locked her there. She in turn obtained a writ of habeas corpus, but the court ruled that her confinement was legal. The law, the judge wrote, acted "for the happiness and honour of both parties" in placing the wife "under the guardianship of the husband, and [enabling] him, for the sake of both, to protect her from the danger of unrestrained intercourse with the world, by enforcing cohabitation and a common residence."

I distributed these documents at the end of the first class on *Wuthering Heights* and asked students to read them all and to return for the second class ready to discuss in small groups how the articles illuminated the novel for them. I assigned one text to each group. We then moved into a full-class discussion of how the archive had changed students' views of the novel.

I should note that this approach marked a sharp shift in my teaching technique (although not in the topics covered). Distributing an archive of primary documents meant not only that I asked students to think about literature in a historicist manner but also that I gave them the tools to achieve this work independently of me. Previously, I had always historicized class discussions myself. If a student raised the issue of Heathcliff confining Isabella, for example, I summarized the law of coverture, which made a husband his wife's moral guardian and allowed him to control her behavior, even to the point of confinement. If someone remarked that, according to Linton, "everything" his wife, Cathy, has "is mine" (248), I explained the Victorian laws governing married women's property. Under the earlier method, I would dole out summaries of Caroline Norton, Barbara Leigh Smith, or the Cochrane case, but I did not turn over the texts to my students. Although I had taken seriously Brook Thomas's challenge to historicize undergraduate English courses, I had not yet given students ownership of historical materials. In the previous model, I was the expert; I explained how the text was embedded in the politics and culture of the mid-nineteenth century. This teaching method mystified historical or legal knowledge as special and technical—something, in short, that was mine alone. Ironically, although my assignments had consistently encouraged students to analyze historical documents in conjunction with literary texts, our classroom discussions had embodied historical analysis only insofar as I (or the scattered history students in the class) provided it.

In contrast, I now put primary materials into students' hands, asking them to analyze issues of marital power and domestic violence in each text and to consider how *Wuthering Heights* treated similar issues. I found that in discussion, in essays, and on exams, the documents became vehicles for transforming students' emotional responses to the novel's gender politics into historicized analyses.

For example, my class immediately related the Cochrane case to the plot of *Wuthering Heights*. The Cochrane decision rests on the logic that a man can imprison his wife to maintain his moral guardianship over her; my students observed that Heathcliff appeals to this logic when he controls Isabella. One wrote, "The fine line between control, custody, and imprisonment is explored when Heathcliff tells Isabella, 'No, you're not fit to be your own guardian, Isabella, now; and I, being your legal protector, must retain you in my custody, however distasteful the obligation may be' " (134). Cecelia Cochrane's experience of being locked in her husband's rooms in Great Castle Street vividly suggested the carceral nature of domestic space, a theme reinforced by Caroline Norton and Barbara Leigh Smith and extensively explored by Emily Brontë in *Wuthering Heights*. As one student noted, "the locked outer gates, locked doors, and crushingly small windows" of the Heights emphasize women's sense of "physical entrapment" and "powerlessness"; another observed that the same forces are at work (less obviously) at the Grange: Edgar, she wrote, represents the "cruel kindness" of patriarchy. Cecelia Cochrane's escape from her marriage threw Isabella's flight from Heathcliff into a new light: previous classes had little to say about Isabella (who pales, literally and metaphorically, beside the more colorful Catherine), but this class returned repeatedly to her escape, which they saw as defying the principle of coverture as well as Heathcliff personally. In the words of one student, "Isabella proves herself to be the only female of the novel who takes on a proactive role as she leaves behind . . . an abusive husband, and smashes their wedding band."

Knowledge of marriage law prompted a student to wonder why Heathcliff does not pursue Isabella: "Even though Heathcliff has every legal right in this period to retrieve her from where she has run to, he doesn't do it." To another, this knowledge brought new meaning to the novel's powerful theme of returning to childhood: "For each wife, the home of her childhood, or her non-married life, is that to which she seeks to return. . . . The childhood home becomes a metaphor for a life free from the imprisonment of the emotional death of a loveless marriage, the civil death of coverture, and death of personal freedom once subjected to the custody of masculine control." To a third student, this knowledge illuminated the strength and rebellion of the female characters: "it seems that neither [Heathcliff] nor Edgar ever manage to 'absorb the existence' of their respective wives," she wrote, quoting Smith's definition of coverture. Finally, a knowledge of married women's property law shed light on the second half of the novel: "Catherine Linton, born in an upper-class family, becomes penniless. . . . Her financial status following her marriage is disclosed when Zillah says to Nelly: 'And what will all her learning and her daintiness do for her, now? She's as poor as you or I—poorer, I'll be bound' " (262).

With similar vividness, "The Luxury of Assault" made visible the nexus of power, class status, money, and domestic violence. While the article used satire to suggest a "gentleman's club" of wife abusers, students instantly remarked on the connection between Heathcliff's acquisition of wealth and his violence: in Emily Brontë's novel, it is not the dispossessed who beat their wives. Moreover, the *Punch* essay prompted students to ask if there was a magistrate anywhere in the novel. Edgar, of course, is a magistrate, but my class recognized immediately that social power structures dictate that he cannot prosecute his sister's husband or his daughter's father-in-law (even if Edgar were well enough to do so). At one point, Joseph threatens to fetch a magistrate, but my students remarked that this threat is taken with as little seriousness as *Punch* readers would have given to the suggestion that they could blacken their wives' eyes for ten shillings. In different ways, the two texts—the novel and the *Punch* article—show that social class factors make prosecuting domestic violence ineffective or impossible: as one student pointed out, Nelly's statement—"There's law in the land, thank God, there is!" (242)—is suffused with irony. In summary, then, the archive of documents was highly effective in leading students to an understanding of men's legal power over women in the nineteenth century.

In future classes, I will also distribute C. P. Sanger's "The Structure of

Wuthering Heights" (1926), a widely reprinted article that clearly explains the inheritance laws underlying the novel's plot. I would do so because class discussion of men's legal power over women inevitably led to students' questions about how land, houses, and money are controlled, lost, and regained in the novel. The laws of inheritance, property ownership, and entail are thus crucial to an understanding of gender and power in the text. Sanger argues that Emily Brontë's complex and accurate knowledge of law underpins Heathcliff's revenge plot. He explains in detail how Heathcliff got his hands on all the property of the Earnshaws and the Lintons. At Mr. Earnshaw's death, Wuthering Heights (which is a farm, not an estate, and thus probably owned in fee simple) descends to the son, Hindley. Mr. Earnshaw's personal property would be divided among his children, Catherine and Hindley. Hindley, in turn, drinks and gambles away his money and mortgages the property to Heathcliff in order to raise money for his addictions. At Hindley's death, then, Wuthering Heights falls to Heathcliff as "mortgagee in possession" (Sanger 202). Thrushcross Grange is an estate, not a farm, and therefore entailed. Under the law of entails, Sanger explains, male heirs are preferred to females, and males inherit in order of birth. Hence Edgar Linton inherits the Grange from his parents; since Edgar has no sons, his daughter is passed over in favor of Isabella's son, Linton Heathcliff. In the brief time after his uncle's death and before his own, Linton becomes "tenant in tail in possession" (202). He cannot make a will because he is a minor. After his death, Heathcliff claims the Grange in his wife's name and his son's—and the younger Catherine, who is penniless, cannot dispute his possession. However, Catherine is in fact the only heir of the Linton line, and so after Heathcliff's death she presumably makes her claim to the Grange (by far the more valuable of the two properties). The personal property, of course, is governed by married women's property law as explained by Barbara Leigh Smith: whatever Catherine Earnshaw inherited goes to Edgar Linton; whatever Isabella had, Heathcliff claims when he marries her. Edgar Linton had saved money to provide for his daughter but dies before altering his will; hence when she marries Linton Heathcliff, all her money goes to him, to be willed by him, in turn, to Heathcliff, his father.

As I recently realized during class discussion, students need to understand the novel's complex legal underpinnings (which are not fully explained in the text) in order to grasp Heathcliff's bid for power. Moreover, the laws of inheritance play a crucial role in disabling the novel's women, reducing their choices and options. I would thus add Sanger's article to my collection of handouts, as it provides this vital information as well as confirming that the novel is both based on and focused on legal structures. The topic of women and the law, then, is not a modern issue superimposed on the novel. To the contrary, textual evidence supports the theory that Emily Brontë was preoccupied with women's legal disempowerment with respect to inheritance, property, and coverture.

How did the work on these historical documents fit into the course structure as a whole? Students frequently made use of the documents to help them think about marital power, domesticity, and child custody in *Wuthering Heights* as well as in other nineteenth-century novels on the syllabus: *Adam Bede*, *A Tale of Two Cities*, *The Moonstone*, *The Mayor of Casterbridge*. Moreover, throughout the semester, I reinforced the value of historical research by asking students to give class presentations summarizing their research on specific aspects of novels on the syllabus. I assigned the topics: Elizabeth Gaskell's *Mary Barton* and 1848, *Great Expectations* and the London suburb, *Wuthering Heights* and Liverpool. Thus my archive was supplemented by others, as students provided information and primary documents on other aspects of the texts. I should note that for these presentations, I stated explicitly that I would give higher grades to students whose research successfully grappled with primary materials (newspaper articles, paintings, cartoons, parliamentary debates, etc.). My students noted that the presentations, which set the tone for a class that was insistently historical, were extremely valuable, for the research experience they gained, for what they learned from others' reports, and for the discussions they prompted: "The class presentations were . . . in themselves interesting," wrote one student, "but the discussions they generated were great."

Reviewing my students' discussions and essays on *Wuthering Heights*, I feel that the archive project was a success. As one student commented on the course evaluation, "This approach to literature was a wonderful change from most other classes I've taken in the English department; the incorporation of history to the study of novels greatly enhanced the course."

NOTE

My thanks to the students from English 380-S01 (2003) for permission to tape their provocative discussions of *Wuthering Heights*; my gratitude also to the following students who allowed me to quote from or refer to their work: Susan Dickson, Jasmine Johnston, Ticki Mackenzie, Laura-Lee Pernsky, Samantha Scott.

Evading "the Secret Truth" in *Wuthering Heights*: Film and Visual Illustration in Teaching Critical Theory

Patsy Stoneman

How we read and teach *Wuthering Heights* is crucially affected by the classroom context: the educational level of the students and the novel's place in a program of study. This essay deals with a slightly unusual teaching situation, in which the main focus is not on the novel itself but on the range of possible reading strategies that have, historically, been used to approach it. The context is a module entitled Critical Approaches to Literature, designed to introduce first-year undergraduates to the study of literature at the university level. Rather ambitiously, it attempts a three-fold introduction: to period studies, to genre studies, and to literary theories.

We chose as the focus of study six texts from a variety of genres from the last four hundred years and decided to treat them in reverse chronological order, so that the first lectures could concentrate on genre (What is a poem? How do you read a novel?) and theoretical approaches, while the historical factor would become more prominent as the text became more distant from the present. Because in practice we found that students felt more comfortable beginning with a novel, *Wuthering Heights* is now the first text to be studied. Three lectures are given on each text, by instructors who have made the work a special study; there is also an introduction and a conclusion from the module convener. About two hundred students attend these lectures, however, and so they are followed up by seminars in groups of about ten, led by graduate teaching assistants, who also attend the lectures. The seminars are thus linked to the lectures not only by material provided by the instructors but also by the TAs' personal experiences. A common introductory text, Peter Barry's *Beginning Theory*, provides continuity of approach; and wherever possible, we also recommend a teaching edition of the focal text that includes a selection of critical essays. For *Wuthering Heights* we chose the version edited by Linda Peterson.

The essays in the Peterson volume contain the material I need in my introduction to a range of academic critical practices. Writing my book on derivatives of the novel (*Brontë Transformations*), however, had convinced me that films, spin-off novels, parodies, pop songs, and advertisements can be treated as critical readings of their source (see also Stoneman, *Emily Brontë* 283 and *New Casebook* 285). Students, for their part, often assume that the film adaptation is more or less equivalent to the original and can be substituted for reading the novel. I was anxious, therefore, to include references to the various derivatives not only because visual material livens up lectures but also because I wanted to show that each film or illustration involves critical choices.

Another intuitive response that students bring with them from high school is to look to the author's intention to explain the text. Much current academic criticism, however, assumes what Roland Barthes calls "the death of the author." Barthes rejects the term "author" because it implies a point of absolute origin for the text (in the way that God is "author of our being"). He prefers the term "writer," which suggests that the text is "produced," from an amalgam of previous texts, by a process of labor. Having worked with first-year students, I knew that in my Critical Approaches lectures I must not jump too rapidly into theories that depend on "the death of the author"; I decided, therefore, to devote one session to "the author" and the others to "the text" and "readers." In this essay, I outline each of the lectures, paying special attention to the use of film and other visual material, but I focus particularly on the second lecture, in which I use film clips to justify a deconstructive reading of the novel.

In my first lecture, I ask, "What can we know about an author?" My aim is to upset the assumption that the author is unproblematically there, behind the text, to be appealed to as its source and explanation. The assumption that the author is the origin of the text is not only tenacious, it also takes very varied forms. At one extreme is the Romantic idea of the author as inspired genius, almost independent of context. At the other is the materialist concept of an author whose physical existence is tied to a particular location and circumstances.

I begin with the material actuality of the Brontë sisters. I show slides of what are for many of our students familiar scenes (we are, after all, in Yorkshire): Haworth village, the Parsonage, and the sisters themselves. I concede that they were real people with existences recorded in church and school registers. I then point out, however, that it is only the written records to which we have access and that, in all but the simplest cases, these documents are shaped by the motivations of the writer.

I use this opportunity to talk about how biographies are researched and to suggest that students might test the reliability of biographies by looking at the way in which they identify their sources, but I also observe that even highly accurate biographers always shape their material. Nicholas Marsh, in his useful student guide to *Wuthering Heights*, demonstrates that fourteen biographers, working on the basis of the evidence, have been able to present Emily Brontë as "wild, misanthropic, anorexic, sensitive, self-obsessed, affectionate, hostile, demanding, considerate, self-sacrificing, atheist, superstitious, deluded, suicidal" (181).

The problem of "knowing" the author (and thus "the author's intentions") has been increased by Freudian psychoanalysis, which teaches us that intentions may be unconscious. Philip Wion argues that the famous yearning for oneness in the novel derives from the fact that Brontë's mother died when she was two, before the child had undergone the normal process of separation. Psychoanalyzing the author in this way produces seductively stable readings of the novel but, I suggest, can also be reductive, seeing the text as a set of symptoms pointing back to a single cause.

At the opposite pole from Wion's position is that of Charlotte Brontë, whose Romantic notion of the author as inspired genius comes down to us through her 1850 "Editor's Preface" to *Wuthering Heights*, which is reprinted in almost every modern edition. "The writer who possesses the creative gift," Charlotte Brontë writes, "owns something of which he is not always master—something that at times strangely wills and works for itself" (327). This unknown "something" is not the Freudian unconscious, tied to particular familial relationships, but a universal spirit of imagination. I point out that this transcendental view of the literary process is now out of fashion in academic circles but is still popular in the world at large, and I demonstrate this observation by showing the opening of Peter Kosminsky's 1992 film, *Emily Brontë's* Wuthering Heights.

While the title and credits are showing, we see the figure of a woman walking toward a gothic mansion on a windswept moor. This woman is the author. Even though Emily Brontë's novel is notable for having multiple narrative voices and almost no sense of an authorial presence, Kosminsky brings the author visibly before us and allows us to believe that we are seeing the very moment of conception of her story: "Something whispered to my mind," she says, "and I began to write." This Romantic scene effaces the idea that writing is work or that it feeds on earlier written sources. Instead, the author is a point of origin, inspired by nothing more social or more labor-intensive than a breath of wind.

Wion's author, constrained by maternal deprivation, seems to have little in common with Kosminsky's free-floating genius, but both interpreters envisage an author who is independent of written sources. My aim in this first lecture is to posit that what we think of as Emily Brontë is made up of what she herself wrote and what people wrote about her. Wherever we look for origins, we find texts—family letters, Romantic poems—and I suggest to the students that our job as literary critics is not to look for single points of origin but to take all such texts or "pre-texts" into account. I leave the students with the idea that if they learn to see "the author" as an effect of texts, then they are on the way to accepting "the death of the author" and "the birth of the writer."

The second lecture, focused on "the text," moves from the idea of authorial origin to the words on the page. I begin by introducing a little critical history, pointing out that nineteenth-century readers did believe that the author was the origin of the text and that fiction mirrored real life. Because of the close link between art and life, moreover, fiction could be judged on moral terms. All such assumptions changed, however, with the advent of modernism, which shifted critical attention away from the reality or morality of a text and toward the craft of its writing. I explain that the New Critics of this period were called formalists, because instead of looking in a text for an illusion of reality, they looked for its beauties of form. The introduction of formalism, incidentally, gives me the opportunity to talk about the mechanics of novels and to distinguish among technical terms such as "plot," "story," "narrative," and "structure." This functional section of the lecture is, I hope, a relief for the students from new and difficult critical ideas, but it also allows me to introduce structure as something that depends on patterns (e.g., patterns of imagery), which many different readers recognize. Patterns, in turn, depend on contrasts (e.g., between nature and culture).

I refer to seminal essays on *Wuthering Heights* by C. P. Sanger, David Cecil ("Emily Brontë"), and Dorothy Van Ghent ("Window Figure") and point out that each of them depends on structures of contrast in the novel. Readers find these essays persuasive because they recognize these contrasts from a wider context. We may have met the nature-culture contrast, for instance, in Shakespeare or in fairy tales. *Wuthering Heights* thus emerges as unique, certainly, but also as occupying a place in a web of meanings shared by other texts. I go on to explain that for structuralists, all meanings depend on such binary oppositions. *The Raw and the Cooked*, by the structuralist anthropologist Claude Lévi-Strauss, is a particularly useful reference here since it deals precisely with the nature-culture contrast. My presentation is a fairly sketchy treatment of structuralism, but it establishes what I need in order to talk about deconstruction (see also Stoneman, *New Casebook*).

The deconstructionist Jacques Derrida, I explain, agrees with the structuralists that all meanings depend on binary oppositions, but his crucial observation is that the opposed pairs are never equally balanced (see Derrida; Kamuf). Half the pair is always valued more highly than the other. Derrida is especially concerned with the opposition between presence and absence, which he says underlies the whole of Western philosophical thought. Within this opposition, the positive term, "presence," is so highly valued that it has traditionally been thought of as a quality of God, who is "omnipresent." I remind the students that in the first lecture, we saw how the author is often conceived as being like God, omnipresent in the text, and how Kosminsky made Emily Brontë physically present in his film. If we believe that we can make sense of all the contradictions in a text by knowing the author's intention, we need the author to be present in some way. For formalist or structuralist critics, the presence of structure is thought of as explaining everything. In either case, the critic who can interpret the author's intention or the structures of the text takes on the supposed power and presence of the author or the structures. Derrida therefore sees traditional literary criticism as an attempt to play God, to assert mastery over the text by claiming that we can interpret it and contain its contradictions within an overview. What Derrida wants to do is to resist the pressure to adopt a position of mastery and, instead, to undo these neat interpretations by focusing on the contradictory elements that they have to ignore. This process of undoing is what Derrida calls deconstruction.

Earlier in the lecture I had explained that structures or patterns in a novel depend on the repetition of features: deaths, storms, hearths, and windows.

A deconstructive critic, however, would point out that the repetitions are never exact—the different scenes involving windows, for instance, do not lead us to make the same interpretation of what "inside" and "outside" mean—so that we are never quite allowed to grasp the "central truth" the repetition seems to point to. The novel continually suggests that it is about to reveal its secret but, in the words of J. Hillis Miller, "the secret truth about *Wuthering Heights* . . . is that there is no secret truth" (*Fiction* 51).

Deconstruction is an anti-intuitive way of reading because we all need to make sense of what we read, and in my experience, students resist deconstruction not only because it is difficult but also because they don't see why it's necessary. I explain, therefore, that I am going to use some extracts from film versions of *Wuthering Heights* to show how the films make sense of the novel by overvaluing one half of a binary opposition so that it appears to be the whole—*the* meaning. A deconstructive approach may not save us from this kind of one-sidedness, but it can make us aware of what we are doing when we make sense of a text.

In the opposition between the inside and the outside of houses, it is commonly assumed that Edgar and Isabella belong to the inside and the elder Catherine and Heathcliff belong outside, on the moors. It comes as a surprise to most readers to discover that only two short passages, in chapters 3 and 6, describe Catherine and Heathcliff together on the moors. The two passages refer to the same episode—the episode when they escape from Joseph's persecution to "have a scamper on the moors" (17) and look in on the Linton children; the elder Catherine is less than twelve years old at the time. The only other reference to Catherine and Heathcliff on the moors together comes after Catherine's marriage, and on that occasion Isabella is with them (90). Yet in almost every stage and film representation of the novel, we are shown Catherine and Heathcliff together, as adults, on Penistone Crag. I demonstrate this by showing clips from William Wyler's 1939 film, with Merle Oberon and Laurence Olivier, and from the Kosminsky film, with Juliette Binoche and Ralph Fiennes. Both films show us a pair of grown-up lovers setting up a kind of alternative existence, up on the hills.

Where, then, I ask, does this idea come from, of a grown-up Catherine and Heathcliff experiencing a kind of natural paradise of love and freedom on the hilltops? In the novel, the answer must lie not in what happens (because it doesn't happen) but in the patterns of opposition, which have the power to persuade us and generations of filmmakers that we have seen the meaning of the novel.

As children, Catherine and Heathcliff are shut out from what Catherine describes as Hindley's "paradise on the hearth" at Wuthering Heights and also from the "heaven" they glimpse through the window at Thrushcross Grange (17, 42). In a more conventional novel, we would expect them to yearn to be restored to this privileged inside realm. Instead they are scornful both of Hindley's sweet-talking with Frances and of Edgar and Isabella's squabble over the pet dog. Thus the heaven from which they are excluded is presented as not worth having. Catherine and Heathcliff are cold instead of warm, dark instead of light, outside instead of inside, but they are free from constraint, and they are together.

Catherine and Heathcliff are thus reversing the normal hierarchy of value between outside and inside, and as readers, we are persuaded to follow them. As soon as the reversal is made, however, it seems inevitable that we start to invest the newly privileged term—the outside—with increasingly positive qualities. Instead of the uncomfortable "scamper on the moors," in which Catherine loses her shoes and is bitten by a bulldog, we imagine an alternative heaven on Penistone Crag, which offers both freedom and security, and this is the image the filmmakers make present for us as disclosing the meaning of the novel.

Robert Fuest's 1970 film, with Anna Calder-Marshall and Timothy Dalton, even supplies an alternative hearth fire under Penistone Crag, and in showing this clip, I let the scene run on to demonstrate how the lovers try to freeze time by swearing to one another that nothing will ever change. In Wyler's film, Catherine says, "Heathcliff—make the world stop right here; make everything stop and stand still and never move again." In Fuest's film, she calls down dreadful curses on their heads if they ever leave this place and each other. Both films show the lovers in their alternative realm, the privileged version of the outside, striving to make it permanently present by sheer force of will. These images seek to suppress the other half of the binary opposition—the inside—and to conceal the fact that what we desire (for Catherine and Heathcliff to be together for ever and ever in freedom) is not a social possibility. They cannot live forever around a campfire under a rock. The only way for them to continue occupying this impossible territory outside time and outside society is for them to die, and so we are also led to give death a positive and present value.

In the novel, the lovers die apart in both place and time, but our impulse to invest in the newly privileged outside realm is so strong that many film and stage versions choose to represent the lovers dying together on Penistone Crag. In the novel, Lockwood's last words suggest that the lovers are firmly under the sod, but in the 1939 film, it is Lockwood who sees their ghosts on the moor and Nelly, our most reliable narrator, who endorses the idea that Heathcliff is "not dead—he's with *her*." I show the final minute of this film, which makes the ghostly lovers present for us in a visual image. In addition, I point out that Nelly's words ("he's with *her*"), the swelling music, and the caption announcing "The End" all assure us that we now know what the meaning of the novel is. But critics who aim for this kind of closure are asserting their mastery over the text by freezing it.

The aim of deconstruction, on the other hand, is to resist the temptation to announce "The End" and instead to keep the critical possibilities in play by reminding us, for instance, that death and the outside are not always positive values. I agree that a deconstructive reading is frustrating because it refuses to reach conclusions or to provide answers. By showing that there are no "right" answers to its puzzles, however, deconstruction opens the text to readings that claim to be pertinent rather than true. I talk about this idea in my third lecture.

In this lecture, on readers, I quote Terry Eagleton, for whom literary criticism "is a matter of starting from what we want to do, and then seeing which method and theories will best help us to achieve these ends" (*Literary Theory* 210). My goal here is to empower the students, to show them that what they "want to do" with the text is a question not of finding its secret truth but of finding their own priorities. What they want to do with the text will almost always be determined by something outside the text: by their unconscious desires or by their political convictions.

Linda Peterson's edition includes excellent political readings of the novel, and most of my final lecture is taken up with demonstrating the novel's possible social meanings as suggested by these essays. I reinforce the idea of a variety of readings, however, by including my own analyses of popular disseminations of the text, choosing images as different as possible in their styles of representation. I contrast Laurence Olivier's noble-looking Heathcliff in Wyler's film with Milton Rosmer, in A. V. Bramble's 1920 silent version, who looks like a genuine farm laborer, and I contrast these in turn with a 1989 Japanese comic book showing Heathcliff as a Disney-like juvenile in picturesque rags (Suzuka).

Two book illustrations of the lovers' last embrace show a more thoughtful contrast. Fritz Eichenberg's 1943 lithograph portrays the characters locked together in a mirroring of bodily angles, while a blowing curtain suggests the transcendent "something" that "whispered" to Emily's mind. Peter Forster's 1991 lithograph, clearly alluding to Eichenberg, stresses the social parameters that "outsiders" cannot escape: the lovers fall away from their embrace, the blowing curtain is restrained by an intrusive hand, and both Catherine and Heathcliff have African features.

In the three lectures, I use visual material not simply to illustrate a point but to demonstrate that pictures, like written arguments, interpret the novel. My aim is to move students away from the assumption that knowledge of the author is all that is needed in explaining *Wuthering Heights* and toward an active engagement with the text, in which they are challenged to find and defend patterns of meaning. The film clips of Catherine and Heathcliff on the hilltop are pivotal to this argument, because they show that what we "see" in the novel is the result of our efforts to make present what is only suggested by the novel's patterns.

IMAGINING AND REIMAGINING *WUTHERING HEIGHTS*

Teaching *Wuthering Heights* through Its Film and Television Adaptations

Kamilla Elliott

Between 1920 and 2003, *Wuthering Heights* was adapted to film and television at least twenty-five times in at least eleven countries. While there are many ways to plumb these adaptations pedagogically, this essay emphasizes adaptations as criticism and places such audiovisual criticism alongside literary criticism of *Wuthering Heights*. I have taught this in a variety of ways. In one series of classes, we discussed literary and audiovisual prefaces to the novel, to raise questions of authorship and authenticity. In another, we determined how both literary critical essays and film and television adaptations select and order passages from the novel to create their interpretations. In still another, we juxtaposed literary criticism and film adaptations from similar historical periods to scrutinize shared critical trends and cultural influences; and in yet another, we analyzed recurring interpretive questions that have been answered differently across historical periods, cultures, and media.

These approaches can be undertaken together or separately. I engage them together only in an advanced seminar of undergraduates or first-year graduate students, where the primary purpose is to study interdisciplinary criticism. In such a seminar, *Wuthering Heights* provides a constant, a case study through which to investigate other variables. The novel and its films might occupy as many as six weeks of the seminar. In contrast, in a general seminar on literature and film or the nineteenth-century novel or the Brontës, I use only one or two of the approaches. Finally, when class time is even more restricted, I include in my lectures findings gleaned from the approaches.

Literary and Audiovisual Prefaces to Wuthering Heights

Examining literary, filmic, and televisual prefaces to *Wuthering Heights* raises productive questions of authorship, authoritative editions, and authorized adaptations. For this investigation, we read Charlotte Brontë's 1850 preface to the second edition and Richard J. Dunn's preface to Norton's 1990 critical edition (Sale and Dunn), hear Russell Baker's introduction to the broadcast, in the United States, of London Weekend Television's (LWT) 1998 airing of *Wuthering Heights* (Skynner); view the prologue to Peter Kosminsky's 1992 film, *Emily Brontë's* Wuthering Heights, and examine Luis Buñuel's prefatory title card to his 1953 film of *Wuthering Heights, Abismos de pasión.*[1]

The Norton preface and Baker introduction each claim an authoritative return to authorial origins for their versions of *Wuthering Heights*, asserting that they restore an authenticity lost in prior editions and adaptations. The 1990 Norton edition subtitles itself "authoritative text, backgrounds, criticism." Its preface announces that it has restored the 1847 first edition of the novel, determining that Charlotte Brontë had "assumed privileges" in editing the 1850 edition "that now seem unwarranted" (Sale and Dunn xi).[2] Similarly, Baker asserts that the LWT adaptation "finishes the story just as Emily Brontë wrote it," whereas earlier adaptations had not.[3] In our discussion of the prefaces, we first contextualize the claims in Western ideologies of return to origins, like Christian concepts of rebirth and psychoanalytic returns to childhood, as well as in aesthetic preoccupations with originality. We explore the role of textual editors, considering which of their changes are deemed valid, which are considered "unwarranted," and why. For example, editors typically alter punctuation and spelling according to shifting customs without raising critics' eyebrows, while other changes are frowned on.

Following this inquiry, we debate how far a film or television adaptation can be considered an "edition" of a literary text as opposed to more conventional understandings of adaptation as translation, performance, audiovisualization, or interpretation. In selected reviews of and articles on these adaptations, we ponder which changes have been deemed authoritative, which have not, and ask why. For example, we observe that critics are more willing to accept omissions and abridgments than additions and modernizations and are more likely to praise foreign adaptations than Anglo-American ones.

In the course of these discussions, the issue of fidelity to the text inevitably arises. We connect what I call the "fidelity imperative" to religious and scientific precedents. For example, Judeo-Christian theology insists that the word precedes and shapes phenomenological reality, as in the Genesis creation story, where God speaks ("Let there be light") and the words materialize ("And there was light"), and in the Christian belief that the word is made flesh in Jesus. Analogously, scientific empiricism requires that the phenomenological world prove the truth of verbal hypotheses. These precedents help explain why audiovisual adaptations that do not appear as materializations or proofs of the word are seen as unfaithful and untrue, like graven images or failed experiments.

Concomitantly, we recognize the increasing insistence, during the twentieth century, that film and television adaptations be *un*faithful to their original texts—whether in the name of semiotic impossibility (the widespread belief that words and images are untranslatable), of aesthetic independence (the mandate that values filmmaker originality over fidelity to textual origin), of changing genre and audience requirements, of financial gain, of ideological and political protest, of psychoanalytic latency, or of deconstructive inevitability.

We then engage the question of just how much interpretation goes on in the name of "editing," whether written or audiovisual. We read the novel and view the LWT televization in their entirety and discuss whether the adaptation does or does not finish "the story just as Emily Brontë wrote it." We consider which elements besides plot constitute "the story," how much plot is allowed to be cut in a film that claims to tell "the story just as Emily Brontë wrote it" and, more interesting, what has been added to the adaptation: actors' bodies, props, sets, costumes, videography, music, and lighting, as well as elements of 1990s Anglo-American culture and influences from contemporary literary criticism and cultural theory. Focusing on the elder Cathy's "I *am* Heathcliff" speech (73) as it appears in several films and televizations, we study how vocalization, facial expression, movement, lighting, camera angle, music, costumes, props, and sets create different interpretations of this speech in different adaptations. We also consider how genre and cultural context filter into these significations. For example, the 1939 Hollywood film version of *Wuthering Heights*, directed by William Wyler, creates a sense of doomed, melodramatic love by punctuating the speech with cosmic thunder and a flash of lightning and underscoring it with orchestral music heavy on the violins. By contrast, the cinematic realism and method acting of Robert Fuest's 1970 film highlight impulses of economic and sexual liberation, following trends of the 1960s. The elder Cathy (Anna Calder-Marshall), her hair loose and decked with flowers, engages in rough, impulsive sexual relations with Heathcliff (Timothy Dalton) and speaks about helping him rise socially.

In our study of prefaces, we examine, as well, a practice pervasive among canonical literary adaptations produced in the 1990s: the inclusion of the author's name in the film or television title. We ask what this titular trend lends to claims of authorial authorization and authenticity for adaptations, particularly their bid to differentiate themselves from earlier versions, just as new textual editions of *Wuthering Heights* seek to distinguish themselves from earlier editions. We note how the grammatical construction of the titles diminishes the literary author, making her the possession of the production company or of the director: London Weekend Television's *Emily Brontë's* Wuthering Heights or Peter Kosminsky's *Emily Brontë's* Wuthering Heights.[4] The Kosminsky production goes further to co-opt the author as a character in the film. As the film opens, Emily Brontë (played by an uncredited Sinéad

O'Connor), clad in billowing hooded cape, walks on windswept moors to the ruins of a country house. We hear her thoughts through voice-over:

> First I found the place. I wondered who had lived there—what their lives were like. Something whispered to my mind and I began to write. My pen creates stories of a world that might have been, a world of my imagining. And here is one I'm going to tell. But take care not to smile at any part of it.

We discuss how the casting of the author as a character in a film version of her book disrupts chronologies and hierarchies of origin and adaptation. In this instance, the last step in the chain of adaptation—the film—dramatizes a pretextual space of authorial imagination and inspiration (wonderings and whisperings), presenting the film as more comprehensive of the novel's origins than the novel itself. We note too that the preface equates literary inspiration with filmic preproduction: finding a location, developing characters, commissioning a screenplay ("Something whispered to my mind"), writing a screenplay, and so on.

We then turn to another filmic preface, Buñuel's, to discuss an alternative mode in which an adaptation claims authorial possession. Instead of locating his film in pretextual authorial imagination, Buñuel situates it in the novel's afterlife:

> This picture is based on *Wuthering Heights*, the immortal work of Emily Brontë, written more than one hundred years ago. Its characters are at the mercy of their own instincts and passions. . . . Most importantly, this picture tries to remain true to the *spirit* of Emily Brontë's novel.[5]

In Buñuel's preface, the author is not possessed by the film as embodied character; rather, her novel possesses the film as immortal spirit. We delineate how these different concepts of possession configure relations between a novel and its adaptation. To understand the adaptation better, we examine conflicting views of what constitutes textual spirit (author personality, author intent, transcendent aesthetic genius, authorial style, reader response, the spirit of the times, and more) and observe how claims of fidelity to the spirit of a text seem to mandate *in*fidelity to its letter, allowing for a host of outside agendas and accidents to enter.[6] For instance, being "true to the spirit" of Emily Brontë's "immortal work" for Buñuel meant adapting those aspects of the text that foreground his surrealist credo of *l'amour fou*: sadism, necrophilia, rebellion, and social transgression. He not only selects and omits passages from the novel but also writes additional scenes and dialogue that appear nowhere in Brontë's novel. The film opens with the elder Cathy (Catalina, played by Irasema Dilian) shooting at buzzards to send them "to death's liberty"; the film ends with Heathcliff (Alejandro, played by Jorge Mistral) shot into death's liberty by Hindley (Ricardo, played by Luis Aceves Castañeda). A squealing pig is slaughtered as Heathcliff woos Isabella; a live frog is sacrificed on burning coals as he returns to Wuthering Heights; Wagner's *Tristan and Isolde* permeates the score.

Economic accidents as well as ideological agendas enter into adaptations that claim to be true to a text's spirit. Buñuel had written the screenplay in 1930 but had been unable to find a producer then. In 1953, he was shooting a musical comedy when Oscar Dancigers suddenly offered to produce *Wuthering Heights*. Buñuel leapt at the chance. However, he had to use the actors under contract for the musical comedy. Lilia Prado, who plays Isabel(la), was a rumba dancer. Because of budget limitations, the film had to be shot in just two weeks.

In advanced seminars, we go further to juxtapose these literary and audiovisual prefaces to writings on authors and authorship: to Charlotte Brontë's biographical notice of Ellis Bell in the second edition of *Wuthering Heights*; to reviews of *Wuthering Heights*'s first edition that read the novel as an expression of author character (J. F.; Lewes, Rev.); to Charles Algernon Swinburne's 1883 essay on Emily Brontë, which argues, from an entirely different philosophical viewpoint, that *Wuthering Heights* "is what it is because the author was what she was" (763); and to Roland Barthes's "The Death of the Author" and Michel Foucault's "What Is an Author?"

Literary and Audiovisual Criticism of Wuthering Heights

Transitioning to our next approach to teaching *Wuthering Heights* through its film and television adaptations, I point out to students that both the LWT and Kosminsky adaptations share the title of Harold Bloom's volume of critical essays, *Emily Brontë's* Wuthering Heights. Together, we trace how the critical essays and film or televisual adaptations select and arrange passages of a literary work to create their interpretations. Umberto Eco writes, "In order to transform a work into a cult object one must be able to break, dislocate, unhinge it so that one can remember only parts of it, irrespective of their original relationship with the whole" (198). J. Hillis Miller observes that "each [critic of *Wuthering Heights*] takes some one element in the novel and extrapolates it toward a total explanation" ("*Wuthering Heights*" 50). Film and television adapters have done likewise.

At this stage in the course, students undertake their first major assignment. Each student views one film or television adaptation of *Wuthering Heights* (see the app. to this essay) and reads two critical essays on the novel. Each then identifies and charts the passages adapted in the film or televization and those cited in the two essays. I also ask students to note omissions they consider significant in the shaping of these selections and interpretations. Students subsequently meet in groups of three or four to share their findings in depth before we engage in a class discussion. We look at modes of selection and juxtaposition in critical argumentation, filmic montage, and television editing, paying attention to sound as well as to visual editing. For example, Skynner's 1998 LWT production forges a wordless feminist criticism that resembles many didactic feminist literary critical essays. It offers a narrative of patriarchy-oppressed sisterhood when shots of a delirious Cathy (Orla Brady), screaming as her hair is forcibly cut by her husband and a doctor, are intercut with shots of a stunned, mute Isabella (Flora Montgomery) being forcibly penetrated by her new husband, Heathcliff (Robert Cavanah), in the marriage bed. Here, we discuss contrasts between nonverbal commentaries and verbal criticism.

Cotemporaneous Literary and Audiovisual Criticism of Wuthering Heights

Through this approach, we try to determine whether similar critical impulses occur in cotemporaneous literary criticism and audiovisual adaptations. Students read critical essays written at the time of their selected adaptation. Some students have linked 1930s literary indictments of Nelly's narration and the second half of the novel with Wyler's excision of both in his 1939 film.[7] Students have engaged in fruitful discussions of differences between criticism and excision, drawing on our earlier discussions of editing and interpretation.

We also consider cotemporaneous cultural influences on criticism and adaptations. For example, we observe that the 1939 film refigures Cathy's vacillation between Edgar Linton and Heathcliff as a prescriptive template for the viewer's alternation between earning in the labor force and spending at the motion picture palace. In a similar vein, we see that Paul Nickell's Westinghouse Television Theater's *Wuthering Heights*, made in 1950 postwar America, adapts the novel to foster a tension between desire for what housewives do not have (Heathcliff, romance, new Westinghouse products) and what they do have (Edgar, the 1950s husband, his income). The adaptation arouses desire but channels it toward Westinghouse products. The exuberant libidinal exhibitionism of Fuest's 1970 film, the first adaptation of *Wuthering Heights* released after the relaxation of film censorship laws in 1969, resonates with cotemporaneous critical essays highlighting liberated sexual and romantic expression, particularly the anarchic, socially disintegrating aspects of these expressions.[8]

Transhistorical and Transcultural Critical Issues

Next, in contrast to cotemporaneous juxtapositions, we survey debates on aspects of the novel that have been differently addressed over time and across cultures. For example, throughout the nineteenth century, critics represent

Edgar sympathetically. An 1848 *Britannia* review of the novel depicts Heathcliff as "brutal in his language and sentiments, and cruel in his conduct," whereas "Edgar Linton, [is] in all respects a contrast to Heathcliff . . . very fair and handsome, and naturally of a gentle temper" (Rev. [*Britannia*] 42). While subsequent nineteenth-century reviews increasingly romanticize Heathcliff, they do not villainize Edgar. At worst, he becomes "the kind, weak, elegant Edgar" (Lewes, Rev. [Dunn] 349).

But in most twentieth-century interpretations, Edgar is anything but kind and elegant. Buñuel's 1953 film figures him as a heartless entomologist pinning live, writhing insects to index cards, an emblem of the way he treats his household. Buñuel's film draws on politicized aspects of psychoanalysis, which posits the institutions and individuals who repress as the archvillains of fiction, families, and society alike, from whom unbridled ids, like Heathcliff's and the elder Catherine's, seek liberation.

Similarly, though from a feminist rather than a Marxist point of view, Stewart (Sam Neill), the Edgar character in Jane Campion's *The Piano*, becomes the archvillain of the film, maiming and threatening to rape the Cathy character, Ada (Holly Hunter), while the Heathcliff character, Baines (Harvey Keitel), evolves from a libidinous half-wild man into a tamed Harlequin romance figure dripping affection and domestic support.[9] By contrast, the Wyler film is decidedly antifeminist, representing the elder Cathy (Merle Oberon) as a peevish villain, dying from sheer frustration that she cannot have both men, while depicting Edgar (David Niven) as a dignified, long-suffering husband and romanticizing and glamorizing Heathcliff (Laurence Olivier). In discussion, we hypothesize broader ethical, social, and formal reasons for and implications of these changing character assessments.

Character softenings, we find, are paralleled by interpretive softenings of the novel's narrators, the second generation, and estimations of its status in reviews, literary criticism, and audiovisual adaptations. We discuss whether and how Lockwood, Nelly Dean, and Isabella rationalize, censure, and civilize the words and actions of narrated characters. We ponder critical claims that the novel's second generation tames and heals the destructive actions of the first. We note that while in 1848 an *Atlas* reviewer declares, "We know nothing in the whole range of our fictitious literature which presents such shocking pictures of the worst forms of humanity" (Rev. [*Dunn*] 283), by 1887, a reviewer fears he is resorting to "truisms or plagiarisms" when he claims that *Wuthering Heights* is "the most beautiful romance of the present century" (J. F.). As we posit reasons for these shifting assessments, the class considers how written and audiovisual criticism tame and civilize the novel differently. For example, written criticism has subjected the novel to humanism, psychoanalysis, historicism, structuralism, poststructuralism, and other -isms, in an effort to codify and tame it. Filmic and televisual versions more frequently soften the novel through the star system, glamorization, soft-focus photography, music, censorship, film genres and conventions, and cultural nostalgia for canonical novels and Victoriana.

While few courses allow time to cover all these aspects, they do connect to and build on one another and, separately or together, offer ways to deepen critical thinking about *Wuthering Heights* and to engage both formal and contextual aspects of interpretation across historical periods and media. I look forward to the time when even more international films and televizations of *Wuthering Heights* will be readily available on videocassette and DVD and can be juxtaposed to international written criticism to produce a more intercultural critical understanding of *Wuthering Heights*.

NOTES

[1]For the purpose of this discussion, Dunn's preface to the Norton (2003) edition is less provocative than its predecessor; however, the Norton is a useful course text and one can always distribute a photocopy of the (1990) edition preface.

[2]While the Dunn volume (2003) removes "authorized" from the subtitle, the 2003 Peterson edition subtitle claims the work to be a "complete, authoritative text."

[3]Baker and his research team evidently did not see Kiju Yoshida's *Arashi ga oka* (1988) or Peter Kosminsky's *Emily Brontë's* Wuthering Heights (1992), both of which also dramatize the novel's second generation.

[4]Other 1990s films of canonical literature employing this titular practice include *Bram Stoker's* Dracula (1992), *Mary Shelley's* Frankenstein (1994), *William Shakespeare's* Hamlet (1996), *William Shakespeare's* Romeo and Juliet (1996), and *William Shakespeare's* A Midsummer Night's Dream (1999).

[5]Emphasis as in original.

[6]For a fuller discussion of these issues, see Elliott, ch. 5.

[7]See, e.g., Edgar. The 1939 film does include one or two shots of Nelly's narration.

[8]See, e.g., Apter; Weissman; Frankenberg; and Efron.

[9]Jane Campion has referred to *The Piano* as her "tribute" to *Wuthering Heights*.

APPENDIX
Film and Television Adaptations of *Wuthering Heights*

The adaptations of *Wuthering Heights* are listed chronologically, from earliest to most recent.

Film and television adaptations available on videocassette, DVD, or both

Wuthering Heights. Dir. William Wyler. Perf. Laurence Olivier and Merle Oberon. United Artists, 1939.

———. Dir. Paul Nickell. Perf. Charlton Heston and Mary Sinclair. Westinghouse Television Theater. CBS, 1950.

Abismos de pasión. Dir. Luis Buñuel. Perf. Jorge Mistral and Irasema Dilian. Plexus, 1953.

Wuthering Heights. Dir. Robert Fuest. Perf. Timothy Dalton and Anna Calder-Marshall. MGM, 1970.

Hurlevent. Dir. Jacques Rivette. Perf. Lucas Belvaux and Fabienne Babe. Renn, 1985.

Emily Brontë's Wuthering Heights. Dir. Peter Kosminsky. Perf. Ralph Fiennes and Juliette Binoche. Paramount, 1992.

The Piano. Dir. Jane Campion. Perf. Harvey Keitel, Holly Hunter, and Sam Neill. Miramax, 1993.

Emily Brontë's Wuthering Heights. Dir. David Skynner. Perf. Robert Cavanah and Orla Brady. London Weekend Television-WGBH, 1998.

Wuthering Heights, CA. Dir. Suri Krishnamma. Perf. Mike Vogel and Erika Christensen. MTV, 2003.

Films and televizations available at the Library of Congress Motion Picture Reading Room

Wuthering Heights. McGraw-Hill Text, 1967 [animated].

"Wuthering Heights / House of Dolls." Dir. Philip Leacock. *Fantasy Island* episode. Columbia TV. 1982.

Arashi ga oka [*Onimaru*]. Dir. Kiju Yoshida. Perf. Yusaku Matsuda and Yuko Tanaka. Seiyô Films. Japan, 1988.

Lost adaptations, adaptations located in archives outside the United States, or in archives closed to researchers

Wuthering Heights. Dir. A. V. Bramble. Perf. Milton Rosmer and Colette Brettel. Ideal, 1920 [silent; lost film].

———. Dir. Daniel Petrie. Perf. Richard Burton. 1958 [TV; no production company information available].

Pokpoongea uhunduck. Korea, 1960 [no production company information available].

Wuthering Heights. Script Nigel Kneale. BBC, 1962 [single TV episode].

Dil Diya Dard Liya. Dir. A. R. Kardar and Dilip Kumar. Perf. Dilip Kumar and Waheeda Rehman. Kary. Bombay, 1966.

Morro dos Ventos Uivantes, O. Perf. Altair Lima and Irina Greco. TV Excelsior. Brazil, 1967 [TV miniseries].

Wuthering Heights. Dir. Peter Sadsy. BBC, 1967 [TV miniseries].

Vendaval. Perf. Jonas Mello and Joana Fomm. Brazil, 1973 [TV miniseries].

Wuthering Heights. Dir. Peter Hammond. BBC, 1978 [TV miniseries].

Cumbres borrascosas. Dir. Karlos Velázquez. Perf. Gonzalo Vega and Alma Muriel. Mexico, 1979 [TV miniseries].

Hihintayin kita sa langit [*I'll Wait for You in Heaven*]. Dir. Carlos Siguion-Reyna.

Perf. Richard Gomez and Dawn Zuleta. Philippines, 1991 [no production company information available].

Matsura. Perf. Zahim Albakri and Ellit Suriaty Omar. Antah UTV, Malaysia, 1998 [TV miniseries].

[*Wuthering Heights*.] Dir. Metin Erksan. Turkey [no date or production company information available].

Hearing Class in Class: Using Audio Excerpts to Teach *Wuthering Heights*

Dean de la Motte

Most of today's students are aware—if only by comparing Hugh Grant with Julia Roberts in the film *Notting Hill*—that an English accent differs markedly from an American accent. However, they rarely make fine distinctions between or among the almost infinite variety of accents in Britain, let alone grasp the possible social significance of the variations. The extent of their reaction to language in *Wuthering Heights*, for example, is usually to complain about the difficulty of understanding the old servant Joseph.

It is my contention, however, that the text clearly indicates the importance of language to Brontë's depiction of the different social classes, as well as the interpretive limits of such social markers. Moreover, students need to be reminded that to the novel's early readers, these important distinctions were ubiquitous, so easily grasped that they were, in essence, transparent. Indeed, some of the novel's most powerful passages describe the disruption of this typically easy identification of language with social class, especially in the case of Hareton and Heathcliff.

In this essay, I suggest how Emily Brontë's characters themselves underscore the social conventions by which language—particularly in nineteenth-century England—reveals social class but also how an uncritical reliance on those conventions can lead to confusion. Indeed, a careful examination of the causes of such linguistic disorientation can lead students to a keener appreciation of central themes in *Wuthering Heights*.

As early as the novel's second chapter, Lockwood becomes confused by the apparent discrepancy between aspects of Hareton Earnshaw's appearance and language, and his inability to place the young man neatly into a recognizable social category is a source of considerable discomfort:

> I began to doubt whether he were a servant or not; his dress and speech were both rude, entirely devoid of the superiority observable in Mr. and Mrs. Heathcliff; his thick, brown curls were rough and uncultivated, his whiskers encroached bearishly over his cheeks, and his hands were embrowned like those of a common labourer; still his bearing was free, almost haughty, and he showed none of the domestic's assiduity in attending on the lady of the house. (8)

That Lockwood cannot find "clear proofs of [Hareton's] condition" (8) may be properly viewed as the exception that confirms the rule, here; in a highly stratified society, where social superiority is instantly recognizable through physical appearance and speech, Hareton's ambiguity points to his dual origins as a gentleman farmer's son who has been purposely degraded by Heathcliff. Significantly, late in the novel, young Cathy's rehabilitation of Hareton—at least in the few glimpses we have of it through Lockwood's eyes—centers on language:

> "Con-*trary*!" said a voice, as sweet as a silver bell—"That for the third time, you dunce! I'm not going to tell you, again—Recollect, or I pull your hair!"
>
> "Contrary, then," answered another, in deep but softened tones. "And now, kiss me, for minding so well."
>
> "No, read it over first correctly, without a single mistake."
>
> The male speaker began to read—he was a young man, respectably dressed, and seated at a table, having a book before him. His handsome features glowed with pleasure, and his eyes kept impatiently wandering from the page to a small white hand over his shoulder, which recalled him by a smart slap on the cheek, whenever its owner detected such signs of inattention. (273)

It is important to remind students of the most basic distinctions, now blurred or even lost—those between the "ladies" and "gentlemen" of the landed gentry and the rough "women" and "men" of the peasantry and other working classes. Emily Brontë underscores these differences throughout the novel, as when Nelly Dean identifies the speech of her late master with the current inhabitant of Thrushcross Grange, Mr. Lockwood: "He had a sweet, low manner of speaking, and pronounced his words as you do: that's less gruff than we talk here, and softer" (62). Though at first glance Nelly appears to be speaking of regional differences, we recall that the Lintons have long resided in the area and that their diction is both a direct result and an unmistakable emblem of their social superiority.

The connection between the outward signs of gentility and true social standing is emphasized in the passage in which young Catherine Linton, at her first meeting with Hareton, is thoroughly disoriented at learning that this rough young man is, in fact, her cousin. Her confusion begins when he fails to call her "miss"—as "he should have done, shouldn't he, if he's a servant?" (172), and her bewilderment points up the crucial, usually transparent role language (regional accent, diction, grammar and mastery of vocabulary, including proper social distinctions) plays in the differentiation and perpetuation of the social classes, both in the plot of the novel and in society in general. Because Hareton, her cousin and the son of a gentleman farmer, behaves like a clown, the easy transparency of language as a marker of class is muddied. Cathy and we, as readers, know that something is amiss. Young Cathy, of course, comes to learn what the reader has already witnessed, that Heathcliff has repaid Hindley's degradation of himself two-fold on the unsuspecting Hareton: "Now, my bonny lad, you are *mine*! And we'll see if one tree won't grow as crooked as another, with the same wind to twist it" (165).

Heathcliff's success merely reinforces the importance of language as both source and consequence of social power in *Wuthering Heights* and in the world at large. The book is replete with examples of how speech determines what characters think of one another and, ultimately, who they are. Emily Brontë's innovative use of phonetic renderings of dialect is but the most obvious example.

Brontë's two primary narrators, Mr. Lockwood and Nelly Dean, represent two distinct social classes, and their language is fashioned accordingly. The considerable fastidiousness in Lockwood's choice of vocabulary and manner of speech is echoed only in that of the Lintons, his predecessors at Thrushcross Grange. Nelly, on the other hand, is a literate, thoughtful, but homely narrator, whose diction we expect to find somewhere in the middle regions between servant and master; raised among and employed by the Earnshaws and Lintons, and well-read, she nevertheless lacks all pretense of expression. Indeed, we might see hers as the speech of the growing middle class that will come to dominate England and the industrialized world in the decades to come, as the effete aristocracy declines and the peasantry makes the transition from rural poor to urban proletariat. She even has a cheerful, almost mercantile practicality about her. Students can glimpse all this in a brief, seemingly trivial exchange between Lockwood and Nelly Dean:

> "The clock is on the stroke of eleven, sir."
>
> "No matter—I'm not accustomed to go to bed in the long hours. One or two is early enough for a person who lies till ten."
>
> "You shouldn't lie till ten. There's the very prime of the morning gone long before that time. A person who has not done one half his day's work by ten o'clock, runs a chance of leaving the other half undone."
>
> "Nevertheless, Mrs. Dean, resume your chair; because to-morrow I intend lengthening the night till afternoon. I prognosticate for myself an obstinate cold, at least." (54)

Despite these clear indications, however, I maintain that United States students cannot fully appreciate the relation of language to class unless they hear the novel read aloud. To this end, I use audiocassettes of the novel—notably Patricia Routledge's 1983 version—to allow students to see or, rather, hear the importance of class distinctions as an overarching structural and thematic component of the novel.

I begin with the passage describing young Cathy's first meeting with Hareton, which demonstrates thematically the point I wish to convey. Routledge's brilliant reading of the novel, in which she approximates the age, gender, and emotional and social condition of each character, brings these distinctions vividly to life. In this section of Brontë's novel (172), we hear the voices of

Catherine Linton, Nelly Dean, and Hareton, each of whom has a particular pattern of usage and diction. The genius of Routledge's performance is her uncanny ability to reproduce the accents of the English nobility, the housekeeper Nelly, and the boorish Hareton, as well as of the other characters, of birth high and low.

Once I have introduced this theme, I have students turn back to the pivotal scene of the elder Cathy and Heathcliff's intrusion at Thrushcross Grange (43–44). Here we have Heathcliff recounting within Nelly's narration, but the voices of the Lintons are juxtaposed with that of their servant, Robert, and Routledge's interpretation of the scene is again illuminating, with Robert speaking in the songlike cadence of a Yorkshire domestic and the Lintons with the stilted formality of the ruling elite. We also learn from Heathcliff's account that at least three servants (Robert, John, and Jenny) are present at the scene. The Lintons' very comments, as well as the manner in which they are expressed, betray their concern (bordering on paranoia) with wealth, class—including Heathcliff's uncertain "race"—and, as an expression of these, language. The passage deserves quoting at length:

> " 'What prey, Robert?' hallooed Linton from the entrance.
>
> " 'Skulker has caught a little girl, sir,' he replied, 'and there's a lad here,' he added, making a clutch at me, 'who looks an out-and-outer! Very like, the robbers were for putting them through the window, to open the doors to the gang after all were asleep, that they might murder us at their ease. Hold your tongue, you foul-mouthed thief, you! you shall go to the gallows for this. Mr. Linton, sir, don't lay by your gun!'
>
> " 'No, no, Robert!' said the old fool. 'The rascals knew that yesterday was my rent day; they thought to have me cleverly. Come in; I'll furnish them a reception. There, John, fasten the chain. Give Skulker some water, Jenny. To beard a magistrate in his strong-hold, and on the Sabbath, too! Where will their insolence stop? Oh, my dear Mary, look here! Don't be afraid, it is but a boy—yet the villain scowls so plainly in his face, would it not be a kindness to the country to hang him at once, before he shows his nature in acts, as well as features?'
>
> "He pulled me under the chandelier, and Mrs. Linton placed her spectacles on her nose and raised her hands in horror. The cowardly children crept nearer also, Isabella lisping—
>
> " 'Frightful thing! Put him in the cellar, papa. He's exactly like the son of the fortune-teller, that stole my tame pheasant. Isn't he, Edgar?'
>
> "While they examined me, Cathy came round; she heard the last speech, and laughed. Edgar Linton, after an inquisitive stare, collected sufficient wit to recognise her. They see us at church, you know, though we seldom meet them elsewhere.
>
> " 'That's Miss Earnshaw!' he whispered to his mother, 'and look how Skulker has bitten her—how her foot bleeds!'

> " 'Miss Earnshaw? Nonsense!' cried the dame, 'Miss Earnshaw scouring the country with a gipsy! And yet, my dear, the child is in mourning—surely it is—and she may be lamed for life!'
>
> " 'What culpable carelessness in her brother!' exclaimed Mr. Linton, turning from me to Catherine. 'I've understood from Shielders' " (that was the curate, sir) " 'that he lets her grow up in absolute heathenism. But who is this? Where did she pick up this companion? Oho! I declare he is that strange acquisition my late neighbour made in his journey to Liverpool—a little Lascar, or an American or Spanish castaway.'
>
> " 'A wicked boy, at all events,' remarked the old lady, "and quite unfit for a decent house! Did you notice his language, Linton? I'm shocked that my children should have heard it.' " (43–44)

I also use the passage in which Linton Heathcliff taunts the young Hareton because the latter "does not know his letters" (194), a fact that briefly enables Linton—in the eyes of virtually everyone in the novel "an ailing, peevish creature" (161)—to assert his superiority through learning and, specifically, through language.

While some teachers may prefer to target different passages, I recommend the Routledge recording because no other reader comes close to her ability to capture the shadings of social class. For example, a more recent recording, by Michael Page and Laural Merlington (as Lockwood and Nelly Dean), attempts, somewhat half-heartedly, to do so but fails to attain anything approaching the rich textures of Routledge's version.

Between these excerpts and the helpful endnotes of Ian Jack's edition of the novel (the notes are often translations of Yorkshire dialect, especially as used by Joseph), students are equipped to make significant progress toward an appreciation of language's connection to social class. Such an approach represents a striking way of reminding students that to the novel's early readers, these important distinctions were ubiquitous and immediately recognizable—indeed, so much so that they had a transparency clouded only by the unexpected appearance of aberrations like Heathcliff and, to an even greater extent, Hareton. After listening to the audiocassette, students can return to the text with an auditory impression in their minds, a clear sense of what it is to sound like these characters. The minor confusion that arises from Brontë's innovative transcription of Yorkshire dialect should give way to a far more complex, far richer understanding of the role that language plays in the differentiation and perpetuation of the social classes in nineteenth-century England (notwithstanding Brontë's setting of the novel in the last quarter of the eighteenth century). This understanding, in turn, can enrich their comprehension of Heathcliff's effect on the other characters and of the disruption of the social order that lies at the heart of the novel.

Finally, I point out to students that young Cathy and Hareton's true attachment to each other begins with the gift of a book (276), just as his redemption, as noted, comes through instruction in proper reading and diction. From the reader's perspective, it is language that returns Hareton to his rightful place in the social order. So it is that the social function of language, brought to life by Routledge, dramatically reinforces the central themes and structure of the novel.

Teaching *Wuthering Heights* Intertextually: The Example of Alice Hoffman's *Here on Earth*

Maureen T. Reddy

In teaching *Wuthering Heights* during the past decade, I have found students to be ever more enamored of romance plots and inclined to sympathize uncritically with Heathcliff as a victim while seeing the elder Catherine as entirely unsympathetic. Encouraging more-nuanced readings of the novel has consequently become both increasingly difficult and urgent. In addition to assigning critical articles on *Wuthering Heights* as a way of pointing students toward alternative readings that might open up their responses to the text, I have been approaching the novel intertextually as a useful method of addressing the limitations of a romance reading.

Like many other nineteenth-century novels, *Wuthering Heights* has inspired several recent women novelists, who have either revised elements of Emily Brontë's text in their work or written novels that are direct responses to *Wuthering Heights.* Jane Urquhart's *Changing Heaven* treats Brontë's novel as a meta-romance, exploring its presumed acceptance of the cultural demand that women live only for love, and Angela Carter's *Nights at the Circus* examines male masochism and female objectification in *Wuthering Heights* and many other texts. Maryse Condé's *Windward Heights* (originally published as *La migration des coeurs*) is a strikingly direct rewriting of Brontë's novel, moving the characters to the Caribbean and emphasizing the theme of revenge. It foregrounds race and racism, with Razyé—her Heathcliff character—representative of oppressed blacks and his revenge ultimately thwarted. These three novels, as well as other revisions of or homages to Brontë's—ranging from Luis Buñuel's brilliantly strange film *Abismos de pasión* to Reni Suzuka's Famous Love Comics version of *Wuthering Heights*—offer fascinating possibilities for expanding the interpretive strategies students bring to the work. However, since my course focuses on British and North American narratives by women, some of these revisions do not fit the course parameters. Of the texts that do, Alice Hoffman's *Here on Earth* can fruitfully be paired with *Wuthering Heights.*

Like Condé's *Windward Heights*, Hoffman's novel is a faithful retelling of Emily Brontë's novel. It transposes numerous elements of the first part of the original text—the Catherine-Heathcliff story—to late twentieth-century Massachusetts. Speculating on the question, what if Cathy had lived? Hoffman offers the plot of *Here on Earth* as an answer. I have used Hoffman's book immediately after *Wuthering Heights* in an upper-division English course called Literature by Women. Obviously, with such a broad title, the course requires considerable narrowing. For several years, my focus has been on nineteenth- and twentieth-century narratives by women, in which the desire for freedom, variously defined, is a central theme. In this version of the course one of my major interests is to explore alternatives that women writers have imagined to the all-too-familiar pattern of novels about women ending in marriage or death. That exploration requires us to consider the hold the romance plot has on Western fiction in general and the methods women writers have devised to break the hold. This interest prompted me to build the course around narratives by women that somehow speak to each other. Texts I have used include revisions of earlier texts (e.g., *Jane Eyre* and Jean Rhys's *Wide Sargasso Sea*) and treatments of similar concerns (e.g., Virginia Woolf's *A Room of One's Own* and Cheryl Dunye's film *The Watermelon Woman* or Harriet Jacobs's *Incidents in the Life of a Slave Girl* and Octavia Butler's *Kindred*).

In other portions of the course, I try not to subordinate either one of the paired texts to the other, but in the Brontë-Hoffman pairing, I have deliberately chosen a modern novel that is far less complex and much easier for students to read than the earlier work. My decision was largely determined by the difficulty students have reported in reading *Wuthering Heights*, as well as their tendency to simplify Emily Brontë's novel into a tragic romance. Initially, I anticipated that reading and discussing the Hoffman text would encourage students to look back to *Wuthering Heights* and to see the elements Hoffman ignores. While that has sometimes happened, one problem is that the elements Hoffman ignores tend to be those the students downplay as well. I therefore give reading questions and writing prompts that push students to analyze particular aspects of the texts.

I begin the course with Virginia Woolf's *A Room of One's Own*, moving from there to Charlotte Brontë's *Jane Eyre*. After we have discussed *Jane Eyre* for three or four class meetings, we return to Woolf's discussion of that novel, in which she conflates Jane Eyre and Charlotte Brontë and claims that Jane's and Charlotte's anger mars the book. I ask students to consider Woolf as a reader of Charlotte Brontë and to compare Woolf's response with their own. What does Woolf's criticism of *Jane Eyre* tell us about Woolf? about cultural responses to women's anger generally? Most students do not perceive Jane Eyre's anger as Charlotte Brontë's, nor do they see that anger as problematic; indeed, students frequently argue that both Jane and Charlotte should be angrier than they are and describe the anger they see in *Jane Eyre* as a righteous response to female oppression.

We move from there to Sandra M. Gilbert and Susan Gubar's chapter on *Jane Eyre* in *The Madwoman in the Attic* and then to Jean Rhys's *Wide Sargasso Sea*. In our discussion of Rhys's novel I emphasize the race issues submerged in *Jane Eyre* that *Wide Sargasso Sea* brings to the fore. Jane's inheritance, after all, comes from colonial exploitation, as does at least some of Rochester's wealth, yet that history remains obscured in Brontë's text. We also consider how our experiences of *Jane Eyre* and *Wide Sargasso Sea* are shaped by their first-person narration, with Rhys giving us two narrators (Antoinette-Bertha and the unnamed Rochester character) in place of Brontë's Jane.

By the time we turn to *Wuthering Heights,* then, students have acquired experience in reading intertextually, considering narrative strategies, placing texts in their social and historical contexts, and thinking about the assumptions that might underlie readings different from theirs. Splitting the reading of the novel across a week, I ask students to write brief responses to four questions after completing the first volume and to come to class prepared to discuss their responses and to identify specific passages we might look at as a class. My questions are broad and basic:

1. Consider the narrative frame of the novel. Can we trust any of the speakers? How do we decide?
2. Is Heathcliff pure evil (a "demon")? Why do people claim he is a "gipsy," and what might that term signify? What does his foundling status mean?
3. Compare and contrast the two major sites of the novel (Wuthering Heights and Thrushcross Grange). What is the symbolism of each location?
4. How would you interpret the relationship between Cathy and Heathcliff? Are we meant to read it as a great love?

Unsurprisingly, we do not fully address or resolve any of these questions, but we at least touch on all of them. Having students spend time responding to these questions on their own elevates class discussion beyond what I can expect without study questions. Further, since we have already spent considerable class time exploring similar issues in *Jane Eyre* and *Wide Sargasso Sea*, students feel fairly comfortable focusing on these topics. Usually the first class period on the novel requires attention to the Earnshaw and Linton family trees and to questions of social class. In the United States, we tend to deny social class, or to equate it simply with money, so students sometimes struggle with the complexities of social class in *Wuthering Heights*. The discussion springs naturally from the questions about the two settings of the novel and about narrative frame: the full extent of the irony with which Emily Brontë treats Lockwood is clear only if students recognize his blunders about social class and his comparative status in Yorkshire.

For the second session on the novel, I ask students to complete the book, but I do not give them new study questions. Instead, I ask them to reconsider their responses to the earlier questions in the light of the novel's second volume and to bring in questions of their own for the class to discuss. We spend much of that meeting on student revisions of their responses to the questions. The most striking shift usually occurs in their reading of Heathcliff. Sympathy for Heathcliff as a victim—already undermined by his apparent hanging of Isabella's dog, which always has more impact than his sadistic treatment of human beings—diminishes considerably as students answer question 2 (Is Heathcliff a demon?) on the basis of his subsequent behavior. Interestingly, even the students who begin with the greatest awareness of the way Nelly shapes the story and her highly interested portrayal of characters and events often lose track of her as narrator in the second volume. Many students treat big sections of that part of the novel as if they are presented by a third-person omniscient narrator and assume that Nelly's approbation of the relationship between Hareton and the younger Catherine reflects Emily Brontë's views.

For the third class meeting on the novel, I generally assign Charlotte Brontë's "Biographical Notice of Ellis and Acton Bell" and her preface to the second edition of *Wuthering Heights*, as well as a critical essay on the book. I have used both the Richard J. Dunn edition and the Linda H. Peterson casebook edition of *Wuthering Heights,* because they include several useful essays; Dunn's edition provides much of the chapter on Emily Brontë from Gilbert and Gubar's *The Madwoman in the Attic.* Using this essay works especially well in the course, since students have already read the essay on *Jane Eyre* from *Madwoman,* and the one on *Wuthering Heights* touches on many of the issues they have considered in their readings of the book. Gilbert and Gubar argue that Emily Brontë creates a myth explaining how culture arose and treating the elder Cathy's entry into womanhood as a fall from the freedom of hell. Their readings of Heathcliff (as Cathy's "whip" [Dunn, *Wuthering Heights* 386]) and of the two locations in the text challenge students' prior analyses.

We spend much of the third session discussing Charlotte Brontë as a reader of her sister's work and Gilbert and Gubar as readers of Emily Brontë's novel, comparing these writers' interpretations of *Wuthering Heights* with students' responses. Students are often surprised and disappointed by what they see as Charlotte Brontë's limited understanding of *Wuthering Heights,* which is more distressing to them than Virginia Woolf's problematic reading of *Jane Eyre.* They frequently debate about Charlotte Brontë's descriptions of Nelly ("a specimen of true benevolence and homely fidelity" [326]), Edgar ("an example of constancy and tenderness" [326]), and Heathcliff (who "betrays one solitary human feeling . . . his rudely confessed regard for Hareton Earnshaw" [327]). This discussion generally continues into a fourth class meeting, during which I try to steer students toward some consideration of the second generation in the novel, asking why they have so little interest in that generation and why the Heathcliff-Cathy story seems so much more compelling to them. What does that lack of interest say about us as readers of the novel?

At the end of the fourth session on *Wuthering Heights,* I give students the paper assignment. Because they have not yet read *Here on Earth*, the writing prompt tends to structure their reading of that novel. The assignment consists of some version of the following, on which I ask students to write four to six pages:

> In *A Room of One's Own,* Virginia Woolf famously says that "we think back through our mothers if we are women" (79). Our syllabus this term is grounded in that claim. Although we can trace many influences behind

> Alice Hoffman's *Here on Earth* and should assume that there are others of which we are not aware (and that perhaps even Hoffman herself is not conscious of), it seems clear that one of the literary "mothers" that Hoffman thinks back through is Emily Brontë. Choose some element of *Here on Earth* and examine it in relation to *Wuthering Heights.* What do we gain by reading the two texts against each other that we might miss if we read just one of them? Obviously, this is a huge topic with many possible approaches. How you narrow the topic and what approach you take is up to you.

After the four class meetings on *Wuthering Heights,* we turn to Hoffman's *Here on Earth,* on which we spend two sessions. I ask students to finish the book before the first meeting and to come to class with a list of connections—small or large, in no particular order—that they see between Hoffman's novel and Emily Brontë's. This list making helps move them toward writing their essays as well as preparing for class discussion.

I start the first class on *Here on Earth* by asking students to share items from their lists, beginning with the similarities between the two novels. They include two important houses (Fox Hill and Wuthering Heights, Guardian Farm and Thrushcross Grange) whose functions are highly symbolic and also ambiguous, as well as parallel characters, such as Hollis and Heathcliff, March and elder Cathy, Gwen and young Cathy, Alan and Hindley, Mr. Earnshaw and Judge Murray, Hank and Hareton, Isabella and Belinda, and Richard and Edgar. Students tend to find the similar plot elements remarkable, including the foundling brought home by the rather distant, authoritarian father and then favored by him over his natural children, especially his son; the jealous rage that the son is able to indulge after the father's death, followed by the foundling's eventual revenge; the intense, uncanny relationship between the central characters in their youth, disrupted and then rekindled; and the growing love between the dispossessed children of the next generation. Despite the striking plot similarities, my students respond to the two novels in fundamentally different ways.

We try together to account for the dissimilarity. Students generally agree that Hoffman's novel is more familiar to them than Brontë's: the characters are modern and considerably less strange, and their motives and feelings are spelled out for the readers. Hoffman's narrative strategy underscores that crucial difference, since her novel is told from a third-person omniscient position, eliminating the layers of narration in *Wuthering Heights.* Even students who had seen Lockwood's and Nelly's narration as unproblematic now tend to revise their opinions, recognizing the impact that removing the personal narrators has on our experience of the text (the Nelly character, Judith Dale, has died just as the novel opens; her funeral is the reason March returns to her hometown and reunites with Hollis).

One significant difference between Hoffman's Hollis and Emily Brontë's

Heathcliff never provokes student comments unless I mention it first: the race issue. From his introduction in *Wuthering Heights,* Heathcliff is marked as racially different from the English. Mrs. Earnshaw is horrified that her husband brings "that gipsy brat" home; Mr. Earnshaw says he is "as dark almost as if [he] came from the devil"; and Nelly describes him as "a dirty, ragged, black-haired child" who speaks only "some gibberish that nobody could understand" (31). Some years later, Mrs. Linton cannot believe that Catherine Earnshaw is "scouring the country with a gipsy," and Mr. Linton recognizes Heathcliff as "that strange acquisition my late neighbour made in his journey to Liverpool—a little Lascar, or an American or Spanish castaway" (44). Trying to cheer Heathcliff up when Cathy seems to prefer Edgar to him, Nelly encourages him to fantasize about his origins, saying, "Who knows, but your father was Emperor of China, and your mother an Indian queen" (50). Whatever Heathcliff's origins, the novel repeatedly emphasizes that he is not white, and not English.

In contrast, Hoffman makes Hollis white, not different in appearance from most of the inhabitants in the small town to which Mr. Murray brings him; whiteness is presented as normative and uncomplicated. Hollis's lack of difference gives me an opening to encourage students to consider the meanings of race in *Wuthering Heights* and in *Here on Earth.* How would the former change if Heathcliff were white? And how would the latter change if Hollis were not? These questions lead to a lively discussion, particularly in relation to Jean Rhys's foregrounding of race in *Wide Sargasso Sea* versus Charlotte Brontë's covert coding of Bertha as not white in *Jane Eyre.*

In the second class on *Here on Earth,* I ask students to consider Hoffman as a reader of *Wuthering Heights.* Do they sympathize with her reading of the novel? How does it compare with Charlotte Brontë's reading or Gilbert and Gubar's or their own? Even students who prefer *Here on Earth* to *Wuthering Heights*—and there are always some, most saying they can relate to Gwen in ways that they cannot relate to any character in Emily Brontë's novel—tend to see Hoffman as insufficiently alive to the complexities of the earlier novel. Several students have said that Hoffman is as limited a reader of Emily Brontë's novel as Charlotte Brontë is, albeit for different reasons.

Hoffman's revision of Brontë's novel simplifies each complex issue, tending to reduce its ambiguity. So, for example, when Heathcliff leaves Wuthering Heights and returns years later with money, we never learn how he came by that money but, like Nelly, must rely on speculation and rumor. In contrast, although the townspeople do not know for certain how Hollis obtained his money during his years away, readers are directly told: he was a hit man for racehorses, injuring and killing them so that their owners could collect insurance payments. Similarly, Heathcliff's sadism and capacity for violence are implied more than they are shown in the text, whereas we see Hollis's brutality repeatedly. Hoffman even has one character uncover evidence that Hollis beat his wife, Belinda, and caused her death by refusing to obtain medical attention for her. Hollis wants only to control March, which, being privy to his thoughts and plans, we learn directly from Hollis himself; he is incapable of what most people would be willing to term love. The relationship between March and Hollis thus seems less multidimensional than that between the elder Cathy and Heathcliff.

Students acknowledge that the dynamics of abuse Hoffman centralizes are hinted at in *Wuthering Heights*, but they see her reading as distorted because it only considers abuse. I ask, Is that focus partly a function of different eras? Are we now so alert to the possibility of domestic abuse that we read its potential in any romantic obsession? Is it possible to have an obsession without any hint of abuse? In complaining about Hoffman's oversimplification of the relationship between Cathy and Heathcliff, are we deflecting our sorrow at the loss of great romance narratives? And is *Wuthering Heights* really a romance narrative? March comes across to students as a deceived victim; her awakening to the truth about Hollis occurs too late to redeem her in their eyes. As students express their anger with March, I ask them to consider her as an updated Cathy. Interestingly, March makes students have more sympathy for Cathy, but probably not in the way Hoffman intends. Instead, in contrast to March, Cathy seems less passive, and certainly not a willing victim of an abusive man. On the other hand, Cathy dies—apparently willing herself dead—while March decides to live and extricates herself from her imprisonment by Hollis.

Susanna Justice, one of the few characters in *Here on Earth* who have no model in *Wuthering Heights,* can be credited with helping March wake up and also providing an important reminder of what is missing in the elder Cathy's life: a female friend who takes her side and fights for her. Cathy's solitariness, which few students initially comment on, emerges now as a motif worthy of consideration. In creating Susanna, Hoffman seems to be fulfilling Woolf's prophecy that women writers will finally write seriously about women's relationships instead of remaining trapped in romance plots.

Despite its refusal to obey most of the demands on women novelists, Brontë's novel ends with both death and a promised marriage for its female protagonists, while Hoffman's offers broader possibilities. March escapes Hollis, who then providentially dies in a car crash while trying to bring her back, and Gwen goes back to her father in California, leaving Hank in Massachusetts. Both women's lives are left open: anything might happen, and the options are not limited to marriage or death. Brontë was certainly a more revolutionary, daring novelist than Hoffman, and yet the options she imagines for her female characters are sharply limited. Reading Hoffman's novel immediately after Brontë's virtually forces students to consider that evident conundrum and to attend to the impact of social conditions on authors' imaginations.

BUILDING SKILLS THROUGH TEACHING *WUTHERING HEIGHTS*

Teaching Emily Brontë's Poetry and *Wuthering Heights* in a First-Year Composition Course

Tricia Lootens

Many of the first-year composition students I teach seem driven by anxieties over genre and voice. Haunted by the five-paragraph high school essay and often driven by acute ambivalence toward what they imagine as the magisterial requirements of formal critical prose, such students tend to approach their first college English course with trepidation. In recent years, I've had some success in engaging such anxieties head-on, partly by setting them into relief against a series of gothic readings. The course in question, an introduction to critical writing most often entitled Ghosts, Monsters, and Genres, addresses a shifting series of texts, including Edward Albee's *The Zoo Story*, Elizabeth Bishop's "The Man-Moth," W. H. Auden's "As I Walked Out One Evening," Elizabeth Barrett Browning's "The Runaway Slave at Pilgrim's Point," Robert Browning's " 'Childe Roland to the Dark Tower Came,' " Emily Dickinson's "One need not be a Chamber—to be Haunted—," Henry James's *Turn of the Screw*, Toni Morrison's *Beloved*, Shakespeare's *Hamlet*, Mary Shelley's *Frankenstein*, and Tom Stoppard's *Rosencrantz and Guildenstern Are Dead*. We always read *Wuthering Heights*, and lately we have begun to read selected Emily Brontë poems as well.

I open the first class by handing out "One need not be a Chamber—to be Haunted—" and Brontë's "R. Alcona to J. Brenzaida" ("Cold in the earth—and the deep snow piled above thee"). Genre, I note, may be a surprising third term in our course title, but it is also a suitable one. After all, fear of ghosts and monsters often constitutes a form of genre panic: are they or aren't they human? After discussing how such figures may push us to define humanity by questioning its boundaries, I note that literary genres, too, rely on boundaries that may seem both essential and impossible to define. (Is a novel in verse still a novel? a novel presented in comic book form?) Drawing on William Wordsworth's famous suggestion in the Preface to *Lyrical Ballads*—that publishing poetry calls a sort of "contracted" formal "engagement" into play (596)—I consider genre's operations as a source of productive constraints. This observation sets up a good bridge to addressing the leap from high school to college writing. By speaking of the five-paragraph essay as a beginner's genre, I can honor many students' training, even as I underscore the likelihood that their capacity to write high school English assignments may be a weak predictor of college performance. From here, I often move on to consider the social aspects of the professional writing process, stressing the extent to which published writing tends to reflect a communal production, whether through the intervention of collaborators, editors, grant officers, or other collegial or supervisory readers. These points emphasize students' need to meet increasingly complex demands for documenting sources, even as they help explain why the course requires so much collaborative editing and constant writing, whether of timed responses, brief position papers, essay proposals, joint projects, or multidraft formal papers. My role, I stress, can only be that of a coach; students' private, often idiosyncratic responses to the demands of improving their writing will determine the course's usefulness in the long run.

This final point brings us back to the combined anxiety and exhilaration with which many people greet stories of ghosts and monsters. For students' greatest challenges in writing classes often begin rather than end with learning the specific strategies required by different genres of academic and professional writing. On a deeper level, students need to learn to know themselves as writers, which may well involve developing strategies for negotiating the uncanniness of writing. Roughly translating *das Unheimliche*, or "the uncanny," as "un-home-like," I ask students to think about the process whereby what we may consider to be thoroughly abstract and private intellectual impulses—impulses secret, at points, even from ourselves—take on material form through writing and, in so doing, acquire, at least potentially, the capacity to move beyond our control, outliving our conscious intentions and even our bodies. Writing, I stress, always involves taking risks; as both Emily Brontë's and Emily Dickinson's poetry underscores, the boundaries between ghosts and muses may be thin or nonexistent. With this, we move to Dickinson's "One need not be a Chamber—to be Haunted—" and Brontë's "R. Alcona to J. Brenzaida," to juxtapose the emotional charges of these poems' very different interplay between corporeality and the workings of the mind.[1]

Wuthering Heights sets up much of the course; but to make our writing on the novel work, I use the discussion leading up to our initial diagnostic paper as a means of preparing for the novel. Recently, I have begun our exploration of genre anxieties on two levels: first, by considering students' sense of the challenges of college-level writing and, second, by addressing folk ballads. For our opening assignment, students begin with a fifteen-minute assessment of their writing. I ask them to articulate their current strengths and the specific challenges they expect to face. What writing have they done? What writing would they like to do or will they need to do? How comfortable are they in moving across styles? What sorts of practice might help them develop greater versatility? Our course packet includes dramatically different versions of two or three ballads, both as they appear in the Francis James Child edition and as transcribed from recently recorded performances. Cruel sister ballads, grotesquely comic ballads like the "Twa Corbies," and demon lover ballads can all help set the stage for *Wuthering Heights*, as can the cruel mother ballads more immediately connected to Morrison's *Beloved*. I ask students to read these ballads carefully, composing brief preliminary responses to the following questions: Does it make sense to approach these texts with the familiar questions of who is speaking and why? What, if anything, seems to justify classifying these potentially very different accounts as the same sort of ballad?

This assignment is a tricky move, since the printed texts of ballads often seem somewhat flat; but I have found that it pays off in the end. In one sense, folk ballads represent linguistically straightforward, "starter" texts; in another, they may actually help push students toward breaking free of common high school reading habits. Neither ballad authors nor ballad characters can pretend to have "essential selves," for example; and thus, freed from the temptation to pronounce on what the author meant or to equate all literary power with psychological realism, students can begin to consider more sophisticated approaches. By insisting on the complex resonance of folk forms within canonical literature, moreover, the class can explore the many levels of connection between the spoken and the written word, whether in literary texts or in the students' writing itself.

In our second class, then, I open with a brief history of the ballad, stressing not only the revaluations and appropriations of the folk genre during the late eighteenth- and early nineteenth-century ballad revival but also folk ballads' previous and ongoing existence as collective creations with intimate, unpredictable connections to print culture. Writing about traditional ballads, I tell students, poses particular challenges, for like other folk forms, ballads have no clear points of origin. Developed and developing through a constant accretion of repetition and variation, such works do not even have any correct form. At this point, I play recordings of at least two or three versions of each ballad we have read, pausing for a few seconds between renditions for students to jot down responses. This is a key moment: most students were not expecting the dramatically heightened vitality of the recorded versions. When pressed to speculate on why they find the ballads so much more moving in performance, students tend to stress the impact of modulations in pacing and tone.

They confess to having been especially unprepared for the emotional force of refrains; in reading, they had often simply "bleeped over" these lines.

On the narrowest level, students' surprise at recorded ballads' power can help clarify their own choices in reading or in using repetition. On a broader level, hearing ballads can increase awareness of writing's complex connections to the spoken word. I stress the importance of hearing, not merely silently reading, literary works—most obviously poetry and plays but also other forms, including novels. Before undertaking final revisions on their *Wuthering Heights* paper, I tell students, they will meet with me for individual tutorials, performing their drafts aloud. In the meantime, I suggest they begin practicing in private. Finally, we talk about possible parallels between writing criticism and performing folk ballads. In one sense, I note, ballad singers contain and manipulate the words of songs, subjecting traditional language to the authority of their own idiosyncratic, irreducible voices. In another, the ballad moves—and moves through—the singer. We can think of singing ballads as a form of criticism, I suggest, not least because a fine rendition can move audience members through a work that they may already know quite well, transforming their sense of that work in the process. And though the analogy is not exact, we can also think of the critic as one who both shares and shapes an audience's experience of a potentially well-known text. This, I stress, is one reason that students' work in tracing and articulating the precise origins of their peculiar responses as readers can be so important to their success as critics.

Our next stop on the way to *Wuthering Heights* is with literary ballads, specifically, Wordsworth's "Strange Fits of Passion" and John Keats's "La Belle Dame sans Merci: A Ballad." Much as the folk ballads may pave the way for the often casual brutality of Emily Brontë's literary universe, so, too, the Romantic ballads may foreshadow her novel's narrative shiftiness. Students' written responses focus on questions of narrative voice; our classroom discussions focus on what the literary ballad, as opposed to the folk ballad, offers—and demands of—readers. In discussing the folk ballads, students frequently argue that one specific textual moment, one trope or turn in the action, unites dramatically different variants; and here, too, we look for interpretive cruxes. Working line by line, we consider both the specific effects and the cultural histories of literary form. Discussions of, say, enjambment merge with exploration of the way Romantic poets both evoke and break the "contract" of expectations created by the ballad form. Often students express their investment in generic purity through irritation at changes in the rules; they charge Wordsworth with tricking us into expecting "fits of passion" whose strangeness is not what we had anticipated, or they suggest that Keats cheats by presenting us with a narrator whose perceptions we cannot trust. It matters, we note, that someone in particular crafted these ballads—that they are signed and titled. Yet why and how? Sooner or later, I encourage students to acknowledge, first, that Wordsworth himself is not speaking in "strange fits of passion" and, second, that we can't know what Wordsworth meant, both because it's doubtful that he himself could ever have articulated such a thing and because he's no longer around to ask. "Are these poems about love?" I ask. "About monstrousness? muses? What do the poems say? What can you reasonably make them say?" When discussions of such questions work well, they move between individual students' attempts to articulate and defend specific readings and a common attempt to reach consensus on which passages those readings will have to address. Such practice will become increasingly important as we move toward *Wuthering Heights*.

In the first day's discussion of "R. Alcona to J. Brenzaida," I evaded the question of who, precisely, R. Alcona and J. Brenzaida might be. Now, preparing students to reread that poem, along with "No coward soul is mine" (Gezari 182), I offer a brief description of the Brontës' childhood and an introduction to their writings on Gondal and Angria.[2] We open the next class by discussing what difference, if any, it might make to know that the author of "No coward soul is mine" also wrote Gondal poems. Moving to "R. Alcona to J. Brenzaida," I split the class in half. One group is to argue, by detailed demonstration, for the wisdom of reading the poem as an independent entity; the other, to develop a close reading that relies on imagining R. Alcona and J. Brenzaida as specific fictional characters. With luck, the ensuing discussion opens up suggestive questions concerning context, genre, and lyric address—questions that turn, in part, on the drive to imagine corporeal speakers. Members of the first group, for example, tend to describe "R. Alcona to J. Brenzaida" as a lyric of more or less generic loss and longing. The title, they often argue, is beside the point—as may be the speaker's gender. What matters, as in Wordworth's Lucy poems, is intimate emotional force. In contrast, the second group tends to read the poem as a monologue, arguing that one must know not only the speaker's gender but also her rank. These students, some of whom have initially assumed that the poem's "sterner desires" and "darker hopes" must spring from a male figure, read the poem as a specific meditation on a particular psychic situation, that of a threatened ruler who dares not give way to mourning. Finally, by juxtaposing three versions of the poem, drawn from the C. W. Hatfield and Janet Gezari editions, as well as the *Norton Anthology of English Literature*, we address how readers' conceptions of the historical or corporeal body of a speaker may be determined by editorial decisions concerning the body (or title) of a text. As I underscore the importance of choosing editions carefully, I can stress, one more time, the necessity of quoting carefully as well. We will return to these split readings of Brontë's poetry later, in considering the fruitful tension between mythic and historicist readings of *Wuthering Heights*.

Students' first papers, which focus on some intersection between folk ballads, literary ballads, and "R. Alcona to J. Brenzaida," enter final revisions as we actually begin *Wuthering Heights*. Our initial assignment never varies: students read the novel's first three chapters and analyze what they see as the book's most disturbing moment so far. Precision, I stress, is one of the exercise's points. They should begin by narrowing their choice down to a single moment, a single phrase, or even a single word, then work out from there. Almost invariably, they arrive eager to address Lockwood's nightmare confrontation with the spirit of Catherine. We start, however, on another note, by working through the previous chapters. "What kind of story does Lockwood seem to want to narrate?" I ask. "What role does he seem to imagine himself playing? When and how do you begin to realize that he is in trouble as a narrator? as an agent in the story?" We begin by deploying a skepticism honed by readings of the literary ballads, but as we proceed, we focus on generic differences. Addressing the particular challenges of rereading for writing about novels, for example, we consider various ways of charting personal cartographies through lengthy texts.

Fairly quickly, students note the transparency of Lockwood's attempts to conceal or dissemble anxiety through facetiousness or elevated diction, as well as the grotesque comedy of his actual behavior at the Heights. (As I mention casually, such moves are common in student writing as well.) The rapid progression from "canine mother" to "ruffianly bitch" to leader of a "hive" of "four-footed fiends" (4) is a favorite choice, as is the later image of Zillah coming to the rescue for a second time as Lockwood lies cursing and bleeding from the nose (5), while members of the same pack pin him down, "stretching their paws, and yawning, and flourishing their tails" (13). As we move toward discussion of the students' response papers, I give small groups a few minutes to address two related questions: "How is your chosen moment staged and framed?" and "How can you explain your visceral responses?" Students quickly focus on what some call the "wrist scene" (21). They seem prepared to consider how anxiety over definition shapes their reactions to and judgments of Lockwood's struggle here, and we analyze the book's uneasy conflation of wailing, lost, and ultimately bleeding child with icy-fingered, grabby, invading ghost. Given how focused discussants usually become on the implications of bloody sheets, I generally need to emphasize consideration of how the "wrist scene" might enact the eruption of one sort of narrative into another. Still, once I ask students to explore the way anxieties over reading, writing, and narrative authority suffuse Lockwood's account, they generally need only two or three minutes of group work to engage with the uncanniness of writing in these opening chapters. Carved names nearly always play a key role in the ensuing discussion. Students notice how the apparently archaic "Hareton Earnshaw" (2) of the house's official threshold turns out to name a contemporary, physical (and growling) human presence, even as the illicitly carved variations "*Catherine Earnshaw*," "*Catherine Heathcliff*," "*Catherine Linton*," which mark a more private threshold, give rise first to a moment in which "the air swarm[s] with" written names spelled out in a "glare of white letters" as "vivid as spectres" (15) and then to the vision itself (20). We address Lockwood's dangerous and musty-smelling near-burning of the Testament; his reading of that defaced Bible-diary, which, as some students point out, temporarily and tellingly transforms him from narrator to transcriber; and his dream displacement as authoritative speaker by the nightmare concerning Jabes Branderham. Students emphasize Heathcliff's response to Lockwood's story. If they have not noticed the ambiguities of Lockwood's professed vexation at having caused such "agony" by recounting his "ridiculous nightmare," I point these out (24).

In closing, I return to students' initial question: Just what kind of bloody wrist does Lockwood drag across the window? "Why does categorizing this confrontation seem so imperative?" I ask. "What may make a definitive answer impossible?" If *Wuthering Heights* is perfect for a writing class, I tell them, it is both because the novel seems to demand analysis and because it renders analytic certainty so elusive. Their task will be to develop strong, logical readings, choosing and framing their evidence as effectively as possible. To do so, they will have to commit themselves to a line of interpretation, but they will also need to recognize that all interpretations are provisional. This exercise, I note, is a form of discipline that will stand them in good stead in any sort of serious writing, including scientific writing. They will need to speak their minds precisely and compellingly, even while knowing that, in time, they may need to change their positions. In keeping with this project, they will write a response to every section they read.

The assignments that follow attempt to move students from close reading of interpretive cruxes (and crises) to consideration of the specific challenges the novel presents. Ideally, as discussions develop, very different readings emerge; indeed, as I reassure uneasy students, this diversity is precisely what we are after. Where possible, I reinforce the point by placing student discussions in the context of ongoing critical controversies.[3] Brief writing assignments tend to ask students to present strong readings of individual scenes: Heathcliff and Catherine's first visit to the Grange; Nelly's or Heathcliff's confrontation with the dying Catherine; the younger Catherine's initial imprisonment at the Heights; Heathcliff's confession to Nelly, on meeting Hareton's and the younger Catherine's eyes over a book; or Lockwood's final visit. As we talk about the novel, I establish initial critical positions, insist on specifics, and then complicate and expand our approach. In discussing Nelly Dean's narration, for example, I write on the board, " 'Nelly, I *am* Heathcliff'—Comment" (73). Once students have aired their (usually varied) responses to this claim and defended them through direct citation, we look at two kitchen scenes, both of which end in Heathcliff's flight and the elder Catherine's physical breakdown. The first is, of course, the one in which Nelly plays unwilling confessor to Catherine, silencing her awareness of the presence and departure of Heathcliff (68–73); the second, the one in Thrushcross Grange, where Nelly's talebearing helps transform a quarrel between Catherine and Heathcliff into a violent confrontation between Heathcliff and Linton (98–103).

Here, too, ballads can serve as important access points for analysis. For in order to confess her engagement, Catherine must first interrupt Nelly's singing to Hareton, and momentary though this violation of intimacy is, it foreshadows Nelly's own forced removal from Hareton and the Heights after the elder Catherine's marriage. Beginning with the ballad's performance context, I ask, "Who sings ballads, and to whom? What cultural role is Nelly filling here? What personal role is she filling for Hareton? What might it mean, symbolically, for either, or both, to cut short this singing?" From this moment of interrupted tenderness and cultural transmission, we move to the two quoted lines of the ballad itself. "Why this form of ballad?" I ask. "What do we expect to happen, once the 'mither beneath the mools' hears her babies crying? (67). Why cut the song off before our expectations are tested?" If all goes well, students come to see Nelly's ballad as a multilayered performance—not merely as a song that awakens expectation of the return of the dead but also as a story in which the crying children hearken back to the mourning, newly orphaned child Catherine, even as they prefigure the deprivation of Hareton. Such discussions help students prepare to watch Nelly's behavior, as well as her narrative tone, very carefully.

Students generally begin by wanting to consider Nelly as an agent within the plot, and I honor this impulse. By focusing on Nelly's role as interrupted ballad singer, however, I can help them think about her role as narrator as well. By her own admission, I point out, Nelly has looked into every book in Edgar Linton's presumably well-stocked library. On one level, then, Lockwood's attempt to envision her as a folk informant seems naive. On another level, however, precisely by insisting on Nelly's singing, Brontë's depiction of "Mrs. Dean" underscores possible affinities between Nelly's stories and those of other "old wives." Such points can work well in addressing Nelly Dean's paradoxical role as both an insistent singer of eerie folk ballads and an embattled, perhaps failed speaker for literary realism. By the time she appears, after all, I note, Catherine's icy hand has already erupted into the novel, and with it the claims of a brutal transcendence whose force may well outstrip any social, scientific, or religious law.

As we approach the novel's end, response papers should have trained students to look for suggestive details as a way of engaging with larger concerns. Once more, then, we return to a kitchen scene, and with it, to an interruption of Nelly's ballad singing. Now, however, as students note, Nelly seems to be singing for her own pleasure. "This is 'Fairy Annie's Wedding,' " she tells her hostile fellow servant Joseph, cheerfully defying his call for the Lord to "judge" her for setting up "glories tuh Sattan." On one level, of course, this folk epithalamium looks forward to the marriage of Hareton and the younger Catherine; it voices Nelly's joy at the healing of a breach associated with her first, interrupted song. On another level, however, Nelly's mischievously rebellious performance marks a return to the supernatural world of the earlier ballad's "mither beneath the mools." For in flouting Joseph's religiosity by performing a "bonny tune" that "goes to a dance" (274), Nelly celebrates a fairy wedding, a wild, inhuman union that cannot help evoking the shared, uncanny afterlife of Catherine and Heathcliff. From within the novel, I suggest, Brontë's conclusion might lead one to ask, What kind of universe is this? From our position as critics, the question must partly be, What kind of novel is this? Our uncertainties about the fleshliness of Lockwood's nightmare assault, about the nature and plausibility of Catherine's claim to "be" Heathcliff, about Nelly's role in the death of Catherine, or about the moral or social implications of Heathcliff's vengeance—all arise partly from crises of critical categories; and as Nelly's ballad singing attests, critical and cultural boundary anxieties cannot be easily disentangled.

So far, most classes I have taught have leaned either toward quarantining the novel from the poetry or toward overidentification of the two. My role has been to challenge these leanings: as I suggest ways in which the texts may resonate, I resist attempts to read one work merely as a gloss on another. Partly as a result, the questions I present as points of departure for formal papers vary from term to term. Toward the end of our reading, I usually meet with each student to discuss response papers and begin negotiations for the formal essay. I then pass out a series of questions, presenting these less as topics than as possible catalysts for the formulation of students' investigations. Some options connect the novel and poems: I might ask, for example, how Nelly's role as singer of ballads intensifies or complicates her presence as narrator or whether it makes sense to read Heathcliff's expressed longing to join Catherine in the grave in terms of R. Alcona's desire for J. Brenzaida. Other options encourage students to plot an idiosyncratic course through our more general discussions. (One class, for example, surprised me by homing in on Edgar's retreat to his library as a central moment in the text; another disagreed strongly over the significance of the Heights' abandonment at the novel's close. In both cases, topics emerged in response.)

Finally, I present at least one topic that goes beyond our discussions altogether. We brainstorm possible variations in class. Since most students have become acutely aware of the problems posed by unreliable fictional narrators, we also speculate on the requirements of more or less reliable critical narration. What questions will students absolutely have to address, for example? What scenes, if any? Their job, I stress, is not to retell Emily Brontë's story but to offer their audience a vivid, ambitious, and plausible analysis of the language of *Wuthering Heights*.

As students progress from proposals through drafts, we intersperse workshop, editing, and tutorial time with one final Brontë exercise: a series of detailed discussions of "No coward soul" and "Julian M. and A. G. Rochelle" ("Silent is the House—all are laid asleep" [Gezari 177–81]), focused on what is lost and what gained by juxtaposing the language, plot, characters, and larger preoccupations of this poem with those of *Wuthering Heights*. Is Catherine Heathcliff, in the same way that the speaker of "No coward soul" is the "God within my breast," for example? Ideally, these final sessions give students not only one more chance to disagree but also a safe means of stepping back from, and even rethinking, the readings they are engaged in formulating. With luck, that rethinking process will continue throughout the course. For a few students, I hope, it may last even longer.

NOTES

[1]For this exercise, I prefer to begin with the transcribed manuscript version of Brontë's poem: see Hatfield, 222–23. Gezari reverses Hatfield's editorial choices by offering the poem in its first published form under the title "Remembrance" (8–9), noting the manuscript version as variant (xix; see also 228–30 on the textual history).

[2]In class, I limit my discussion of this context to Ratchford's *Gondal's Queen: A Novel in Verse by Emily Jane Brontë*, and to Gezari's more skeptical treatment (xv–xxxii; xxix–xxxii).

[3]As *Wuthering Heights* comes early in the semester, I assign no criticism. I do, however, use Dunn's edition of *Wuthering Heights*, which allows me to point interested students toward accessible, suggestive discussions by J. Hillis Miller, Gilbert and Gubar, Nussbaum, and Haire-Sargeant.

Teaching *Wuthering Heights* through Close Reading / Teaching Close Reading through *Wuthering Heights*

Paul Vita

The first two essays that I assign in most undergraduate literature classes are exercises in close readings, usually phrased, "in one or two paragraphs, discuss the effect of a short passage from . . ." or "in a page or two, analyze a few sentences from . . . to say something about the novel as a whole." There's nothing original here, I admit. A Google search with the key words "close reading assignment" will call up links to hundreds of similar assignments. And, I suspect, many instructors know that an essay due during the second week of the term helps winnow out a student or two from an overenrolled literature section. The real motivation behind this assignment, however, is to ensure that students get practice analyzing the language of literary texts. With so many approaches to *Wuthering Heights* to choose from, there's something to say for looking at the issues the novel raises inductively—that is, teaching the novel through close readings.

I structure most class discussions around a series of close readings. I ask students to read aloud a passage from the text and then I pose questions about its potential significance. With *Wuthering Heights* in mind, then, rather than opening our first discussion with biographical background or thematic issues, I ask a student to read the first sentence aloud: "1801—I have just returned from a visit to my landlord—the solitary neighbour that I shall be troubled with" (1). Comments range widely, but at least one student, at some point, mentions that the first relationship between characters is an economic one, between landlord and tenant. When I ask about the meaning and etymology of the word *landlord*, the focus of the discussion shifts to the owning and renting of property. I keep the class focused on this issue for as long as I can, since it is one we return to in later classes, and ask students to point out other references to property and inheritance in the first four chapters, the first day's reading assignment. From Heathcliff's proprietary claim on the first page, "Thrushcross Grange is my own, sir," to the dialogue between Nelly Dean and Lockwood that opens her narrative, students come to see that the houses of the novel aren't simply settings with symbolic significance; they establish social relations. And if all goes well, from property we move to other aspects of ownership and possession.

The novel's opening sentence leads to other issues as well, especially when students consider the printed date "1801." Some venture comments on why this date is important or why dates in general are important (or turn out to be not as important as we thought). At least one student locates the plot of the novel historically against the industrial revolution and Napoleonic wars. I wait it out, though, until someone notes that the printed year, by announcing the novel as a journal of sorts, raises issues related to the structure of the narrative. Like the physically remote Yorkshire moors, the temporal setting separates the actions of the narrative from the reader. I attempt to link this sense of distancing with passages that betray Lockwood's tone and limited perspective as narrator, just as, later, his interruptions after Nelly takes over the narrative are telling. Similarly, there are plenty of specific episodes that complicate Nelly's dual role as character and narrator. What is essential to establish and not difficult for students to grasp is how the story is filtered through these two narrators—how, even when following the text closely, the reader is distanced from the events of the novel by the two unreliable narrators.

For me and for the students, preparation is a matter of bringing passages into class that pose questions, that strike us as significant or noteworthy. Since an issue, idea, or theme is often on the table as we turn to different parts of the text, the process is not purely inductive, but I find myself reminding students to support any claim they make with textual evidence. If we are looking at the statements by Catherine or Heathcliff that reflect on, say, their paradoxical love-hate relationship, students can and do refer to episodes without our actually turning to the specific passage. But once we read a passage, be it a short sentence or several paragraphs, I lead the discussion through a series of questions, such as "What is unusual about the language here?" or "Do any words or phrases strike you as curious or important?" And I follow up by asking about the potential meanings of a word, the significance of a phrase, and the relation of this passage to similar ones elsewhere in the novel. While these questions may lead to digressions from the topic at hand, they force the students to build interpretations based on the language of the text.

This way of directing discussions on *Wuthering Heights* appears straightforward, I hope, partly because I am using the phrase "close reading" very loosely. It's a term that comes from the New Criticism of the 1940s and 1950s, and more contentious academics may regard its practice as polemical. In simplest terms, what's at stake is text versus context. The scholars now recognized as New Critics—I. A. Richards, John Crowe Ransom, Cleanth Brooks, among others—transformed the study of literature at universities with what seems today the not-so-startling claim that the meaning of a poem can be found in the words of the poem itself. They rejected the apparently vague humanistic approach to literature then current in the academy, that great poetry was a means to appreciating the genius who wrote it or understanding the spirit of the age in which it was written.

The next generations of critics balked at some of the New Critics' more ambitious claims: that the author's intention or social situation has nothing to do with the meaning of a literary work and that every text should be treated as a coherent, autonomous, even organic whole. They also objected to attributing the transcendent, universal quality of a poem to the tensions brought about by ambiguous words and phrases. One need not identify oneself as a poststructuralist, materialist, or new historicist to question these assertions. Nonetheless, today even the most politicized theorists of literature grant that the attention to language brought about by this new approach has given readers a sound method of interpretation. Indeed, as overviews of the history of literary criticism repeatedly point out, the very critics who derided the practices of the New Critics are most often exemplary close readers themselves.[1]

The more relevant issue, really, is whether or not a theoretical approach initially applied to poetry can be used in teaching a nineteenth-century novel. One cannot weigh every word of *Wuthering Heights*, tease out every ambiguity page by page within the confines of three or four class meetings. Inevitably, the intensive focus on selected passages in isolation distorts the meaning of the text, placing undue emphasis on certain themes and slighting others. I am afraid there's no way around this problem, which is not unique to teaching through close reading: it's the challenge we face when we teach novels—indeed, literature in general. The solution rests in the extent to which individual instructors are forthright with their students (and themselves) about their approaches to literature. Clearly, one can't cover everything, and there's something to say for teaching students in an introductory class a process of how to interpret, rather than teaching them specific interpretations. Although there is the risk that some students may take away from the discussion a disconnected series of readings, even misreadings, they are nevertheless being challenged to make sense of the novel and not their lecture notes.

There's an even more pressing concern. While *Wuthering Heights* may not pay the sort of explicit attention that other Victorian novels do to social issues of the period, isn't some backgrounding in order? Aren't we, as teachers, obliged to explain how a relatively young female novelist is manipulating the conventions of gothic romance, satirizing forms of religion, and, inadvertently or not, promulgating a certain class ideology while she investigates, if not subverts, gender stereotypes? My short answer would be, well, yes, but that we need to exercise caution in the undergraduate classroom. The more complex issue is when and how, which again relates to what's the best use of class time. Indeed, I have found that passage analysis in class not only allows me to introduce recent and modern trends in literary scholarship but also helps students recognize the potential for multiple interpretations and approaches.

I have also found that a little context goes a long way. Informed close readings are not simply verbal exercises but a means of exploring social conditions of the past while making the text relevant to readers today. For example, early in volume 2, after Catherine's death, Nelly admits to a predilection that most undergraduates would find unusual—sitting with corpses. When she asks Lockwood, "Do you believe such people *are* happy in the other world, sir? I'd give a great deal to know," he remarks, "I declined answering Mrs. Dean's question, which struck me as something heterodox" (146). Students often need a definition of *heterodox*; I use it, along with other verbal clues, to identify the tone of this short interchange. Nelly's earnest question, though, and Lockwood's stiffly formal comment can lead to a discussion about religion as represented (or not) in the novel; I set the topic in the context of the more general concern over faith and doubt in the nineteenth century. Is Emily Brontë using Lockwood as a device here, to anticipate objections from readers? Nelly's description of the dead Catherine's "perfect peace" (145) can also generate a discussion about shifting cultural attitudes toward death and the dead body, an issue that engages undergraduates since few eighteen-year-olds in my classes have seen a corpse. Eventually, though, I steer the conversation back to the effect of this narrative interruption. What does it emphasize? How is it connected to other references to the afterlife in the novel? And why doesn't Lockwood answer the question?

What I guard against are dismissive assumptions that explain away a potentially rich and interesting issue: that the novel is the way it is because, oh, Emily Brontë was psychologically unstable or excessively morbid, comments I have encountered in class; or that what seems strange to us today was probably considered normal back then. When students make references to nineteenth-century British culture and society, I encourage them to qualify their remarks with phrases like "as represented in the novel." If they can't, I ask them where they would go to substantiate their claims. In other words, one can practice close reading without unquestioningly embracing New Criticism's focus on the central unity of a text or assuming that ambiguous issues are the *only* issues to be raised.

Ambiguity, many will recognize, is one of the buzzwords of New Criticism, but I treat the potential for competing meanings in a work as a central issue that *Wuthering Heights* addresses, not as a literary critical issue. Analyzing the language of the novel, however, requires a specialized vocabulary, which I reinforce by phrasing questions that incorporate literary terms (metaphor, irony, etc.), stressing that these terms enable us to discuss novels more precisely. Getting students to identify figures of speech and instances of irony is where I start, since the exercise often draws their attention to Brontë's extraordinary use of imagery. But I remind students that just pointing out that a group of words is a metaphor is not making a point: they need to say something about the suggested comparison, discuss how it contributes to the tone, relates to other parts of the novel, disrupts readerly expectations, and so forth. There is often a protracted silence after I ask, "What's the effect of this metaphor?" And while I usually have the patience to wait it out (not always), one way to avoid this situation is to give students practice through in-class writing. For me, such practice takes the form of passage identification and analysis quizzes, which are, again, old standards in the undergraduate literature class that ultimately derive from and reinforce close reading practices.

I begin or break up a class with these exercises, distributing half sheets of paper onto which I've cut and pasted a few passages from the novel. The directions ask students to identify where each passage falls in the story, who's speaking to whom about what, and why the passage is significant. I emphasize that I'm most interested in the significance, although the questions about location and speakers let me know who's keeping up with the reading. For the past few semesters, I've included on one of these quizzes Heathcliff's discovery of Isabella's infatuation, how his stare reduces her first to "the object of discourse," then to "a strange repulsive animal" and "a centipede from the Indies" (93). Students grumble when I threaten to take off points for not identifying the speaker as Lockwood, who narrates through Nelly, a technicality subject to debate, I suppose, but intended as a reminder that they are reading a multivoiced narrative. The class has plenty to say about this simile, from its relation to other animal imagery to its foreshadowing of Heathcliff's cruelty. Although I've never had an undergraduate articulate a postcolonial reading unprompted, someone usually points out the exotic origins of this centipede; the image can be used as an entrée into how British imperialism has infiltrated even the isolated households of *Wuthering Heights*.

Through class discussions and quizzes, then, I stress a process for analyzing the text by encouraging students to focus on individual words and to investigate potential meanings, to explore the effects of figurative language, and to consider how the specific interpretations relate to the novel as a whole and to other large issues. It's the same process I ask them to follow in writing the out-of-class essays. Students are accustomed to marking passages that puzzle or interest them as they are reading the novel to prepare for class, so they don't have much trouble settling on the passage they want to write about. A few are perennial favorites, whether we've had the time to discuss them in class or not: Lockwood's dream, the various heaven-hell speeches, and the final paragraph of the novel. I don't hesitate to make suggestions, and since time in the classroom is always precious, I frequently find myself telling students that the passage they have pointed out (or, to be frank, I have pointed out) would be a good one to discuss in an essay.

I repeatedly remind students that the essay is just a few paragraphs, not something that follows the traditional structure of English papers. They can forgo the introductory and concluding paragraphs, I tell them, and focus on what they want to say about the language of the text. Stronger, more intuitive readers tend to have no problem working from details and phrasing their essays in a way that shows sensitivity to other interpretations and arguments. The weaker ones often spend too much space setting up their passage through plot summary and offer only a paraphrase followed by a list of disparate ideas, or they quickly shift to other parts of the novel. These essays need to undergo revision, ideally after a writing conference, in which students focus on generating ideas about the language of the text and shaping them into coherent paragraphs (see app. at the end of this essay). Students will frequently turn to a passage already discussed in class. This doesn't concern me, since they usually have something more to say or want to stress a certain perspective;

the weaker ones (especially those in a required literature class) demonstrate that they understand the process, even if they are only re-creating it.

Assigning this sort of close reading exercise has a number of practical advantages. For students who want or need direction, it appears to provide a topic, while really it is a very open assignment. It also trains students to write about literature and to get to a closer understanding of the novel, especially if the assignment is given more than once. If students summarize the plot, fail to quote the text, or use past tense, they quickly realize they have done so; thus the exercise reinforces conventions of writing about literature. The temptation to plagiarize isn't there for such a short assignment; it's easier just to write the paragraphs. Finally, instructors can expand the assignment into a longer essay on the novel by having students analyze other passages and relate them all to a thesis.

This assignment, as well as the other activities I have been describing, works well not only in an introductory literature class but also at other levels because it forces students to base arguments on the text. Even graduate students, who may have embraced a methodology and theoretical stance, can reassess the extent to which their method of interpretation or theory applies to *Wuthering Heights.* While no doubt part of "old-fashioned New Criticism," as J. Hillis Miller has pointed ("Teaching" 51), close reading makes responding to a novel a performative activity. It enables readers to engage with the language of the text and to recognize their share in making sense of *Wuthering Heights*.

NOTE

[1]For two overviews of the extent to which close reading informs and is practiced by later critics, see Dubois; Abrams; Hošek and Parker's *Lyric Poetry*.

APPENDIX

Sample Student Essays by Anthony Fior

The two drafts appended here, one written before and one after a writing conference, respond to the exercise instruction "Discuss a short passage from *Wuthering Heights* to say something about the novel as a whole." Written by Anthony Fior,[1] a political science major at Saint Louis University's Madrid Campus, the drafts are about average for students enrolled in this required first-year literature course. They illustrate, perhaps better than anything else, a shift from listing subjective impressions to generating a close reading of Emily Brontë's text.

Draft 1: *Wuthering Heights* Essay

> I hasped the window; I combed his black long hair from his forehead; I tried to close his eyes—to extinguish, if possible, that frightful, life-

> like gaze of exultation, before any one else beheld it. They would not shut—they seemed to sneer at my attempts, and his parted lips and sharp, white teeth sneered too! (298)

Emily Brontë crafts dark and cold images in *Wuthering Heights* to cultivate a novel that embodies and expresses what it means to be grotesque. Near the end of the story, Mrs. Dean climbs the gloomy stairs of Wuthering Heights to find Heathcliff dead. Through imagery and diction, Brontë creates an emotional and gothic feeling for the reader. In her diction of "black," "frightful," and "life-like," the reader is drawn to an immediate mysterious and unpleasant description of Heathcliff. As his "frightful" gaze compels her to close the eyes in hopes of smothering the cruel and foul image, Heathcliff's face exudes a sense of life in death. Moreover, an "exultation" is normally evoked for joyous and glorious events, whereas Brontë utilizes it here to bring forth neither joy nor glory, but horror and darkness. In addition, "sneer" rouses and makes reference to the sneers and terror of the devil, the most foul and evil of all beings. And Brontë's depiction of Heathcliff's "sharp, white teeth" only reinforces her desire to construct sly and sinister images throughout the novel. Nonetheless, Brontë's diction fosters cold, dark, and wicked imagery that is prevalent throughout the work and generates an unparalleled grotesque and foul piece of English fiction.

Draft 1 shows that Anthony Fior understood the assignment and ventured a general claim. It conveys pleasure in language, even if the diction is somewhat forced. However, it also illustrates weaknesses I see in many student papers.

I opened our conference by praising Anthony warmly for looking at specific words and thinking about their context. I then asked how he wrote the paper. He admitted that he had trouble "coming up with ideas," which explains its listlike organizational structure, forced transitions, and non sequiturs. Rather than develop a reading, he shifted from one part of the passage to the next, a common strategy for students writing this kind of essay.

In response to his comment, we looked at sentence 4, in which he first attempts to analyze the text. I pointed out that he interpreted Brontë's use of "life-like" as "mysterious" and "unpleasant" and asked him what else he could say about the adjective. Nelly's animation of Heathcliff's corpse, which Anthony linked to suggestions of the supernatural, was the major topic of our conference. This discussion enabled him to come up with a more specific interpretation and thus a more focused topic sentence.

We ended by opening the *MLA Handbook* to the sample paper and works-cited list (Gibaldi 320–21); it took Anthony less than a minute to see how to follow the conventions of documentation.

While his second draft is still rough, its focus on the supernatural helps direct his reading. The essay implicitly recognizes some of the paradoxes of Emily Brontë's language and their effect on the reader. And although some of Anthony's interpretations could have been articulated more precisely, his success here demonstrates that he is prepared to write longer essays that argue a reading supported by textual evidence.

Draft 2: Darkness in Diction:
Emily Brontë's *Wuthering Heights*

Emily Brontë crafts grotesque images in *Wuthering Heights* to cultivate the eerie sense that Heathcliff, even at his death, is not human and to evoke the supernatural. Upon her discovery of Heathcliff's corpse, Mrs. Dean tells Lockwood and the reader her reaction:

> I hasped the window; I combed his black long hair from his forehead; I tried to close his eyes—to extinguish, if possible, that frightful, life-like gaze of exultation, before any one else beheld it. They would not shut—they seemed to sneer at my attempts, and his parted lips and sharp, white teeth sneered too! (298)

Like Mrs. Dean, the reader is drawn to and repulsed by an immediate mysterious and gruesome description of Heathcliff. His gaze is "frightful" and "life-like," like a ghost's or demon's from another world, or even a vampire's. This gaze compels Mrs. Dean to close the eyes in hopes "to extinguish" it, as if Heathcliff were still alive. Even in death, Heathcliff still seems to defy and control, to have emotions. His face exudes a sense of "exultation," a word that normally evokes joy and glory, but "exultation" is more of an emotion of horror and darkness in Mrs. Dean's description. In addition, Heathcliff still "sneered," which rouses more fear in Mrs. Dean and the reader. His "sharp, white teeth" suggest vampire qualities that reinforce Brontë's desire to construct an unparalleled grotesque and foul image, Heathcliff as a living corpse. Finally, the room that Heathcliff dies in also relates to ghosts and the supernatural. The window Mrs. Dean "hasped" is the window that Cathy's ghost tried to enter at the beginning of the novel. Brontë is suggesting that Heathcliff's spirit may have left the room through the open window. Using Nelly Dean as a narrator (and Lockwood too), the wicked, dark image of Heathcliff has an impact on the reader that further contributes to how the novel makes the love between Catherine and Heathcliff a love that goes beyond death.

APPENDIX NOTE

[1]Anthony Fior's writing used with permission.

Using Collaborative Learning to Teach the Themes of Education, Ignorance, and Dispossession in *Wuthering Heights*

Laraine Fergenson

At Bronx Community College, City University of New York, where I have taught *Wuthering Heights* in a course entitled Writing on Prose Fiction, most students are members of New York's minority groups, quite a few are recent immigrants, and many are single parents. My students understand the value of education and see it as a means to rise into the middle class. But although they want to read complex books and to learn the vocabulary that will help them succeed in college, they nevertheless find *Wuthering Heights* difficult, citing its complex structure, profusion of characters (who, as one student noted, "all have the same names"),[1] and the northern English dialect spoken by Joseph as barriers to their understanding of the work. To bridge the divide between the terrain of this Victorian novel and the realities of my students' lives, I discuss themes that have relevance to them and make use of collaborative learning—that is, the work-group method.

Reginald Watson's essay emphasizing the "blackness" and "otherness" (452) of Heathcliff is helpful in introducing a theme that resonates with my students. Watson sees Heathcliff as a marginalized figure who, constantly reminded that he "has no place in civilized society" (458), responds by undermining the social order that has rejected him and cost him the unbearable loss of his love. *Wuthering Heights* also lends itself to a discussion of the themes of child rearing, both positive and negative, and the related themes of dysfunctional families and domestic violence—topics that my students find compelling.

Two related themes with importance to the students I teach are education and its opposite, enforced ignorance as a means of oppression. Since most of my students are the first in their families to attend college (as I was), the theme of education, which they see as a way into the middle class, is of consuming interest to them, so exploring it as a major force in driving the plot of *Wuthering Heights* motivates students to overcome the novel's challenges.

I first present the background and themes of the novel in a fairly traditional lecture-discussion format, but once this ground is covered, the class begins collaborative work, following a method that was presented by Kenneth Bruffee at a faculty development workshop held at our college.[2] I divide the class into groups of four to six students. The members of each group select two leaders: a moderator and a recorder-reporter (also called the spokesperson). It is important that the moderator, the student who keeps the group on task and decides when to move from one point to another, not be the recorder-reporter also; these two leadership roles ought to be separate, because it is distracting for one student to do the note taking and writing while simultaneously leading the group's discussion. Furthermore, dividing the leadership responsibilities gives more students a chance to play active roles. The recorder-reporter writes down the group's ideas and then explains them to the rest of the class when, after about twenty minutes, the groups stop their individual work and share what they have developed.

This method has many advantages. In a large class, it provides a means by which all the students can become fully engaged in a discussion. It also fosters autonomy and independent learning. Some instructors may choose to assign students to permanent groups, intentionally putting reticent students together as a way of encouraging them to participate, because they will not be able to rely on talkative students to carry the ball for them. This technique might get good results, but I have usually found it best to let the students group themselves and choose their leaders. I stress, however, that the leadership roles should shift around during the semester so that each student has a chance to be moderator and recorder-reporter at least once.

The collaborative groups can work in many ways. When the class has just begun *Wuthering Heights* and most of the students have not yet read beyond the first few chapters, the groups can be instructed to find a passage that contains descriptive language and explain how the language renders the characters or scene described. Sometimes the students are asked to find three words that were not previously in their vocabulary, explain their meanings, and show how they are used by Emily Brontë. Since *Wuthering Heights*, like most Victorian novels, is rich in SAT or ACT words and since some of our students must take standardized tests if they wish to continue their education beyond the associate degree our college offers, this exercise is helpful.

Later on, when the class has read further into the novel, the groups can analyze themes. All the groups may discuss the same questions, or I might assign different tasks to different groups, putting the group numbers and their respective goals on the chalkboard. Using this method, my classes have traced the all-important theme of education in *Wuthering Heights*. One group might analyze the role played by young Cathy in inspiring Hareton to become educated, while another might look for examples of Nelly's role in educating her nurslings. Through such discussions, my students share their insights into the theme of education.

Within the context of the group work and in discussions that involve the class as a whole, we bring out the following themes in *Wuthering Heights*. The first one has to do with the effects of the denial of education. Even more than the brutal beatings Hindley inflicts on his adopted brother, it is the cessation of Heathcliff's education that most torments him and turns him into a villain thirsting for revenge, for his lack of education leads to his loss of Catherine and sets the whole tragedy in motion. Catherine says it would "degrade" her to marry him (as her brother has degraded him), and this speech, overheard by Heathcliff (71), sends him away. When he returns, three years later,

Catherine is already married to Edgar, and Heathcliff can only destroy what semblance of happiness the couple has—destroy Catherine by harrowing her already riven soul and then wreak his vengeance on the surviving Earnshaws and Lintons. Heathcliff takes revenge on Hindley in the person of Hindley's son, Hareton, by making the boy, despite his early promise, into an uneducated lout. Heathcliff brags to Nelly Dean:

> If he were a born fool I should not enjoy it half so much—But he's no fool; and I can sympathise with all his feelings, having felt them myself—I know what he suffers now, for instance, exactly—it is merely a beginning of what he shall suffer, though. And he'll never be able to emerge from his bathos of coarseness and ignorance. (193)

Although Heathcliff despises his son, Linton Heathcliff, he takes pains with the boy's education, explaining to Nelly, "I've engaged a tutor . . . to come three times a week, from twenty miles distance, to teach him what he pleases to learn" (184), and he takes a bitter pleasure in overhearing young Cathy and Linton mocking the uneducated accent of the rough, illiterate Hareton (194–95).

As Heathcliff has noted, Hareton does suffer, tormented by his cousins' disdain. Young Cathy, discovering that Hareton is illiterate, asks, "Is he all as he should be?" (194). The relevance of Cathy's question is wider than she intends. She is asking if he is mentally retarded, but, in fact, Hareton, denied an education and dispossessed of his property, is not "all as he should be." Significantly, Cathy has asked Hareton to explain the writing over the door of Wuthering Heights. It reads, "1500 Hareton Earnshaw" (2), for this house is the ancestral residence of the Earnshaw family, wrested from the hapless Hindley and the ignorant Hareton by Heathcliff. Hareton's inability to read the inscription is symptomatic of the way he fails to understand that he has been dispossessed of his birthright by his father's bitter enemy (and his enemy too, although he does not recognize Heathcliff as such). Thus the denial of education is interwoven with the themes of dispossession and revenge in the novel. Education plays a role not only in eventually preparing Hareton to take his place as Catherine's husband and to knit together the bonds of love and trust that have been torn asunder in the older generation but also in restoring the property rightly belonging to Hareton and Cathy.

To Cathy's inquiry about the inscription, Hareton first responds, "It's some damnable writing. . . . I cannot read it." Cathy replies, "Can't read it? . . . I can read it . . . It's English . . . but I want to know why it is there" (194). Her reply unconsciously probes the mystery of Heathcliff's usurpation of Wuthering Heights and foreshadows his usurpation of her home, Thrushcross Grange, as well. Hareton, by conquering his illiteracy, will become a worthy husband for Cathy, and by their love for each other, which grows as Cathy teaches him, the two dispossessed orphans will conquer their familial enemy and unite their estates, restoring them to the families who had owned them before Heathcliff's intercession. In this way, the two reverse the process that Hindley begins when he denies an education to Heathcliff.

Ironically, Cathy, who initially prompts Hareton to overcome the prejudice against "book-larning" (194) that Heathcliff has inculcated in him, almost extinguishes his desire for intellectual improvement by her scorn for his early attempts. When he asserts that he can now read the inscription over the door of his ancestral home, she says with a sarcasm that he does not at first catch, "Wonderful. . . . Pray let us hear you—you *are* grown clever!" Although he reads the name of his ancestor, which, significantly, is also his name, he fails to read the numbers and the date that reveal his long-standing claim on the property. At this stage, Cathy ridicules him as a "dunce," all the while "laughing heartily at his failure." Nelly, to whom Cathy is relating this dialogue, interjects a rebuke to the effect that Hareton's "praiseworthy ambition" should not be met with contempt. She adds, "He was as quick and as intelligent a child as ever you were, and I'm hurt that he should be despised now, because that base Heathcliff has treated him so unjustly" (220). This pattern is repeated when Cathy, having lost her father, her property, and her husband, cruelly mocks Hareton's continued attempts at acquiring literacy. Even Lockwood feels moved to defend Hareton:

> "Mr. Hareton is desirous of increasing his amount of knowledge," I said, coming to his rescue. "He is not *envious* but *emulous* of your attainments—He'll be a clever scholar in a few years!" (267)

But Cathy only laughs at Hareton's plight: "Yes, I hear him trying to spell and read to himself, and pretty blunders he makes! I wish you would repeat Chevy Chase, as you did yesterday—It was extremely funny!" (267). Unable to bear Cathy's scorn, Hareton renounces his attempt to educate himself.

His reaction is not surprising to anyone who has experience with students whose previous education has been problematic: such a student becomes a reluctant—even resistant—learner. Cathy, at length regretting her cruelty, offers a book to Hareton, but he answers with a threat to "break her neck" (276). She leaves the book for him to pick up, but he refuses to take it. Nelly reports, "I saw she was sorry for his persevering sulkiness and indolence—her conscience reproved her for frightening him off improving himself—she had done it effectually" (276–77). Although Cathy is initially discouraged by Hareton's stubbornness, through persistence and some ingenious teaching techniques she eventually succeeds in undoing the damage she has wrought. In the final triumph of love over hate, she overcomes Hareton's resistance and persuades him to learn with her. In educating the man she is to marry, she prepares him to assume his rightful place as master of his ancestral property. Thus a woman with the power to forgive and share her education defeats the revenge of a man with no power to forgive, who has attempted to destroy the child of his enemy through the denial of education.

Since most of my students are women, reflecting the general trend at urban community colleges, feminist issues are also an important concern. I sometimes point out that despite the important role education plays in saving Hareton from Heathcliff's design, it can constitute a problem for women. As Sandra M. Gilbert and Susan Gubar have noted, Catherine Earnshaw's education in the genteel feminine arts is actually the means by which she is deprived of her sense of self: "Just as triumphant self-discovery is the ultimate goal of the male *Bildungsroman*, anxious self-denial, Brontë suggests, is the ultimate product of a female education" (276). Hareton's education leads to self-discovery and liberation, but Catherine Earnshaw's "education," when she stays with the Lintons at Thrushcross Grange, estranges her from her true self. As an ironic consequence of the "ramble at liberty" (41), which Heathcliff and Catherine undertake as an act of rebellion, the two wild creatures are separately snared and diminished. Heathcliff is further excluded from the Earnshaw-Linton society and decisively separated from Catherine and thus from his access to the lessons she has been conveying to him, as well as to the power of her company. When Catherine, who has been bitten by the guard dog, is recognized, she is welcomed as a guest and remains at the Grange. While her physical wounds heal, she receives a crash course in gentility, becoming the object of a plan of reform that turns her from a "wild, hatless little savage" into a "very dignified person," well dressed and genteel (46). As Gilbert and Gubar note, "Catherine's education in ladylike self-denial causes her dutifully to deny her self and decide to marry Edgar" (276).

Gilbert and Gubar relate the negative aspects of education to Emily Brontë's "traumatic experiences at the Clergy Daughters school and elsewhere" and also to the generally repressive way in which women were educated in the nineteenth century (275). Laura Morgan Green has noted that there was a great opening of education to women during the nineteenth century and that Emily Brontë was no doubt aware of this movement. But Brontë might have mistrusted it somewhat because the instruction was not aimed at empowering women but was seen as a way of making them better governesses, better able to serve as transmitters of education than to make it work for themselves. Within the world of *Wuthering Heights*, education confers power on the male characters, but women may be weakened by it, or at least not helped. Although Nelly Dean has done considerable reading in the library at Thrushcross Grange (55), she is still a servant. Female miseducation is exemplified by Isabella, whose fancied love for Heathcliff is, as he himself recognizes, a "delusion" engendered by reading romantic novels. Heathcliff, not under the sway of such books but educated enough to be aware of their influence, coldly diagnoses the roots of Isabella's attraction to him, saying that she has been "picturing in me a hero of romance" (133). Here, a kind of education ruins Isabella and gives Heathcliff the means to destroy the whole Linton family.

Since students themselves may feel that they have been miseducated by their previous experiences, both in life and in public schools, it is helpful to introduce as a topic for discussion the idea that education can have both positive and negative effects, can alienate as well as empower. An instructor may point out that the idea of education as debilitating rather than empowering for women is belied by Cathy, whose education helps Hareton recognize his name and realize his true identity. Tellingly, Cathy has been educated by her adoring father and not by a hired tutor. Compensating for his grief at the loss of his wife, Edgar consoles himself with the upbringing of their beautiful and intelligent daughter: "He took her education entirely on himself, and made it an amusement: fortunately, curiosity and a quick intellect urged her into an apt scholar; she learnt rapidly and eagerly, and did honour to his teaching" (167). Education, like love, can be constructive or destructive, nourishing or famishing, self-affirming or self-denying. The education in gentility that the elder Catherine receives at Thrushcross Grange destroys her identity, her independence of spirit, and her fierce, wild pleasure in life; but the education of her daughter at the same place allows young Cathy to endure and overcome the tyranny of Heathcliff. Having accused Hareton of goading Heathcliff to destroy her precious books, she defiantly avers, "I've most of them written on my brain and printed in my heart, and you cannot deprive me of those!" (267). Miseducation can lead to the destruction of the female self and eventually of a whole family, but true education can resurrect the family and save the self.

Finally, education can be seen as having an almost magical power in effecting the transformation of Heathcliff from a rough "ploughboy" (85) into the apparently cultivated man who returns with money and a certain amount of polish: "A half-civilized ferocity lurked yet in the depressed brows and eyes full of black fire, but it was subdued; and his manner was even dignified, quite divested of roughness" (84–85).

Since Nelly cannot explain Heathcliff's rise, my students, judging from his skill at gambling, surmise that gaming was his way of acquiring wealth, but for them and for me the more intriguing unanswered question concerns "the means he took to raise his mind from the savage ignorance into which it was sunk" (80). In his teens, after Hindley had deprived Heathcliff of any lessons, the boy "lost the benefit of his early education," and his "personal appearance sympathised with mental deterioration" (59–60). Hindley's tyrannical regime of "continual hard work, begun soon and concluded late, had extinguished any curiosity [Heathcliff] once possessed in pursuit of knowledge, and any love for books or learning" (60).

Nelly, when telling Lockwood about Heathcliff's intellectual degradation, says:

> He struggled long to keep up an equality with Catherine in her studies and yielded with poignant though silent regret: but, he yielded completely; and there was no prevailing on him to take a step in the way of moving upward, when he found he must, necessarily, sink beneath his former level. (60)

Yet just three years later, the returning Heathcliff passes for a gentleman whose countenance, Nelly tells us, looked "intelligent, and retained no marks of former degradation" (84). We never learn how this transformation has come about, for it occurs in the larger world beyond the purview of Nelly. Lockwood speculates:

> Did he finish his education on the Continent? Or did he get a sizer's place at college? or escape to America, and earn honours by drawing blood from his foster country? or make a fortune more promptly, on the English highways? (80)

To clarify the quotation, it is helpful to present historical and biographical material explaining that a sizar was an impoverished student of intellectual promise admitted to a university at reduced fees and that, moreover, holding a sizar's place was the means by which Emily Brontë's father effected his upward social mobility. Patrick Brontë's pride in his intellectual achievements can be seen in the inscriptions he wrote on his prize books, awarded for his excellent academic work while a sizar at St. John's College in Cambridge. On the title page of the *Iliad*, Patrick noted, "My Prize Book, for having kept in the *first class* at St. John's College—Cambridge—P. Brontë, A. B. To be retained—semper—" (qtd. in Barker, *Brontës* [1994] 10). Obviously, education loomed large in the life of Emily's father, and no doubt he conveyed its importance to his children. In *Emily Brontë: The Artist as a Free Woman,* Stevie Davies says of Patrick, "He had learned to love books with a passionate enthusiasm engendered by the difficulty of getting access to them, and passed that hunger on to his children" (4). In fact, his upward social mobility—Davies calls him a sort of "embodied social revolution"—from blacksmith to schoolteacher to the clergyman of the Haworth curacy, makes instructive background for students who look to education to better their own lives (Davies, *Heretic* 368).

Lockwood imagines Heathcliff as possibly a robber (a highwayman) or a soldier in America during the Revolutionary War, earning "honours by drawing blood from his foster country," but whether the "foster country" would be

England or America is unclear, an ambiguity that underscores Heathcliff's anarchic violence and his status as an outsider. Whatever the means, Heathcliff succeeds in bettering himself and effectively counteracts the ignorance to which Hindley has tried to consign him. Perhaps he has never wholly lost "the benefit of his early education"; after all, even during the period of his deepest degradation, his speech is never marked by the heavy local accent that makes Joseph's speech comical—and to most of my students, unintelligible—and renders Hareton's early attempts to connect with Cathy so pathetic. Once implanted, education does not die, the text implies, but remains as the basis for further improvement.

There are, of course, many themes in *Wuthering Heights* that appeal to students. In some semesters I have chosen Love, Loss, and Revenge as the advertised subtitle of the course. Nevertheless, when we begin our collaborative learning and I mention education and the denial of education as elements that motivate the characters and drive the plot of *Wuthering Heights*, the intensity of my students' response matches that of their desire to overcome the many obstacles they face in obtaining an education. It is a measure of the novel's timeless appeal that it can work on so many levels and reach students of such diverse backgrounds.

NOTES

[1]My student's comment reflects the observation made by Stevie Davies in *Emily Brontë: Heretic*: "If the meaning of the novel is anything but plain, this is partly due to its calculated assault on difference as the groundwork of communication. . . . There are . . . too few names to go round" (190).

[2]Bruffee's published work on peer tutoring and collaborative learning is well known. It includes "Collaborative Learning and the 'Conversation of Mankind' " and *Collaborative Learning: Higher Education, Interdependence, and the Authority of Knowledge*. The collaborative method is also discussed in Bean.

NOTES ON CONTRIBUTORS

Suzy Anger is associate professor of English at the University of British Columbia. She is the author of *Victorian Interpretation* (2005) and the editor of *Knowing the Past: Victorian Literature and Culture* (2001). She has published essays on nineteenth-century British literature.

Frances Beer is professor of English at Atkinson College and the Graduate Programme in English, York University, Canada. Her publications include *Women and Mystical Experience in the Middle Ages* (1992), an edition of Charlotte Brontë's *Mina Laury* (1995), and an edition of *The Juvenilia of Jane Austen and Charlotte Brontë* (1986). She is coeditor of *Canadian Woman Studies: An Introductory Reader* (2000) and presented a paper, "Addiction and the Brontës," at the 2004 meeting of the American Brontë Society.

Dean de la Motte is dean of the faculty and associate professor of comparative literature at Belmont Abbey College. He is coeditor of *Making the News: Modernity and the Mass Press in Nineteenth-Century France* (1999) and of *Approaches to Teaching Stendhal's* The Red and the Black (1999). He has also contributed essays to the MLA Approaches to Teaching volumes on *Madame Bovary* and *Old Goriot*.

Kamilla Elliott is a lecturer in the department of English and creative writing at Lancaster University, where she teaches Victorian literature and the interdisciplinary study of literature and film. Her book *Rethinking the Novel/Film Debate* (2003) features an extended discussion of *Wuthering Heights* adapted to film and television.

Laraine Fergenson is professor of English, emerita, and former coordinator of the writing program at Bronx Community College, City University of New York. She has published textbooks on writing and essays on American and British literature, including an essay in *Approaches to Teaching Thoreau's* Walden *and Other Works* (1996). She is a contributing editor to the *Heath Anthology of American Literature* and a poet, whose works have appeared in Ball State University Forum, the *CEA Bulletin*, and elsewhere.

Catherine R. Hancock teaches composition and literature at Lewis University. She is the author of " 'It Was Bone of Her Bone, and Flesh of Her Flesh, and She Had Killed It': Three Versions of Destructive Maternity in Victorian Fiction," published in *Literature Interpretation Theory* (2004). She is currently at work on a book that explores the impact of domestic violence on the family in Victorian fiction.

Terri A. Hasseler is an associate professor and chair of the department of English and cultural studies at Bryant University. She has published articles on feminist theory, postcolonial theory and literature, Victorian imperial culture, and women's travel literature in India. She is currently working on a project that examines the impact of business culture on higher education, particularly on the mentoring of women academics and questions of dissent.

Tamar Heller, assistant professor of English and comparative literature at the University of Cincinnati, is author of *Dead Secrets: Wilkie Collins and the Female Gothic*

(1992), a contributor to *Approaches to Teaching* Jane Eyre (1993), and coeditor of both *Approaches to Teaching Gothic Fiction* (2003) and *Scenes of the Apple: Food and the Female Body in Nineteenth- and Twentieth-Century Women's Writing* (2003). She edited Rhoda Broughton's *Cometh Up as a Flower* for the series *Varieties of Women's Sensation Fiction* (2004).

Diane Long Hoeveler is professor of English and coordinator of women's studies at Marquette University. She is the author of *Gothic Feminism* (1998) and *Romantic Androgyny* (1990) and coeditor of *Interrogating Orientalism* (2006). She has coedited *Approaches to Teaching* Jane Eyre (1993), *Approaches to Teaching Gothic Fiction* (2003), *Comparative Romanticisms* (1998), *Women of Color* (2001), and *The Historical Dictionary of Feminism* (rev. ed., 2004). She is editor of *Wuthering Heights* (2002).

Paula M. Krebs is professor of English at Wheaton College, Massachusetts. She is the author of *Gender, Race, and the Writing of Empire: Public Discourse and the Boer War* (1999) and coeditor of *The Feminist Teacher Anthology: Pedagogies and Classroom Strategies* (1998).

Sue Lonoff is senior associate of the Derek Bok Center at Harvard University and a member of the Harvard Extension School faculty. She is the editor of *Charlotte Brontë and Emily Brontë: The Belgian Essays* (1996) and delivered the Brontë Society Annual Lecture at Haworth in 2003. She is the author of *Wilkie Collins and His Victorian Readers* (1982), as well as articles on Victorian literature and on pedagogy. She is currently working on a book about Marguerite Yourcenar.

Tricia Lootens, associate professor of English at the University of Georgia, is the author of *Lost Saints: Silence, Gender, and Victorian Literary Canonization* (1996). Her publications include essays on nineteenth-century British and American women poets, Victorian patriotic poetry, and approaches to teaching the gothic. Her current project, "Privatizing the Poetess," is a book-length study of race, national sentimentality, and fantasies of nineteenth-century femininity.

Carine M. Mardorossian is associate professor of English at the State University of New York, Buffalo, where she specializes in postcolonial and feminist studies. Her essays have been published in *Ariel, College Literature, Signs, Hypatia, Callaloo,* and the *Journal of Caribbean Literatures*. She is the author of *Reclaiming Difference: Caribbean Women Rewrite Postcolonialism* (2005).

Beth Newman is associate professor of English at Southern Methodist University. She is the author of *Subjects on Display: Psychoanalysis, Social Expectation, and Victorian Femininity* (2004) and editor of an edition of *Jane Eyre* (1996). She is preparing an edition of *Wuthering Heights*.

Barry V. Qualls, dean of humanities and professor of English at Rutgers University, New Brunswick, is the author of *The Secular Pilgrims of Victorian Fiction: The Novel as Book of Life* (1982) and of articles and reviews on nineteenth-century English literature and on the Bible and its literary impact.

Maureen T. Reddy is professor of English and women's studies at Rhode Island College. Her books include *Traces, Codes, and Clues: Reading Race in Crime Fiction*; *Race in the College Classroom: Pedagogy and Politics* (coedited with Bonnie TuSmith);

and *Sisters in Crime: Feminism and the Crime Novel* (1988). She is working on a book on race and nation in Irish popular culture.

Leilani Riehle is currently at work on the book "Inner Beauty: English Women's Fiction and the Metaphorics of Feminine Appearance, 1792–1850," as well as a project that explores the rage for historical fiction set in the Romantic and Victorian periods. She is an independent scholar working in Los Angeles.

Patsy Stoneman is an emeritus reader in English at the University of Hull, United Kingdom. She edited Wuthering Heights*: A New Casebook* (1993) and *Emily Brontë:* Wuthering Heights*: A Reader's Guide to Essential Criticism* (2nd ed., 2000). She wrote the introduction to the Oxford World's Classics edition of the novel (1995). She is author of *Elizabeth Gaskell* (1987) and a monograph, *Brontë Transformations: The Cultural Dissemination of* Jane Eyre *and* Wuthering Heights (1996). She currently holds a Leverhulme Emeritus Fellowship to facilitate the editing of eight Victorian stage plays based on *Jane Eyre*.

Lisa Surridge is associate professor of English at the University of Victoria, Canada. She has published articles on animals and violence in *Wuthering Heights* (*Brontë Society Transactions*, 1995) and on theatricality in *Villette* (*Victorian Newsletter*, 1995). She is the author of *Bleak Houses: Marital Violence in Victorian Fiction* (2005).

Paul Vita teaches at Saint Louis University's Madrid campus, where he chairs the department of English and communication. He has published articles on Victorian responses to death and commemoration in the *Australasian Victorian Studies Journal*, *Nineteenth-Century Contexts*, and *Victorian Review* and is currently writing on the reception of Victorian novels in Spain.

SURVEY PARTICIPANTS

The following scholars and teachers helped in the preparation of this book by contributing essays, responding to the teacher survey, or participating in both activities. Their assistance has been invaluable.

Suzy Anger, *University of British Columbia*
Stephen Arata, *University of Virginia*
Frances Beer, *York University*
Dean de la Motte, *Belmont Abbey College*
Kamilla Elliott, *Lancaster University*
John P. Farrell, *University of Texas*
Laraine Fergenson, *Bronx Community College, CUNY*
Barbara T. Gates, *University of Delaware*
Janet Gezari, *Connecticut College*
Catherine R. Hancock, *Aurora University*
Terri A. Hasseler, *Bryant University*
Tamar Heller, *University of Cincinnati*
Diane Long Hoeveler, *Marquette University*
Rob Jacklosky, *College of Mount Saint Vincent*
John Kearney, *Lebanon Valley College*
Paula M. Krebs, *Wheaton College (MA)*
Drew Lamonica, *Louisiana State University*
George Levine, *Rutgers University*
Jonathan Loesberg, *American University*
Sue Lonoff, *Harvard University*
Tricia Lootens, *University of Georgia*
Carine M. Mardorossian, *State University of New York, Buffalo*
Deborah Denenholz Morse, *College of William and Mary*
Beth Newman, *Southern Methodist University*
Patrick R. O'Malley, *Georgetown University*
Barry V. Qualls, *Rutgers University*
Maureen T. Reddy, *Rhode Island College*
Leilani D. Riehle, *University of California, Los Angeles*
Elizabeth Sabiston, *York University*
Patsy Stoneman, *University of Hull*
Lisa Surridge, *University of Victoria, Canada*
Herbert Tucker, *University of Virginia*
Kathleen Vejvoda, *Bridgewater State College*
Paul Vita, *Saint Louis University, Madrid Campus*

WORKS CITED

Editions of *Wuthering Heights*

Dunn, Richard J., ed. *Wuthering Heights*. 4th ed. New York: Norton, 2003.

Feltham, Irene M., ed. *Wuthering Heights*. New York: Amsco, 1970.

Heywood, Christopher, ed. *Wuthering Heights*. Peterborough: Broadview, 2002.

Hoeveler, Diane Long, ed. *Wuthering Heights*. New Riverside Edition. Boston: Houghton, 2002.

Jack, Ian, ed. *Wuthering Heights*. 1995. Introd. and notes by Patsy Stoneman. Oxford World's Classics. Oxford: Oxford UP, 1998.

Marsden, Hilda, and Ian Jack, eds. *Wuthering Heights*. Oxford: Clarendon, 1976.

Newman, Beth, ed. *Wuthering Heights*. Peterborough: Broadview, 2007.

Nestor, Pauline, ed. *Wuthering Heights*. Pref. Lucasta Miller. 1995. London: Penguin, 2003.

Peterson, Linda H., ed. Wuthering Heights: *Case Studies in Contemporary Criticism*. 1992. Rev. ed. New York: Bedford-St. Martin's, 2003.

Sale, William M., Jr., and Richard J. Dunn, eds. *Wuthering Heights*. 3rd ed. New York: Norton, 1990.

Ward, Candace, ed. *Wuthering Heights*. Mineola: Dover, 1996.

Wuthering Heights. Notes by Baruch Hochman. New York: Bantam, 1981.

Wuthering Heights. Introd. Alice Hoffman. New York: Signet, 2004.

Wuthering Heights. Introd. Diane Johnson. New York: Modern Library, 2000.

Wuthering Heights. Introd. Daphne Merkin. Notes by Tatiana M. Holway. New York: Barnes, 2005.

Audio, Film, and Video Resources

(See also the listing in Elliott, this volume, pp. 133–35.)

Audiocassette Versions

Wuthering Heights. Read by Michael Page and Laural Merlington. Brilliance, 2001.

Wuthering Heights. Read by Patricia Routledge. Cover to Cover, 1983.

Film and Television Adaptations

Bramble, A. V., dir. *Wuthering Heights.* Ideal, 1920.

Buñuel, Luis, dir. *Abismos de pasión*. Perf. Jorge Mistral and Irasema Dilian. Plexus, 1953.

Campion, Jane, dir. *The Piano*. Perf. Harvey Keitel, Holly Hunter, and Sam Neill. Miramax, 1993.

Fuest, Robert, dir. *Wuthering Heights*. Perf. Timothy Dalton and Anna Calder-Marshall. MGM, 1970.

Kosminsky, Peter, dir. *Emily Brontë's* Wuthering Heights. Perf. Ralph Fiennes and Juliette Binoche. Paramount, 1992.

Krishnamma, Suri, dir. *Wuthering Heights, CA*. Perf. Mike Vogel and Erika Christensen. MTV, 2003.

Nickell, Paul, dir. *Wuthering Heights.* Perf. Charlton Heston and Mary Sinclair. Westinghouse Television Theater. CBS, 1950.

Rivette, Jacques, dir. *Hurlevent*. Perf. Lucas Belvaux and Fabienne Babe. Renn, 1985.

Skynner, David, dir. *Emily Brontë's* Wuthering Heights. Introd. Russell Baker. Perf. Robert Cavanah and Orla Brady. London Weekend Television-WGBH, 1998.

Yoshida, Kiju, dir. *Arashi ga oka* [*Onimaru*]. Perf. Yusaku Matsuda and Yuko Tanaka. Seiyô Films, 1988.

Wyler, William, dir. *Wuthering Heights.* Perf. Laurence Olivier and Merle Oberon. United Artists, 1939.

General Works

Abraham, Nicholas. "Notes on the Phantom: A Complement to Freud's Metapsychology." Trans. Nicholas Rand. *Critical Inquiry* 13 (1987): 287–89.

Abrams, M. H. *A Glossary of Literary Terms*. 7th ed. Fort Worth: Harcourt, 1999.

Alexander, Christine, and Jane Sellars. *The Art of the Brontës*. Cambridge: Cambridge UP, 1995.

Alexander, Christine, and Margaret Smith, eds. *The Oxford Companion to the Brontës*. Oxford: Oxford UP, 2003.

Allott, Miriam. *The Brontës: The Critical Heritage*. London: Routledge, 1974.

———. *Emily Brontë:* Wuthering Heights, *a Casebook*. London: MacMillan, 1970.

Althusser, Louis. "Ideology and Ideological State Apparatuses." *"Lenin and Philosophy" and Other Essays*. Trans. Ben Brewster. New York: Monthly Review, 1971. 127–86.

An American Werewolf in London. Dir. John Landis. Perf. David Naughton, Jenny Agutter, Griffin Dunne. Universal, 1981.

Apter, T. E. "Romanticism and Romantic Love in *Wuthering Heights.*" *The Art of Emily Brontë*. Ed. Anne Smith. London: Vision, 1976. 205–22.

Armstrong, Nancy. *Desire and Domestic Fiction: A Political History of the Novel*. New York: Oxford UP, 1987.

———. "Emily's Ghost: The Cultural Politics of Victorian Fiction, Folklore, and Photography." *Novel* 25.3 (1992): 245–67.

———. *Fiction in the Age of Photography: The Legacy of British Realism*. Cambridge: Harvard UP, 1999.

———. "Imperialist Nostalgia and *Wuthering Heights.*" Peterson, *Wuthering Heights* [1992] 428–49.

Arnold, Matthew. *The Complete Prose Works of Matthew Arnold*. Ed. R. H. Super. Vol. 6. Ann Arbor: U of Michigan P, 1960–72.

Asancheyev, Alex. "The Narrative Structure of *Wuthering Heights.*" Paper for English 290, Wheaton Coll. Dec. 2002.

Barker, Juliet. *The Brontës*. New York: St. Martin's, 1994.

———. *The Brontës: A Life in Letters*. New York: Viking, 1997.

———. "The Haworth Context." *The Cambridge Companion to the Brontës*. Ed. Heather Glen. Cambridge: Cambridge UP, 2002.

Barry, Peter. *Beginning Theory: An Introduction to Literary and Cultural Theory*. Manchester: Manchester UP, 1995.

Barthes, Roland. "The Death of the Author." *Image-Music-Text*. Trans. Stephen Heath. New York: Noonday, 1977. 142–48. Rpt. in Richter [2000] 253–57.

Bean, John C. *Engaging Ideas*. San Francisco: Jossey-Bass, 2001.

Beeton, Isabella. *Mrs. Beeton's Book of Household Management*. 1861. New York: Farrar, 1969.

Benjamin, Walter. "The Work of Art in the Age of Mechanical Reproduction." *Film Theory and Criticism*. Ed. Gerald Mast and Marshall Cohen. Trans. Harry Zohn. New York: Oxford UP, 1976. 612–34.

Bentley, Phyllis. *The Brontës and Their World*. London: Thames, 1969. Rpt. as *The Brontës*. Folcroft: Folcroft, 1975.

Berg, Maggie. Wuthering Heights*: The Writing in the Margin*. New York: Twayne, 1996.

Bersani, Leo. *A Future for Astyanax: Character and Desire in Literature*. New York: Little, 1976.

Bettelheim, Bruno. *The Uses of Enchantment: The Meaning and Importance of Fairy Tales*. New York: Knopf, 1976.

Bleich, David. *Subjective Criticism*. Baltimore: Johns Hopkins UP, 1978.

Bloom, Harold. "Elegiac Conclusion." Richter [2000] 225–33. Rpt. of epilogue. *The Western Canon*. New York: Harcourt, 1994. 483–94.

———, ed. *Emily Brontë's* Wuthering Heights. Modern Critical Interpretations. New York: Chelsea, 1987.

Boone, Joseph. *Tradition Counter Tradition: Love and the Form of Fiction*. Chicago: U of Chicago P, 1987.

Botting, Fred. *Gothic*. London: Routledge, 1996.

Brontë, Charlotte. "Biographical Notice of Ellis and Acton Bell." Jack, *Wuthering Heights* 319–23.

———. "Editor's Preface to the New Edition of *Wuthering Heights*. Jack, *Wuthering Heights* 324–27.

———. *Jane Eyre*. 1847. Ed. Richard Nemesvari. Peterborough: Broadview, 1999.

Brontë, Emily. "R. Alcona to J. Brenzaida." Rpt. as "Remembrance." *Norton Anthology of English Literature*. 7th ed. Vol. 2. Ed. M. H. Abrams and Stephen Greenblatt. New York: Norton, 2000. 1421.

Brooks, Cleanth. *The Well Wrought Urn: Studies in the Structure of Poetry*. New York: Harcourt, 1947.

Browning, Elizabeth Barrett. *Aurora Leigh*. Aurora Leigh *and Other Poems*. Introd. Cora Kaplan. London: Women's, 1978.

Bruffee, Kenneth. *Collaborative Learning: Higher Education, Interdependence, and the Authority of Knowledge*. Baltimore: Johns Hopkins UP, 1993.

———. "Collaborative Learning and the 'Conversation of Mankind.' " *College English* 46 (1984): 635–52.

Burns, Bonnie. "Nostalgia, Apostrophe, *Wuthering Heights*: The Queer Destiny of Heterosexuality." *Nineteenth Century Feminisms* 1 (1999): 81–94.

Bush, Kate. "Wuthering Heights." *The Whole Story*. EMI America, 1986.

Carter, Angela. *Nights at the Circus*. New York: Viking, 1986.

Cecil, David. *Early Victorian Novelists: Essays in Revaluation*. Chicago: U of Chicago P, 1958.

———. "Emily Brontë and *Wuthering Heights*." *Early Victorian Novelists*. London: Constable, 1934. Rpt. in Allott, *Casebook* 135–43.

Chew, Samuel. *Byron in England: His Fame and after Fame*. Toronto: Longman's, 1924.

Child, Francis James, ed. *English and Scottish Ballads*. Boston: Houghton, 1880.

Chitham, Edward. *The Birth of* Wuthering Heights*: Emily Brontë at Work*. New York: St. Martin's, 1998.

———. *The Brontës' Irish Background*. Basingstoke: Macmillan, 1996.

———. *A Life of Emily Brontë*. Oxford: Blackwell, 1987.

Cobbe, Frances Power. "Wife-Torture in England." *Contemporary Review* 32 (1878): 55–87.

Condé, Maryse. *Windward Heights*. Trans. Richard Philcox. New York: Soho, 2000.

Crowley, Sarah. "Pop Goes the Culture." Paper for English 290, Wheaton Coll. Dec. 2002.

Dacre, Charlotte. *Zofloya; or, The Moor*. Ed. Adriana Cracuin. Peterborough: Broadview, 1997.

Daley, A. Stuart. "A Chronology of *Wuthering Heights*." Dunn, *Wuthering Heights* 357–61.

David, Deirdre. *Intellectual Women and Victorian Patriarchy*. Ithaca: Cornell UP, 1987.

Davies, Stevie. *Emily Brontë: The Artist as a Free Woman*. Manchester: Carcanet, 1983.

———. *Emily Brontë: Heretic.* New York: Harvester, 1988.

DeLamotte, Eugenia. *Perils of the Night: A Feminist Study of Nineteenth-Century Gothic.* New York: Oxford UP, 1992.

Derrida, Jacques. "Structure, Sign, and Play in the Discourse of the Human Sciences." *The Structuralist Controversy: The Languages of Criticism and the Sciences of Man.* Ed. Richard Macksey and Eugenio Donato. Baltimore: Johns Hopkins UP, 1972. 247–72.

Dickens, Charles. *Oliver Twist.* 1837–38. Oxford World's Classics. Oxford: Oxford UP, 1999.

Dickinson, Emily. "One Need Not Be a Chamber—to Be Haunted—." *The Complete Poems of Emily Dickinson.* Ed. Thomas H. Johnson. Boston: Little, 1960. 333.

Dobell, Sydney. "Currer Bell." *Palladium* (Sept. 1850). Rpt. in Dunn, *Wuthering Heights* 161–75.

Dubois, Andrew. Introduction. *Close Reading: The Reader.* Ed. Frank Lentricchia and Andrew Dubois. Durham: Duke UP, 2003. 1–40.

Eagleton, Terry. *Literary Theory.* Oxford: Blackwell, 1993.

———. *Myths of Power: A Marxist Study of the Brontës.* Basingstoke: Macmillan, 1975. Rpt. as "Myths of Power: A Marxist Study of *Wuthering Heights.*" Peterson, *Wuthering Heights* [1992] 399–414; [2003] 394–410.

Eco, Umberto. "*Casablanca*: Cult Movies and Intertextual Collage." *Travels in Hyperreality.* Trans. William Weaver. New York: Harcourt, 1983. 197–211.

Efron, Arthur. "'Paunch,' *Wuthering Heights*, and the Body." *Paunch* 40–41 (1975): 166–71.

Eichenberg, Fritz, illus. *Wuthering Heights.* New York: Random, 1943.

Eliot, George. *The Mill on the Floss.* 1860. Oxford World's Classics. Oxford: Oxford UP, 1998.

Elliott, Kamilla. *Rethinking the Novel/Film Debate.* Cambridge: Cambridge UP, 2003.

Ellis, Markman. *The History of Gothic Fiction.* Edinburgh: Edinburgh UP, 2000.

Ellis, Sarah. *The Daughters of England: Their Position in Society, Character, and Responsibilities.* New York: Appleton, 1842.

———. *The Wives of England: Their Relative Duties, Domestic Influence, and Social Obligations.* New York: Langley, 1843.

———. *The Women of England, Their Social Duties, and Domestic Habits.* London: Fisher, 1839.

Fermi, Sarah. Rev. of *Wuthering Heights*, ed. Linda H. Peterson. *Brontë Studies* 29 (2004): 89–91.

Fetterley, Judith. Introduction. *The Resisting Reader: A Feminist Approach to American Fiction.* Bloomington: Indiana UP, 1981.

Fior, Anthony. "Darkness in Diction: Emily Brontë's *Wuthering Heights.*" Paper for English 230–01, Saint Louis Univ., Madrid Campus. 2003.

Fish, Stanley. "Is There a Text in This Class?" Richter [1994] 573–85.

Fiske, John. "British Cultural Studies and Television." *Channels of Discourse, Reassembled.* Ed. Robert C. Allen. 2nd ed. Chapel Hill: U of North Carolina P, 1992. 285–323.

Forster, Peter, illus. *Wuthering Heights.* London: Folio Soc., 1991.

Foucault, Michel. "What Is an Author?" Trans. Donald F. Bouchard and Sherry Simon. *Language, Counter-Memory, Practice: Selected Essays and Interviews*. Ed. Bouchard. Ithaca: Cornell UP, 1977. 113–38.

Frankenberg, Ronald. "Styles of Marxism, Styles of Criticism: *Wuthering Heights*: A Case Study." *The Sociology of Literature: Applied Studies.* Ed. Diana Laurenson. Monograph 26. Keele, Staffs.: Keele UP, 1978: 109–44.

Freud, Sigmund. *The Interpretation of Dreams*. Freud, *Standard Edition*. Vol. 4.

———. *New Introductory Lectures*. Freud, *Standard Edition*. Vol. 22.

———. *The Standard Edition of the Complete Psychological Works of Sigmund Freud.* Trans. James Strachey. 24 vols. London: Hogarth, 1953–74.

Gaskell, Elizabeth. *The Life of Charlotte Brontë.* 1857. Ed. and introd. Alan Shelston. Harmondsworth: Penguin, 1975.

Gates, Henry Louis, Jr. "Canon-Formation, Literary History, and the Afro-American Literary Tradition." Richter [2000] 175–82.

Gavett, Gretchen. "Gender and Narration: A Queer Reading of *Wuthering Heights*." Paper for English 290, Wheaton Coll. Dec. 2002.

Gérin, Winifred. *Emily Brontë: A Biography*. Oxford: Clarendon, 1971.

Gezari, Janet, ed. *Emily Jane Brontë: The Complete Poems*. London: Penguin, 1992.

Gibaldi, Joseph. *MLA Handbook for Writers of Research Papers.* 6th ed. New York: MLA, 2003.

Gilbert, Sandra M., and Susan Gubar. "Looking Oppositely: Emily Brontë's Bible of Hell." Gilbert and Gubar, *Madwoman* 248–308. Excerpted in Dunn, *Wuthering Heights* 379–94.

———. *The Madwoman in the Attic: The Woman Writer and the Nineteenth-Century Literary Imagination.* New Haven: Yale UP, 1979.

Graff, Gerald. *Beyond the Culture Wars: How Teaching the Conflicts Can Revitalize American Education*. New York: Norton, 1992.

Green, Laura Morgan. *Educating Women: Cultural Conflict and Victorian Literature.* Athens: Ohio UP, 2001.

Greenblatt, Stephen. "Resonance and Wonder." *Modern Literary Theory*. Ed. Philip Rice and Patricia Waugh. 4th ed. London: Arnold, 2001. 305–24.

Guillory, John. "The Canon as Cultural Capital." Richter [2000] 218–24.

Hafley, James. "The Villain in *Wuthering Heights*." *Nineteenth-Century Fiction* 13 (1958): 199–215.

Haire-Sargeant, Lin. "Sympathy for the Devil: The Problem of Heathcliff in Film Versions of *Wuthering Heights*." Dunn, *Wuthering Heights* 410–27.

Hatfield, C. W., ed. *The Complete Poems of Emily Jane Brontë*. New York: Columbia UP, 1941.

Heller, Tamar. *Dead Secrets: Wilkie Collins and the Female Gothic*. New Haven: Yale UP, 1992.

———. Introduction. *Cometh Up as a Flower*. Ed. Heller. *Varieties of Women's Sensation Fiction*. Andrew Maunder, gen. ed. Vol. 4b. London: Pickering, 2004.

———. "*Jane Eyre*, Bertha, and the Female Gothic." *Approaches to Teaching* Jane Eyre. Ed. Diane Long Hoeveler and Beth Lau. Approaches to Teaching World Lit. 42. New York: MLA, 1993. 49–55.

———. "Materials." Hoeveler and Heller 3–31.

Hirsch, E. D. "Objective Interpretation." *PMLA* 75 (1960): 463–79.

Hoeveler, Diane Long. *Gothic Feminism: The Professionalization of Gender from Charlotte Smith to the Brontës.* University Park: Pennsylvania State UP, 1998.

———. "*Wuthering Heights* and Gothic Feminism." Hoeveler, *Wuthering Heights* 433–46.

Hoeveler, Diane, and Tamar Heller, eds. *Approaches to Teaching Gothic Fiction: The British and American Traditions.* Approaches to Teaching World Lit. 79. New York: MLA, 2003.

Hoffman, Alice. *Here on Earth.* New York: Berkley, 1998.

The Holy Bible, Containing the Old and New Testaments, King James Version. New York: American Bible Soc., 1999.

Hošek, Chaviva, and Patricia Parker, eds. *Lyric Poetry: Beyond New Criticism.* Ithaca: Cornell UP, 1985.

Jacobs, Carol. "*Wuthering Heights*: At the Threshold of Interpretation." *Boundary 2: A Journal of Postmodern Literature and Culture* 7.3 (1979): 49–72.

Jacobs, Harriet. *Incidents in the Life of a Slave Girl.* New York: Cambridge UP, 1996.

J. F. Rev. of *Wuthering Heights*, by Emily Brontë. *Temple Bar* 81 (1887): 562. Rpt. in *The Brontë Sisters: Critical Assessments.* Ed. Eleanor McNees. Mountfield, East Sussex: Helm Information, 1996. 34.

Jowett, Benjamin. "On the Interpretation of Scripture." *Essays and Reviews: The 1860 Text and Its Reading.* Ed. Victor Shea and William Whitla. Charlottesville: U of Virginia P, 2000. 477–593.

Kahane, Claire. "The Gothic Mirror." *The (M)Other Tongue: Essays in Feminist Psychoanalytic Interpretation.* Ithaca: Cornell UP, 1985. 334–52.

Kamuf, Peggy, ed. *A Derrida Reader: Between the Blinds.* New York: Columbia UP, 1991.

Keats, John. "La Belle Dame sans Merci: A Ballad." *The Poems of John Keats.* Ed. Jack Stillinger. Cambridge: Harvard UP, 1978. 357–59.

Lacey, Candida Anne, ed. *Barbara Leigh Smith Bodichon and the Langham Place Group.* New York: Routledge, 1987. 23–35.

Lambourne, Lionel. *Victorian Paintings.* London: Phaidon, 1999.

Laplanche, Jean, and Bertrand Pontalis. "Fantasy and the Origins of Sexuality." *Formations of Fantasy.* Ed. Victor Burgin, James Donald, and Cora Kaplan. London: Metheun, 1986. 5–44.

Leavis, Q. D. *Lectures in America.* New York: Pantheon, 1969.

Leighton, Angela. "Famous First Lines." *TLS* 15 Jan. 1993: 24.

Leitch, Vincent B., et al., eds. *The Norton Anthology of Theory and Criticism.* New York: Norton, 2001.

Levi-Strauss, Claude. *The Raw and the Cooked.* Trans. John Wightman and Doreen Wightman. New York: Harper, 1969.

Levy, Anita. *Other Women: The Writing of Class, Race, and Gender, 1832–1898*. Princeton: Princeton UP, 1991.

Lewes, George Henry. "The Lady Novelists." *Westminster Review* July 1852. Rpt. in *A Victorian Art of Fiction: Essays on the Novel in British Periodicals, 1851–1860*. Ed. John C. Olmstead. New York: Garland, 1979. 39–51.

———. Rev. of *Wuthering Heights,*by Emily Brontë, and *Agnes Grey*, by Anne Brontë. *Leader* 28 Dec. 1850: 953. Rpt. in Sale and Dunn, *Wuthering Heights* 325–27; Dunn, *Wuthering Heights* 348–49.

Lonoff, Sue, ed. and trans. *Charlotte Brontë and Emily Brontë: The Belgian Essays*. New Haven: Yale UP, 1996.

"The Luxury of Assault." *Punch* 3 (1842): 161.

Marsh, Nicholas. *Emily Brontë:* Wuthering Heights *(Analysing Texts)*. Basingstoke: Macmillan, 1999.

Marx, Karl, and Friedrich Engels. *The German Ideology*. Trans. S. Ryazanskaya. Moscow: Progress, 1968.

Meyer, Susan L. *Imperialism at Home: Race and Victorian Women's Fiction*. Ithaca: Cornell UP, 1996.

———. " 'Your Father Was Emperor of China, and Your Mother an Indian Queen': Reverse Imperialism in *Wuthering Heights*." Meyer, *Imperialism* 96–125. Rpt. in Peterson, *Wuthering Heights* [2003] 480–502.

Michie, Elsie. *Outside the Pale: Cultural Exclusion, Gender Difference, and the Victorian Woman Writer*. Ithaca: Cornell UP, 1993.

Mill, John Stuart, and Harriet Taylor. "The Case of William Burn." *Morning Chronicle* 17 Nov. 1846. Rpt. in Robson and Robson 24: 952–54.

———. "The Suicide of Sarah Brown." *Morning Chronicle* 28 Oct. 1846. Rpt. in Robson and Robson 24: 916–19.

Miller, D. A. "*Cage aux Folles*: Sensation and Gender in Wilkie Collins's *The Woman in White*." *Representations* 14 (1986): 107–36.

Miller, J. Hillis. *Fiction and Repetition in Seven English Novels*. Cambridge: Harvard UP, 1982.

———. "Teaching *Middlemarch*: Close Reading and Theory." *Approaches to Teaching Eliot's* Middlemarch. Ed. Kathleen Blake. Approaches to Teaching World Lit. 30. New York: MLA, 1990. 51–63.

———. "*Wuthering Heights*: Repetition and the 'Uncanny.' " Miller, J. H., *Fiction* 42–72. Rpt. in Dunn, *Wuthering Heights* 361–78.

Miller, Lucasta. *The Brontë Myth*. London: Cape, 2001.

Moore, Thomas. *Life of Byron*. London, 1830.

Moorman, F. W. *Yorkshire Dialect Poems (1673–1915) and Traditional Poems*. London: Sidgwick, 1916. 2 Aug. 2004 <http://www.hyphenologist.co.uk/songs/ydp.html#Preface%20to%20Etext>.

Morrison, Toni. "Black Matter(s)." Richter [2000] 310–22.

Mulvey, Laura. "Visual Pleasure and Narrative Cinema." *Screen* 16.3 (1975): 6–18.

Murray, Janet, ed. *Strong-Minded Women and Other Lost Voices from Nineteenth-Century England*. New York: Pantheon, 1982.

Nestor, Pauline. Introduction. Nestor, *Wuthering Heights* [1995] vii–xxi.

Newman, Beth. " 'The Situation of the Looker-On': Gender, Narration, and Gaze in *Wuthering Heights*." *PMLA* 105 (1990): 1029–41.

Newsome, David. *The Victorian World Picture*. New Brunswick: Rutgers UP, 1997.

Nietzsche, Friedrich Wilhelm. "On Truth and Lies in a Nonmoral Sense." *Philosophy and Truth: Selections from Nietzsche's Notebooks of the Early 1870's*. Trans. Daniel Breazeale. Atlantic Highlands: Humanities, 1979. 79–97.

———. *The Will to Power*. Trans. Walter Kaufmann and R. J. Hollingdale. New York: Vintage, 1968.

Norton, Caroline. *Lady Caroline Norton's Letter to the Queen on Lord Chancellor Cranworth's Marriage and Divorce Bill*. Excerpt rpt. in Peterson, *Wuthering Heights* [2003] 295–99. Rpt. in *Selected Writings of Caroline Norton: Facsimile Reproductions*. Introd. and notes by James A. Hoge and Jane Marcus. Delmar: Scholars' Facsimiles, 1978. Sec. 7.

Nussbaum, Martha. "*Wuthering Heights*: The Romantic Ascent." Dunn, *Wuthering Heights* 394–410.

O'Brien, Erin. "Reception of *Shirley* and *Jane Eyre*." Paper for English 290, Wheaton Coll. May 2003.

Poovey, Mary. *Uneven Developments: The Ideological Work of Gender in Mid-Victorian England*. Chicago: U of Chicago P, 1988.

Pykett, Lyn. "Changing the Names: The Two Catherines." Pykett, *Emily Brontë* 86–98. Rpt. in Peterson, *Wuthering Heights* [2003] 468–77.

———. *Emily Brontë*. New York: Barnes, 1989.

———. "Gender and Genre in *Wuthering Heights*: Gothic Plot and Domestic Fiction." Pykett, *Emily Brontë* 71–85.

Rabinowitz, Peter. "Canons and Close Reading." Richter [1994] 218–21.

Radcliffe, Ann. *The Mysteries of Udolpho*. Ed. Bonamy Dobrée. Oxford: Oxford UP, 1966.

Radway, Janice. "Introduction to *A Feeling for Books*." Richter [2000] 199–210.

Ratchford, Fannie E. Gondal's Queen*: A Novel in Verse by Emily Jane Brontë*. Austin: U of Texas P, 1955.

Re Cochrane (1840) 8 Dowling 633.

Reed, Michael D. "The Power of *Wuthering Heights*: A Psychoanalytical Examination." *Psychocultural Review* 1 (1977): 21–42.

Rev. of *Wuthering Heights*, by Emily Brontë. *Atlas* 22 Jan. 1848: 59. Rpt. in Sale and Dunn, *Wuthering Heights* 299–301. Rpt. in Dunn, *Wuthering Heights* 282–84.

Rev. of *Wuthering Heights*, by Emily Brontë. *Britannia* 15 Jan. 1848: 42. Excerpted in Sale and Dunn, *Wuthering Heights* 305–07; Dunn, *Wuthering Heights* 288–91.

Rhys, Jean. *Wide Sargasso Sea*. 1966. New York: Norton, 1982.

Rich, Adrienne. *Of Woman Born: Motherhood as Experience and Institution*. New York: Norton, 1976.

Richter, David. H., ed. *Falling into Theory*. 1994. Rev. ed. New York: Bedford, 2000.

Rivkin, Julie, and Michael Ryan, eds. *Literary Theory: An Anthology*. Oxford: Blackwell, 1998.

Robson, Ann P., and John M. Robson, eds. *The Collected Works of John Stuart Mill.* 33 vols. Toronto: U of Toronto P, 1963–91.

Roper, Derek, ed. *The Poems of Emily Brontë*. With Edward Chitham. Oxford: Clarendon, 1995.

Russ, Joanna. "Somebody's Trying to Kill Me and I Think It's My Husband: The Modern Gothic." *The Female Gothic*. Ed. Juliann E. Fleenor. Montreal: Eden, 1983. 31–56.

Rutherford, Andrew, ed. *Lord Byron: The Critical Heritage*. London: Routledge, 1970.

Sale, William M., Jr. "Emily Brontë's History of Gondal." Sale and Dunn, *Wuthering Heights* 376–80.

Sanger, C. P. "The Structure of *Wuthering Heights*." 1926. Rpt. in *Critical Essays on Emily Brontë.* Ed. Tom Winnifrith and Thomas John Winnifrith. New York: Hall, 1997. 132–43.

Saussure, Ferdinand de. *Course in General Linguistics*. Trans. Roy Harris. LaSalle: Open Court, 1986.

Scholes, Robert. "A Fortunate Fall?" Richter [2000] 111–19.

Schorer, Mark. "Fiction and the Analogical Matrix." *The World We Imagine: Selected Essays*. London: Chatto, 1968. 24–45.

Shelley, Mary. *Frankenstein*. Ed. M. K. Joseph. Oxford: Oxford UP, 1998.

Shelston, Alan. Introduction. Gaskell, *Life* 9–36.

Showalter, Elaine. *A Literature of Their Own*. Princeton: Princeton UP, 1977.

Simmons, Batholomew. "The Bridegroom of Barna." *Blackwood's Edinburgh Magazine* Nov. 1840: 680–704. Rpt. in Hoeveler, *Wuthering Heights* 393–433.

Sinclair, May. *The Three Brontës*. London: Hutchinson, 1933.

Smith, Margaret, ed. *The Letters of Charlotte Brontë, with a Selection of Letters by Family and Friends.* 3 vols. Oxford: Oxford UP, 1995–2004.

Stoneman, Patsy. *Brontë Transformations: The Cultural Dissemination of* Jane Eyre *and* Wuthering Heights. Hempstead: Harvester Wheatsheaf-Prentice, 1996.

———, ed. *Emily Brontë:* Wuthering Heights. Readers' Guides to Essential Criticism. Basingstoke: Palgrave Macmillan, 2000.

———. Introduction. Jack, *Wuthering Heights* [1998] vii–xxxvi.

———, ed. Wuthering Heights*: A New Casebook*. Basingstoke: Macmillan, 1993.

Suzuka, Reni. *Wuthering Heights.* Famous Love Comics 2. Tokyo: Telehouse, 1989.

Swinburne, Charles Algernon. "Emily Brontë." *Athenaeum* 16 (1883): 762–63.

Thomas, Brook. "The Historical Necessity for—and Difficulties with—New Historical Analysis in Introductory Literature Courses." *College English* 49 (1987): 509–22.

Thompson, F. M. L. *The Rise of Respectable Society: A Social History of Britain, 1830–1900*. Cambridge: Harvard UP, 1988.

Tillotson, Kathleen. *Novels of the 1840s*. Oxford: Oxford UP, 1984.

Tompkins, Jane. "Masterpiece Theater: The Politics of Hawthorne's Literary Reputation." Richter [2000] 137–47.

Tyson, Lois. *Critical Theory Today*. New York: Garland, 1999.

Urquhart, Jane. *Changing Heaven*. Toronto: McClelland, 1990.

Van Ghent, Dorothy. "Dark 'Otherness' in *Wuthering Heights*." Allott, *Casebook* 177–83.

———. *The English Novel: Form and Function*. New York: Rinehart, 1953.

———. "The Window Figure and the Two Children Figure in Wuthering Heights." *Nineteenth-Century Fiction* 7.3 (1952): 189–97. Rpt. in Van Ghent, *English Novel* 153–70.

Visick, Mary. "The Gondal Saga." Hoeveler, *Wuthering Heights* 308–24. Rpt. of *The Genesis of* Wuthering Heights. By Mary Visick. Hong Kong: Hong Kong UP, 1948.

Von Sneidern, Maja-Lisa. "*Wuthering Heights* and the Liverpool Slave Trade." *ELH* 62.1 (1995): 171–97. Rpt. in Hoeveler, *Wuthering Heights* 366–90.

Walters, Karla K. Victoria Listserv. 26 June 2002, week 4. <victoria@listserve.indiana.edu>.

Watson, Reginald. "Images of Blackness in the Works of Charlotte and Emily Brontë." *CLA Journal* 44 (2001): 451–70.

Weissman, Judith. " 'Like a Mad Dog': The Radical Romanticism of *Wuthering Heights*." *Midwest Quarterly—a Journal of Contemporary Thought* 19 (1978): 383–97.

Wiegman, Robyn. *American Anatomies: Theorizing Race and Gender*. Durham: Duke UP, 1995.

Wilde, Oscar. "The Critic as Artist." *Complete Works of Oscar Wilde*. New York: Harper, 1989. 1009–59.

Wilks, Brian. *The Brontës*. New York: Viking, 1975.

———. *The Illustrated Brontës of Haworth*. London: Willow, 1986.

Wimsatt, William K., Jr., and Monroe C. Beardsley. "The Intentional Fallacy." *The Verbal Icon: Studies in the Meaning of Poetry*. Lexington: U of Kentucky P, 1954. 3–20.

Winnifrith, Tom, ed. *The Brontës*. CD-ROM. Woodbridge: Primary Source Media, 1997.

Wion, Philip K. "The Absent Mother in Emily Brontë's *Wuthering Heights*." *American Imago* 42 (1985): 143–64. Rpt. in Peterson, *Wuthering Heights* [1992] 315–29; [2003] 364–78.

Wise, Thomas James, and J. Alexander Symington, eds. *The Brontës: Their Lives, Friendships and Correspondence*. Shakespeare Head Brontë. 4 vols. Oxford: Blackwell, 1932.

Wollstonecraft, Mary. *Maria; or, The Wrongs of Woman*. Ed. Anne K. Mellor. New York: Norton, 1994.

Woolf, Virginia. *A Room of One's Own*. New York: Harcourt, 1957.

Wordsworth, William. "Preface to *Lyrical Ballads* (1802)." Wordsworth, *Major Works* 595–615.

———. "Strange Fits of Passion Have I Known." Wordsworth, *Major Works* 148.

———. *William Wordsworth: The Major Works.* Ed. Stephen Gill. New York: Oxford UP, 1984.

Zipes, Jack, ed. *The Great Fairy Tale Tradition*. New York: Norton, 2001

INDEX OF NAMES

Modern Language Association of America

Approaches to Teaching World Literature

Joseph Gibaldi, series editor

Achebe's Things Fall Apart. Ed. Bernth Lindfors. 1991.
Arthurian Tradition. Ed. Maureen Fries and Jeanie Watson. 1992.
Atwood's The Handmaid's Tale *and Other Works*. Ed. Sharon R. Wilson, Thomas B. Friedman, and Shannon Hengen. 1996.
Austen's Emma. Ed. Marcia McClintock Folsom. 2004.
Austen's Pride and Prejudice. Ed. Marcia McClintock Folsom. 1993.
Balzac's Old Goriot. Ed. Michal Peled Ginsburg. 2000.
Baudelaire's Flowers of Evil. Ed. Laurence M. Porter. 2000.
Beckett's Waiting for Godot. Ed. June Schlueter and Enoch Brater. 1991.
Beowulf. Ed. Jess B. Bessinger, Jr., and Robert F. Yeager. 1984.
Blake's Songs of Innocence and of Experience. Ed. Robert F. Gleckner and Mark L. Greenberg. 1989.
Boccaccio's Decameron. Ed. James H. McGregor. 2000.
British Women Poets of the Romantic Period. Ed. Stephen C. Behrendt and Harriet Kramer Linkin. 1997.
Brontë's Jane Eyre. Ed. Diane Long Hoeveler and Beth Lau. 1993.
Emily Brontë's Wuthering Heights. Ed. Sue Lonoff and Terri A. Hasseler. 2006.
Byron's Poetry. Ed. Frederick W. Shilstone. 1991.
Camus's The Plague. Ed. Steven G. Kellman. 1985.
Cather's My Ántonia. Ed. Susan J. Rosowski. 1989.
Cervantes' Don Quixote. Ed. Richard Bjornson. 1984.
Chaucer's Canterbury Tales. Ed. Joseph Gibaldi. 1980.
Chopin's The Awakening. Ed. Bernard Koloski. 1988.
Coleridge's Poetry and Prose. Ed. Richard E. Matlak. 1991.
Conrad's "Heart of Darkness" and "The Secret Sharer." Ed. Hunt Hawkins and Brian W. Shaffer. 2002.
Dante's Divine Comedy. Ed. Carole Slade. 1982.
Defoe's Robinson Crusoe. Ed. Maximillian E. Novak and Carl Fisher. 2005.
DeLillo's White Noise. Ed. Tim Engles and John N. Duvall. 2006.
Dickens' David Copperfield. Ed. Richard J. Dunn. 1984.
Dickinson's Poetry. Ed. Robin Riley Fast and Christine Mack Gordon. 1989.
Narrative of the Life of Frederick Douglass. Ed. James C. Hall. 1999.
Early Modern Spanish Drama. Ed. Laura R. Bass and Margaret R. Greer. 2006
Eliot's Middlemarch. Ed. Kathleen Blake. 1990.
Eliot's Poetry and Plays. Ed. Jewel Spears Brooker. 1988.
Shorter Elizabethan Poetry. Ed. Patrick Cheney and Anne Lake Prescott. 2000.
Ellison's Invisible Man. Ed. Susan Resneck Parr and Pancho Savery. 1989.
English Renaissance Drama. Ed. Karen Bamford and Alexander Leggatt. 2002.

Works of Louise Erdrich. Ed. Gregg Sarris, Connie A. Jacobs, and James R. Giles. 2004.

Dramas of Euripides. Ed. Robin Mitchell-Boyask. 2002.

Faulkner's The Sound and the Fury. Ed. Stephen Hahn and Arthur F. Kinney. 1996.

Flaubert's Madame Bovary. Ed. Laurence M. Porter and Eugene F. Gray. 1995.

García Márquez's One Hundred Years of Solitude. Ed. María Elena de Valdés and Mario J. Valdés. 1990.

Gilman's "The Yellow Wall-Paper" and Herland. Ed. Denise D. Knight and Cynthia J. Davis. 2003.

Goethe's Faust. Ed. Douglas J. McMillan. 1987.

Gothic Fiction: The British and American Traditions. Ed. Diane Long Hoeveler and Tamar Heller. 2003.

Hebrew Bible as Literature in Translation. Ed. Barry N. Olshen and Yael S. Feldman. 1989.

Homer's Iliad *and* Odyssey. Ed. Kostas Myrsiades. 1987.

Ibsen's A Doll House. Ed. Yvonne Shafer. 1985.

Henry James's Daisy Miller *and* The Turn of the Screw. Ed. Kimberly C. Reed and Peter G. Beidler. 2005.

Works of Samuel Johnson. Ed. David R. Anderson and Gwin J. Kolb. 1993.

Joyce's Ulysses. Ed. Kathleen McCormick and Erwin R. Steinberg. 1993.

Kafka's Short Fiction. Ed. Richard T. Gray. 1995.

Keats's Poetry. Ed. Walter H. Evert and Jack W. Rhodes. 1991.

Kingston's The Woman Warrior. Ed. Shirley Geok-lin Lim. 1991.

Lafayette's The Princess of Clèves. Ed. Faith E. Beasley and Katharine Ann Jensen. 1998.

Works of D. H. Lawrence. Ed. M. Elizabeth Sargent and Garry Watson. 2001.

Lessing's The Golden Notebook. Ed. Carey Kaplan and Ellen Cronan Rose. 1989.

Mann's Death in Venice *and Other Short Fiction*. Ed. Jeffrey B. Berlin. 1992.

Medieval English Drama. Ed. Richard K. Emmerson. 1990.

Melville's Moby-Dick. Ed. Martin Bickman. 1985.

Metaphysical Poets. Ed. Sidney Gottlieb. 1990.

Miller's Death of a Salesman. Ed. Matthew C. Roudané. 1995.

Milton's Paradise Lost. Ed. Galbraith M. Crump. 1986.

Molière's Tartuffe *and Other Plays*. Ed. James F. Gaines and Michael S. Koppisch. 1995.

Momaday's The Way to Rainy Mountain. Ed. Kenneth M. Roemer. 1988.

Montaigne's Essays. Ed. Patrick Henry. 1994.

Novels of Toni Morrison. Ed. Nellie Y. McKay and Kathryn Earle. 1997.

Murasaki Shikibu's The Tale of Genji. Ed. Edward Kamens. 1993.

Pope's Poetry. Ed. Wallace Jackson and R. Paul Yoder. 1993.

Proust's Fiction and Criticism. Ed. Elyane Dezon-Jones and Inge Crosman Wimmers. 2003.

Novels of Samuel Richardson. Ed. Lisa Zunshine and Jocelyn Harris. 2006.

Rousseau's Confessions *and* Reveries of the Solitary Walker. Ed. John C. O'Neal and Ourida Mostefai. 2003.

Shakespeare's Hamlet. Ed. Bernice W. Kliman. 2001.

Shakespeare's King Lear. Ed. Robert H. Ray. 1986.

Shakespeare's Othello. Ed. Peter Erickson and Maurice Hunt. 2005.

Shakespeare's Romeo and Juliet. Ed. Maurice Hunt. 2000.

Shakespeare's The Tempest *and Other Late Romances.* Ed. Maurice Hunt. 1992.

Shelley's Frankenstein. Ed. Stephen C. Behrendt. 1990.

Shelley's Poetry. Ed. Spencer Hall. 1990.

Sir Gawain and the Green Knight. Ed. Miriam Youngerman Miller and Jane Chance. 1986.

Spenser's Faerie Queene. Ed. David Lee Miller and Alexander Dunlop. 1994.

Stendhal's The Red and the Black. Ed. Dean de la Motte and Stirling Haig. 1999.

Sterne's Tristram Shandy. Ed. Melvyn New. 1989.

Stowe's Uncle Tom's Cabin. Ed. Elizabeth Ammons and Susan Belasco. 2000.

Swift's Gulliver's Travels. Ed. Edward J. Rielly. 1988.

Thoreau's Walden *and Other Works*. Ed. Richard J. Schneider. 1996.

Tolstoy's Anna Karenina. Ed. Liza Knapp and Amy Mandelker. 2003.

Vergil's Aeneid. Ed. William S. Anderson and Lorina N. Quartarone. 2002.

Voltaire's Candide. Ed. Renée Waldinger. 1987.

Whitman's Leaves of Grass. Ed. Donald D. Kummings. 1990.

Woolf's To the Lighthouse. Ed. Beth Rigel Daugherty and Mary Beth Pringle. 2001.

Wordsworth's Poetry. Ed. Spencer Hall, with Jonathan Ramsey. 1986.

Wright's Native Son. Ed. James A. Miller. 1997.